Motherlove in
Shades of Black

Motherlove in Shades of Black

The Maternal Psyche in the Novels of African American Women

GLORIA THOMAS PILLOW

Foreword by Geneva Smitherman

McFarland & Company, Inc., Publishers
Jefferson, North Carolina, and London

Abridged variations of a portion of the material in chapters 1, 2, and 6 appeared as articles with the following titles under the author's former name, Gloria T. Randle, in the following publications, respectively:

"Between the Rock and the Hard Place: Mediating Spaces in Harriet Jacobs' *Incidents in the Life of a Slave Girl*." *African American Review*, winter 1999; 23 pp.

"Mates, Marriage, and Motherhood: Feminist Visions in Pauline Hopkins' *Contending Forces*." *Tulsa Studies in Women's Literature*, Vol. 18, No. 2, fall 1999; 26 pp.

"'Knowing When to Stop': Loving and Living Small in the Slave World of *Beloved*." *CLA Journal*, Vol. XLI, no. 3, spring 1998; 21 pp.

LIBRARY OF CONGRESS CATALOGUING-IN-PUBLICATION DATA

Pillow, Gloria Thomas.
    Motherlove in shades of black : the maternal psyche in the novels of African American women / Gloria Thomas Pillow ; foreword by Geneva Smitherman.
    p.   cm.
    Includes bibliographical references and index.

    ISBN 978-0-7864-3533-3
    softcover : 50# alkaline paper

    1. American fiction — African American authors—History and criticism. 2. American fiction — Women authors — History and criticism. 3. African American mothers in literature. 4. Love, Maternal, in literature. 5. Mother and child in literature. 6. African American mothers — Psychology. I. Title.
    PS153.N5P53   2010
    813'.0093552 — dc22   2010017289

British Library cataloguing data are available

©2010 Gloria Thomas Pillow. All rights reserved

No part of this book may be reproduced or transmitted in any form or by any means, electronic or mechanical, including photocopying or recording, or by any information storage and retrieval system, without permission in writing from the publisher.

Front cover: Linda Carole. *Mother Love*. Acrylic on upholstery fabric. 20" × 30". 2003.

Manufactured in the United States of America

McFarland & Company, Inc., Publishers
  Box 611, Jefferson, North Carolina 28640
    www.mcfarlandpub.com

To Mom and Dad,
loved and treasured beyond words.

Acknowledgments

Thank you, God, for bountiful blessings.

Deepest thanks to my extraordinary family, including extended and new family, and to my cherished circle of friends — who, together, compose the finest support system anyone could have. Mom and dad, your exquisite motherlove and fatherlove have enriched countless lives. Thanks to sisters Margaret and Patricia for constant encouragement and Claudia, fearless and thoughtful editor. Angie, Grace, Lish, Rufus — your gifts were essential.

Thank you, Cameron High School in Nashville, Tennessee, and (then–) Clark College in Atlanta, Georgia, for essential lessons in and out of school and for wonderful times, whose memories and imprint will last a lifetime.

Thanks to the University of Chicago for a rich postgraduate experience — those seven years just flew by! Thank you, Professors Elizabeth Alexander, Ken Warren, and, especially, Bill Veeder for excellent guidance. Thanks, MIKE: you were a great study group.

I am so appreciative for the interaction with my students in years past, especially at Michigan State University, who kept the dialogue, the questioning, and the thinking fresh and dynamic.

Geneva, generous spirit, you and your exceptional writing inspire me.

Claudith, you are an enduring blessing.

Phil, you've always been there, all my life.

Thank you to Dr. Jimmy Graham and Dr. Christopher Holloway, for helping me to meet health challenges with some measure of grace.

Thomas, my heart: life with you is golden.

Contents

Acknowledgments vii

Foreword by Geneva Smitherman 1

Introduction 3

1. Linda Brent: Through a Glass, Darkly   9
   Incidents in the Life of a Slave Girl

2. Sappho Clark: Double Exposure   36
   Contending Forces

3. Irene Redfield: Smoke and Mirrors   63
   Passing

4. Maud Martha: Gray, Lined in Silver   87
   Maud Martha

5. Celie: Emergent Light   111
   The Color Purple

6. Sethe: Beyond the Pale   138
   Beloved

Chapter Notes   169

Bibliography   177

Index   187

Foreword

by Geneva Smitherman

Well, my girl GloJean done finally did it, done brought this *magnum opus* to fruition. And what a delectable treat she has given us. *Motherlove in Shades of Black* is a master narrative on the psychology of the Black mother.

Like many of my sistas, I have long possessed an intellectual ambivalence about psychoanalytic theory. What could this racist, sexist ideology tell us about mothers like Langston Hughes's for whom life in Amerikkka "ain't been no crystal stair"? The motherstory, in life and in literature, bequeathed to us by our literary foremothers, is fraught with psycho-social contradictions, many questions, and few answers in our quest to understand what is "good enuf mothering." Dr. Gloria Jean Thomas Pillow, through her wise use of the psychoanalytic paradigm, makes it plain as she vigilantly and brilliantly separates the wheat from the chaff. *Motherlove in Shades of Black* is a major achievement.

Since the time of Freud, the profound failing of psychological investigation has been its glaring myopia about cultural realities as well as its own firmly ingrained biases. Check out the irony. On the one hand, we have a discipline dedicated to insight about and healing of the human psyche; yet it has been historically unaware of or, worse, cavalier about, its own racism, sexism, homophobia, and other prejudices. On the other hand, the great strength of psychoanalysis lies in its ability to understand and articulate the complex workings of the inner mind, to help us make sense of the human condition.

Employing an extremely close reading of the text, Pillow illuminates what is written in the lines and what hovers between, around, underneath them — you know, the deep structure. She taps into psychological inquiry to inform her inner portraits of each mother and uses socially and culturally constructed reality to situate the race and gender dynamics of the historical era in the work. Having had the privilege of observing Pillow's classrooms, I am delighted to see her provocative, interactive teaching style reflected in the tone of *Motherlove*. She offers a hypothesis, then builds a case, step by logical step, only to invite the reader/student/scholar to question it, dissect it, re-analyze it, even subvert it. One's analysis, or counter-analysis, can be traditional or ground-breaking, predictable or unexpected, historically accepted or the "road less traveled"—but it must always be based on carefully formed, perceptive insights. Pillow's own analyses of the mothers peel away layer after layer in search of that kernel of deepest, purest truth, the closest approximation of what actually happens on the mother's psychic level, shedding striking light on behaviors that might otherwise be seen as inexplicable, incredible—like Sethe killing her two-year-old daughter in Morrison's *Beloved*.

Now, look, let's keep it real. I know I ain't the only one, especially among sista-mothers, who just could not wrap her mind around this murderous act. Yeah, I know, we be vibbin on our foremothers and forefathers, "Before I be a slave, I be buried in my grave." But that was "I," not the child of "I." So, is this woman just plain crazy? Where does the madness truly begin, and how can it end? After reading Pillow's fresh, compelling analysis, the *aha* moment came upon me. We actually see and feel how Sethe's mind works to make this happen, as my girl GloJean reconstructs the psychological portrait of the maternal self.

Motherlove is not only a textbook for students, and it sure is not just for academics. Produced by a scholar who doesn't worship at the shrine of polysyllabic jargon and linguistic obtuseness that, unfortunately, characterize much of literary scholarship today, this book has been written with a powerful clarity and eloquence. It is a work for all questioners who want to know and understand why we be "doin the thangs we don't do." How do we each contribute to the inhumanity, and the humanity, of this world? Dr. Gloria Jean Thomas Pillow makes it clear that we are all "mothers," with a responsibility to learn the "lessons of the Blood" and anything else that will help us nurture the next generation. For literature, like language, is not just an exercise in comprehension; we don't study or read it just to get the "right" answer to questions that arise. At its best, it inspires thought and action. It connects us to each other in the best sense of the word. This is the genius of *Motherlove*.

Geneva Smitherman, Ph.D., is a University Distinguished Professor of English at Michigan State University. A renowned sociolinguist and author, her latest work is *Word from the Mother: Language and African Americans*.

Introduction

> Inside, two boys bled in the sawdust and dirt at the feet of a nigger woman holding a blood-soaked child to her chest with one hand and an infant by the heels in the other.... She'd gone wild.... The woman — something was wrong with her.—*Beloved*, Toni Morrison

Yes, something is terribly wrong. A mother is killing her children. The reader has come to know Sethe as a serene and gentle woman and a profoundly loving mother. Her constant subjectivity, however, is apparent at the point at which the narrator defers to the limited perceptions of Schoolteacher, the vicious slavemaster who has come north to re-enslave Sethe and her children. This shift of sensibility addresses the all-important question of agency: Exactly who or what is crazy here? Schoolteacher's judgment that "something [is] wrong with her" does not even begin to penetrate all that is *really* wrong, the profound dysfunction that actually exists, and the incredible challenges faced by African American mothers in the slave culture of *Beloved*. The issues central to this inquiry as a whole concern the role of the mother, the psychology of mothering, and what constitutes "good-enough" mothering in a world circumscribed by oppression. Sethe, arguably the most well-known mother in all of African American literature today, invites consideration of other mothers whose accounts, while not so dramatic, powerfully illuminate the underanalyzed dynamic of mothering under varying conditions of oppression. In order to nurture their children, these mothers' navigation of the pervasive mine fields of race and gender barriers made tightrope walking an art form.

"The child shall follow the condition of the mother." This foundational law of slavery designated a perverse matrilineal construct based on powerlessness, the manifest aim of which was to insure the perpetuation of an enslaved race from the wombs of Black women. Burdened with this legacy,

Introduction

Black mothers have nonetheless historically struggled to grasp fulfillment — for their children, if not themselves. The story of the African American mother is extraordinary. And her literature, so long disregarded, represents her faithfully.

My study attempts to further an understanding of mothering as represented in African American women's literature, primarily through psychological analysis of the forces that create the unique tensions of her life, her strategies for survival and achievement, and the character of the nurturing she gives her children. A discreet body of psychoanalytic theory informs my analysis, while the primary texts, in turn, inform the relative usefulness, and the limits, of the theory in critical interpretation of the literature. Throughout, the term "internal" refers to the individual's psychic structure; "external" connotes one's outer environment, including home, community, and society.

This inquiry examines six works published between 1861 and 1987: Harriet Jacobs's *Incidents in the Life of a Slave Girl*; Pauline Hopkins's *Contending Forces*; Nella Larsen's *Passing*; Gwendolyn Brooks's *Maud Martha*; Alice Walker's *The Color Purple*, and Toni Morrison's *Beloved*. All paint a vivid portrait of race and gender politics at particular moments in nineteenth- and twentieth-century America.

The gender bias inherent in patriarchal society compounds the devaluation of all women, thus making the African American woman's experience unique: racism compounded by sexism cannot be measured by a simple equation. Black women do not face "double" the oppression experienced by either Black men or White women. The subtleties and complexities of American *-isms* are not so straightforward. The effects of institutionalized oppression of Black people, and the persistent subordination of women, are critical to understanding the Black mother's worldview — both socially and psychologically — as represented in African American women's literature.

Although the mother is a crucial figure in psychological study, little attention has been accorded the African American mother in either psychoanalytic theory or the Western literary canon. At the very least, this circumstance has left undiscovered the quiet grace, dignity, and heroism that so many of these women have displayed since arriving in this country in the degraded state of slavery. It is an exciting undertaking to participate — in whatever small measure — in a movement that redresses a blatant omission in American studies, and to illuminate the incredible spirit embodied in legions of African American women in general, and in African American mothers in particular. Closely examined, these apparently unremarkable mothers are often shown to function with extraordinary strength and dignity. However, their efforts cannot be fully appreciated without an understanding of their psychological make-up. This analysis must be undertaken not only in and of itself, but also through the lens of external factors that impact the mother's psyche; these issues are inseparable from the nature of their mothering.

While psychoanalysis and psychiatry have historically held postures that perpetuate racial bias—what Suman Fernando refers to as "the psychiatrisation of Black protest against oppression"—noteworthy practitioners of the disciplines have also individually sanctioned and promoted racism since their development. Fernando offers as an example Stanley Hall, founder of the *American Journal of Psychiatry*, who, in his widely accepted 1904 study *Adolescence*, characterizes African and other non-white peoples as immature children who "live a life of feeling, emotion and impulse," a depiction that has become ingrained in the discipline; Carl Jung postulated in the 1920s that Black people have "probably a whole historical layer less" in their brains than do Whites.[1] In the first volume of the *Psychoanalytic Review* (1914), Arrah B. Evert argues that while Black people lack the psychological intricacy necessary for achieving a truly buried complex, they have nonetheless an inherent tendency toward degenerative insanity.[2] Sigmund Freud contributed significantly to the racist and sexist ideology inherent in psychoanalysis. He declared, for example, that narcissism inhabits the realm of the immature and the self-centered—that is, typically, "perverts, homosexuals, and women."[3]

As Barbara Johnson has observed, there are clearly "mutual resistances between psychoanalysis and African American literature."[4] At the same time, a psychological perspective often brings new and exciting insights to bear on often under-studied texts. Given the limitations of the theory, it is important that its applicability to works dealing with race and gender are thoughtful and measured.

Maternal figures are important both within and without texts in African American women's literature. One of the distinct traits of the tradition that most interests me is the quest for a nurturing source, perhaps best expressed in the title of Alice Walker's 1983 "womanist" prose, *In Search of Our Mothers' Gardens*. Black women's writing illuminates the generally shadowy presence of the mother that has hovered at the margin of the narrative while emphasis fixes on her offspring. While male writers have sought (and fought) their literary, spiritual, and biological fathers, and many White women writers define themselves artistically as separate from their mothers, Black women conversely seek to embrace a maternal past.[5] Marianne Hirsch sees in a great deal of this writing a "daughterly tradition in relation to a complicated maternal past."[6] Mary Helen Washington describes this identification with the maternal as the "connection between the Black woman writer's sense of herself as part of a link in generations of women, and her decision to write."[7] This matrilineal link is more than spiritual. It has resulted in the very tangible rediscovery of literary "mothers" by their "daughters." Alice Walker's crucial role in the revitalization of Zora Neale Hurston's work, Claudia Tate's efforts to reanimate Pauline Hopkins's posthumous career, and Deborah McDowell's revisionary assessment of Nella Larsen's novels constitute some of the linkages that have occurred between contemporary African American women writers and their predecessors.

Another aspect of a matrilineal approach among African American women is the complexity of feelings between Black mother and daughter in fact and in fiction, particularly given external pressures, balanced against the "tremendously powerful need to present to the public a positive image of Black womanhood."[8] As a result, very little study has been accorded the psychological aspect of the Black mother in literature. This omission has been in some cases by design. E. Frances White asks, "How dare we admit the psychological battles that need to be fought with the very women who taught us to survive in this racist and sexist world? We would feel like ungrateful traitors."[9] Yet it is precisely the psychology of the Black mother that I want to explore: the profound love and courage of women who raise their families amidst the malignant strictures of their external world is rarely diminished upon close analysis. And when mothering is *not* triumphant — as in *Passing*, a case of profound and conspicuous failure — understanding the reasons for such deficiency provides a valuable cultural perspective that must be confronted rather than avoided.

The literature calls not only the individual, but society at large as well into accountability by illuminating the hegemony of social dysfunction by which racial and gender relations are driven. The psychological issues involved in the African American woman's ability to mother her children in a "healthy" environment require scrupulous examination of both her external and internal spheres. The self's ability to defend against damaging situations and perceptions — both internal and external — and the critical need to overcome, or at least to learn to negotiate, cultural as well as personal psychic illness in order to produce healthy individuals, families, and societies, is the persistent motif that I pursue through African American women's literature.

Introduction

A personal objective of my study is to try to discover, through the literature, ways in which enlightenment and healing can take place. As a nation, and as a culture, of high and admirable ideals but many unsound and disempowering practices, we have created our own legacy of distress and bequeathed it to the current generation. Race and gender practices — among others — that damage the individual, the community, and the universe must be discussed, written about, challenged, and defeated. We desperately need to break destructive cycles and provide for a healthier community whose members can all thrive and reach for possibility. Our children, both biological and symbolic, are depending on us.

CHAPTER 1

Linda Brent: Through a Glass, Darkly

A complete portrait of this mother — or, for that matter, of this woman — is difficult to conceptualize, because her autobiography conceals even as it reveals: *Incidents in the Life of a Slave Girl* reports only certain "incidents," as noted in the title, not a complete story. This self-portrait is one of incredible complexity and depth and a nexus of contradictions. As painful candor at some moments intersects with profound silence and opaqueness at others. This quiet, melancholy woman is also known for her determined, rebellious nature. She seems to exist between the lines, both indefinable and indecipherable, elusive as air: is she cunning or guileless? Humbly apologetic or angrily defiant? Slave or free? Dead or alive? Mother or child? This is a portrait in chiaroscuro, skillfully shaded, dominated by deep shadow. D.W. Winnicott's theories on good-enough mothering cast some degree of light onto the obscured face of the painting.

Incidents in the Life of a Slave Girl[1] is an extraordinary document — not, as some skeptics have charged, in the sense of the unbelievable nature of its storyline. While Jean Fagan Yellin's conclusive findings tabled at last recurring questions of authorship and authenticity,[2] what I find especially remarkable about Harriet Jacobs's story is the unfolding of her ability to creatively construct sites of temporary refuge where none exist; to discover space where there is none; to identify, over and again, an area of possibility in that narrowest of wedges between the rock and the hard place.

Jacobs's text, presented in the name of her pseudonym, Linda Brent,[3] reflects an unwavering ability to locate, as crisis approaches, viable mediating spaces between the tensions that threaten her and her children's well-being. While these spaces are flawed and grossly inadequate, they serve the immediate purpose of allowing her to function in relative mental health while imprisoned in a pitiless and hostile culture that constantly threatens her sanity and even her life. The depth of Jacobs's creativity is particularly apparent in the often graphically portrayed maternal issues that arise; that is, the deficient and surrogate mothering she herself received, and, in partial consequence, the sporadic mothering that she provides to her own two children. With continual reference to her psychological state, this study also considers the seven-year interval in her grandmother's garret, a masterful portrait of one individual's desperate determination to carve a space larger than that taut and narrow chasm into which she has been born — a realm that contains possibility.

This deliberately crafted text is emphatically gender-specific, its title inscribing at once the author's race, gender, status, and voice. Most likely the first slave narrative to be published by a woman in this country,[4] its title word "girl" situates adolescence as the critical stage of her life and also as the focus of the text. Briefly, Brent's narrative follows her development from childhood. She was born to mulatto parents, orphaned at 13, and "owned" by the abusive Dr. and Mrs. Flint. Refused permission to wed her true love, Linda finally accepts a liaison with a prominent citizen rather than yield to the insistent advances of the abhorrent Dr. Flint. She bears two children, Ellen and Benny, by her admirer, Sands. Brent's grandmother hides her when Brent feigns escape in order to divert Flint's attention from the sale of her children to recapturing her. Concealing herself in her grandmother's attic for seven years, Brent finally escapes. She obtains a position with the Bruce family in New York and eventually gains custody of her children. A free woman as she writes her narrative, Brent continues to care for her now-widowed employer's children and home. Her son Benny resides with her brother in California, and Ellen is away at boarding school.

Though Brent and her children gain their freedom, she suffers still, at the end of her narrative, from physical and psychic effects of her enslavement. Most importantly, she has failed to reunite her widely scattered family members. This disappointment evokes a resolution that is hardly the happily-ever-after ending that critics as scrupulous as John Blassingame have characterized it to be.[5] A sense of privation and melancholy pervades the final pages. In addition to the painful memories of the past, Brent is an unfulfilled mother in the present. "The dream of my life is not yet realized. I do not sit with my children in a home of my own" [513].

The powerful and profoundly perverted institution of slavery defined life for the Africans brought to America and for their descendants. One of its basic tenets was that "the child shall follow the condition of the mother," which insured that, through the matrilineal line, their debased status would continue into perpetuity, providing an infinite supply of free labor for the developing new territory. But while herself a slave, Brent finds within herself the courage to see that her children escape that awful existence, one way or another. This, and not the quality of her mothering, is her triumph.

Peculiar Times, Shadowy Mothering

Psychotherapist D.W. Winnicott characterizes the "good-enough" mother as "one who makes active adaptation to the infant's needs."[6] By her own admission, Jacobs's mothering was a sporadic and flawed endeavor. Yet she maintains throughout her narrative that her children are the most important elements in her life. This apparent maternal contradiction is better understood through (1) an understanding of the formidable claims of the institution of slavery against the African American family; (2) psychological inquiry into the frame of mind of this very young mother, and (3) adjustments that must be made in the psychological concept of "good-enough" mothering when the mother's hostile environment jeopardizes her very existence and severely constrains her ability to nurture her children.

In contrast to the commonly separated slave family, Brent's was unusual in that during her early childhood her nuclear family lived intact on one plantation. Further, the prominent myth of the happy plantation family, perpetuated through the reality (and the South's propagandistic images) of Black and White children playing together in the foreground masked, for the slave child, the reality of Black adults laboring in the background. This youthful illusion of early freedom would typically create a tremendous upheaval in the psyche once the slave comprehends her status. The trauma of Brent's new awareness of her life station is compounded by a critical concurrent event: the death of her mother when she is six years old. Only then does she begin to understand "that I was a slave" (343). The juxtaposition of these two major events will be shown to affect Brent's psychic development in critical ways.

The mother is distinguished by psychoanalyst Sigmund Freud as "unique, without parallel, established unalterably for a whole lifetime as the first and strongest love-object and as the prototype of all later love relations."[7] Nancy Chodorow particularizes the maternal role toward the daughter, suggesting that a gender bond solidifies the daughter's early relationship with her mother, so that "women develop a sense of self continuous with others."[8] Brent's proud image of her mother, whom she remembers as a woman whose slave status did not diminish her regal bearing, persists throughout the narrative. The abrupt end of Brent's mother's care cuts off the construction, from her mother's example, of the psychic tools that she is in the process of amassing in these crucial formative years in order to counsel and protect herself against her external world. In perhaps instinctive awareness of this incomplete internalization process, Brent embarks upon a continuous search for an external maternal figure.[9] Brent's first attempt at mediation, while still a young child, is a viable compromise between her forlorn state of motherlessness and maternal care — a mediating object to help buffer her against the raging storm of institutional slavery. The surrogate nurturing Brent subsequently receives, however, inevitably prefigures the mothering that she later gives: fragmented, inconsistent, undependable, and inadequate.

Two surrogate mothers are connected to Brent by what Hortense Spillers refers to as "the 'threads cable-strong' of an incestuous, interracial genealogy."[10] Spillers's exposition on the psychoanalytic dimension attached to institutional slavery informs the complex and profoundly contradictory impulses existing in relationships between slave and slaveowner, and makes it possible to understand young Brent's attachment to her "kindly" White plantation mistress. The mistress is referred to as the foster sister of Brent's mother, since they were both breast-fed by Brent's grandmother. While such an image promotes the idea of a familial bond, the reality of their shared nursing is less heartwarming. Brent's almost parenthetical notation that her own mother was weaned at three months, to ensure that the White baby would have plentiful milk, deeply ironizes the nostalgic tone of this section of the narrative. After her mother's death, Brent is sent to live in the plantation home, so that even her physical location situates her as the child more of the mistress than of her own father. Brent further describes a scene that would only strengthen the notion that she is, in fact, the mistress's child: "My mistress was so kind to me.... I would sit by her side for hours, sewing diligently, with a heart as free from care as that of any free-born white child" [343].

The affectionate mistress even teaches young Brent to read and write.

1. Linda Brent: Through a Glass, Darkly

Yet, instead of freeing Brent upon her death, as promised, the mistress wills the twelve-year-old girl to a five-year-old niece. In order to salvage her idealized memory of that surrogate mother, Brent falls back upon that classic defense mechanism — denial — and deliberately recalls only happy days spent in this woman's care, saying, "I loved her; for she had been *almost like a mother* to me" (343, emphasis mine). Yet in willfully trading Brent's freedom for the whim of a five-year-old relative, the mistress shows a paucity of maternal instincts toward Brent and provides Brent with her first experience in a long history of betrayal by White women. More importantly, she represents a second instance of maternal abandonment, leaving the child to find her own way without a line of defense.

Aunt Nancy is not only a beloved figure; she is also, importantly, Brent's mother's *twin* sister, and therefore perhaps the perfect — certainly the most appropriate — maternal figure for the young girl after the mother's death. Brent underscores the importance of Aunt Nancy in her life by declaring her aunt to be "at the beginning and end of everything" (347). Yet this compelling statement resists both clarity and elaboration as Brent presents her aunt as a curiously shadowy presence, an elusive figure rarely mentioned within the pages of the text. Although she devotes one very brief chapter to this woman who "supplied a mother's place" (463), Brent discloses almost nothing about their obviously close relationship ("The bond between us was very strong.... She always encouraged me.... She sent me word never to yield" [463]), but instead concentrates on the grueling and humiliating slave labor, directed primarily by Mrs. Flint, that consumes all of Aunt Nancy's time and energy and severely restricts her accessibility to Brent. Brent does disclose that forced heavy labor soon destroys Aunt Nancy's young body (causing a succession of doomed premature birthings and finally sterility, among other conditions) and ultimately proves to be the direct cause of her early death. Otherwise, Brent patently avoids further elaboration. Her haunting silence on the subject of Aunt Nancy suggests profound despair and even smoldering rage over the loss of this most perfect surrogate — the precise mirror image of her deeply lamented mother. Although Brent does not remain motherless, so to speak, after Aunt Nancy's death, it may be argued, as evidenced by her later psychic state while hiding in her grandmother's garret, that each loss — particularly this most acutely felt deprivation — only intensifies her need for an enduring maternal figure.

Brent remembers her father as a strong, skilled, intelligent man, charged by slaveholders with "spoil[ing] his children, by teaching them to feel that they were human beings" (345). Brent is orphaned at thirteen when her father dies. The symbol of her parents' resting-place evokes an image of desolation and blight, echoing as well a profound sense of abandonment: "A black stump sat at the head of my mother's grave. [My father's] grave was marked by a small wooden board, bearing his name, the letters of which were nearly obliterated" (416–17). The black stump, the only remains of a tree that her father had planted, and his "nearly obliterated" name on the gravestone are striking symbols of the impotence, threat of castration, and severed ancestral line that slave fathers endured. Unable to protect his wife or daughters from the slaveholder's sexual appetites, the father's name stands to be obliterated when his wife bears a child, and his seed supplanted by that of the master's.

Now without either parent, Brent finds sanctuary with her maternal grandmother. She retains a child's recollection of a warm, safe, "grand big" haven in a perilous world: "There we always found sweet balsam for our troubles. She was so loving, so sympathizing! ... There was a grand big oven there, too" (351–2). Clearly the most constant and influential person in the girl's life, Brent's grandmother is a freed slave who yet lives on the plantation and who, with deep affection, provides loving care to her grandchildren. Yet her nurturing, while crucial to Brent's development, is not uniformly beneficent. Hazel Carby characterizes the grandmother as "[embodying] aspects of a *true* womanhood; the source of a strong moral code in the midst of an immoral system ... pure and pious, a fountainhead of physical and spiritual sustenance."[11] But the grandmother is a far more complicated figure than Carby suggests. While the grandmother clearly understands on one level that her authority is compromised by the system of slavery ("She promised to be a mother to her grandchildren, so far as she might be permitted to do so" [345]), on a deeper level she labors under psychological impulses that enable her to reject this reality. Such rigid attachment to a moral code that is constantly, invariably, sabotaged by the imperatives of slavery imposes an incredible psychological burden upon her granddaughter.

Brent's grandmother's uncompromising righteousness has the power to subdue, at times, even Dr. Flint, the immoral plantation owner. Importantly, however, it also intimidates her granddaughter, who admits that she feared and loved the formidable older woman in equal portions. The grandmother is simultaneously guilty of egregious lapses in judgment and a covetous kind of mothering: she once "loans" her capricious mistress $300 dollars — money that she has painstakingly amassed and hoarded in order to buy her children out of slavery, money that she never sees again — for a pair of silver candelabrums. When her son Benjamin escapes from slavery, rather than rejoice over his freedom, the grandmother deeply mourns him, almost as though he had died. The most serious contradiction in the grandmother's value system is her strict moral code on the one hand, and her belief that the "master" must be obeyed on the other. While grandmother condemns out of hand any act of immorality on the part of the slaves, at the same time she urges obedience of the laws of slavery. The older woman confides to Brent that she, too, had once railed against slavery, but that she has learned instead to pray to God when she feels burdened, and to suffer in silence. Psychologically, it seems more likely that, having given up the fight against slavery on some level, the grandmother uses religion as a justification for her surrender to the more powerful forces against her. This is not to say that the grandmother is not a sincere believer; only that she relies on religion, as do most slaveholders, to explain the peculiar way of the world: "Most earnestly did she strive to make us feel that [our enslavement] was the will of God ... [that] we ought to pray for contentment" (351).

Brent's philosophical differences with her grandmother surface early on. Echoing yet subtly altering her grandmother's admonishment to "pray for contentment," Brent advises her brother that slave children could not expect to be happy; only by being good could they hope for any sort of contentment. She vehemently opposes her grandmother's acceptance of slavery as God's will. The grandmother is at once Brent's ideal and her nemesis — on the one hand an exemplary model whom she can never hope to emulate; on the other, an unrealistic, disempowering model to whom she is deeply attached but from whom she unconsciously wants to break free. Brent's frustration with and philosophical disconnection from her grandmother find voice in a sort of overcompensation as she repeatedly idealizes her guardian throughout the text:

> The kind grandmother ... the good grandmother ... the brave old woman ... that blessed old grandmother ... the kind-hearted old woman ... the good, patient old friend ... the poor old sufferer ... the dear old grandmother ... [340, 360, 439, 444, 448, 452, 467, 471, 474, *passim*].

The overdetermined characterization, in concert with Brent's consistent use of definite articles (e.g., "the," "that") rather than the more intimate possessive "my," suggest a distancing from her grandmother that subtly undermines their strong bond of kinship and understanding. When Brent irrevocably defies her grandmother's principles, she does so with a canny acceptance of the limitations of the older woman's moral code vis-à-vis the realities of her prohibitive external world. Still, all these surrogate mothers — her mistress, Aunt Nancy, and especially her grandmother — provide Brent with crucial nurturing during her pre-adolescent years and constitute the essential difference between her having, and not having, a mother figure.

I have specifically referenced mothering in relation to parental nurturing because slave fathers are, more often than slave mothers, generally absent figures during their children's upbringing. Uncharacteristically, Brent has been allowed to live with both her mother and father — whom she remembers as a strong, intelligent man — until her mother dies. Like her mother, Brent's father dies at a crucial time in her life — the advent of adolescence, the period that she characterizes as most dangerous for slave girls. The earlier loss of her mother, coupled with her father's death and the slavemasters' refusal to allow her to mourn him, engender a spirit of angry rebellion in Brent that is not to be assuaged by her grandmother's invocation of God's will. "I was ordered to go for flowers ... while the dead body of my father was lying within a mile of me.... My heart rebelled against God" (345).

Ultimately, Brent is forced to parent herself. And perhaps this was the reality for all slave children, orphaned or not, since their parents were also subject to the slaveowner's will. The kindly veteran's advice to the woeful hero in *Invisible Man* ("Be your own father, young man."[12]) is the path upon which Brent embarks. It is most significant psychologically that she never fully relinquishes the only partially formed, yet internalized ideal of her biological mother. This dynamic provides her with the most authentic means of keeping her mother close, even in death.

"The Usual Fate of Slave Girls"

The process by which Brent herself becomes a mother, and the second instance of her creating a mediating space where no space exists, is the central focus of her narrative. The story that she *must* tell — as the authorial tone reflects — is the same one she is loath to disclose. While the slave woman is subject to violence at any time, Brent focuses upon the crucial period of adolescence. "At 14," she writes, "the war of my life had begun" (353). Brent charges slave culture with not only rampant abuse, but also of meticulously concealing the secrets of its corruption. She is specifically referring to that "usual fate of slave girls" which is, of course, their absolute powerlessness with regard to sexual exploitation by those who call themselves "master." In fact *Incidents* is the *only* slave narrative that focuses specifically on the sexual vulnerability of slave girls and women.[13]

Alternately pleading and defending her case and those of her sisters, Brent argues that, because the values of slave culture are so severely perverted, the slave woman should not be judged by the same standards as are free white women. Speaking directly to her assumed audience of White women, she reminds them that, while their lives have always been sheltered and protected both by family and by law, the opposite is true for the slave girl. Neither Brent's fate, nor her will, is in her hands: Just like any other God-fearing woman, she insists, "I wanted to keep myself pure" (384). The picture of security that surrounds White women — which Brent underlines with phrases such as "sheltered," "protected," and "purity" — mocks the tyranny that young slave women face and illuminates the perversity of a system that provides only one type of education for slave girls, even during their preteen years.

> She will become prematurely knowing in evil things. Soon she will learn to tremble when she hears her master's footfall. She will be compelled to realize that she is no longer a child [361–2].

For the female slave, knowledge has nothing to do with formal education which, in any case, was denied by law to the enslaved. Rather, it is associated with adult sexual (mis)behavior, loss of innocence, danger, and debasement.

The institution of slavery tended on the one hand to blur gender lines — placing women in traditional "masculine" roles such as performing heavy labor and men in the "feminine" role of subservience. On the other hand, Brent's narrative challenges Deborah Grey White's view that "female slave bondage was not better or worse, or more or less severe, than male bondage, but it was different."[14]

> Slavery is terrible for men; but *it is far more terrible for women*. Superadded to the burden common to all, *they* have wrongs, and sufferings, and mortifications peculiarly their own [405, emphasis mine].

Brent's argument is acutely gendered: When her uncle Benjamin is sold, "we thanked God that he was not [a girl]" (357). Brent later relates that "when they told me my new-born babe was a girl, my heart was heavier than it had ever been before" (405).

> The slave girl is reared in an atmosphere of licentiousness and fear. The lash and the foul talk of her master and his sons are her teachers.... The profligate men who have power over her may be exceedingly odious to her. But resistance is hopeless [382].

Brent's use of the third person universalizes the plight of slave girls at the same time that it distances her from this very personalized account. Every example she offers above reflects her own experience. The slaveowner's methodology describes psychological, more even than physical, intimidation, much like strategies used against prisoners of war — such as sleep and food deprivation, a punishment/reward cycle, and repetition of desired learning — to "break" the young female slave. At this point the collapse of a previously maintained narrative distance signals a deep authorial tension as Brent attempts to articulate her personal story. Abrupt tone changes underline a shift from the general to the specific as "the slave girl" is particularized to Brent herself and the institution of slavery is replaced by Dr. Flint as the embodiment of evil. The disease metaphor — "violent outbreaks," "contagious," "all-pervading corruption," "pollution," "poisonous grasp"— that she has elsewhere used to characterize the *dis-ease* of an entire slave culture (361, 378, 382, 384, 404) now specifically represents Flint: *he* is the "plague," the "vile monster" (352, 361).

Flint is the model that Brent references in the above excerpt, the lecherous slavemaster who bribes and whispers "foul talk" to the helpless slave girl. His methods are crude but cunning, and he apparently derives more pleasure from the power he exerts and the fear he instills than from outright physical assault. As a final straw, Dr. Flint's banishment of Brent's intended, a free-born carpenter whom she loved with all the wholesome passion of a first, youthful love, precipitates the loss of her adolescence and emotional innocence. His competition dispatched, Flint moves in, so to speak, for the kill. Brent's anthropomorphic image of Flint's predatory character eerily heightens the effect of his ruthless appetite: "[Dr. Flint's] restless, craving, vicious nature roved about day and night, seeking whom to devour" (352). Flint as a roving, beastlike cannibal ("seeking whom to devour") holds chilling psychological implications, his perversity arguably attached to an infantile orality based upon destructive impulses projected outward in service of the satisfaction of his own passions.[15] Brent's fear that Flint will eat her alive certainly suggests sexual anxiety.

At fifteen Brent stands alone between two widely disparate moral poles: Flint's corrupt overtures and threats position themselves squarely against the moral principles that Brent's grandmother instilled in her. At this vulnerable stage, Brent's grandmother's home offers only limited security. Unwilling or psychologically un*able* to deal with her granddaughter's predicament, the grandmother continues to preach the essential virtues of chastity and morality on the one hand and to admonish her granddaughter to obey her master on the other. Such mixed messages place Brent in an impossible position with regard to Dr. Flint. The ensuing friction between Brent and her grandmother is untempered by the sort of mediating influence that a mother could feasibly provide — a sympathetic generational connection that could understand both the grandmother's idealistic, unrealistic moral stance and the young girl's very real predicament.

Brent's growing desperation ("resistance is hopeless") is fueled by a crushing inability to locate any refuge from sexual jeopardy. Even if her parents were alive or if she were "married" (the law prohibited slaves from marrying in a legal sense), neither the parents nor the husband of a slave have power under the law to protect her from the slaveholder's prerogative. While she recognizes that her redoubtable grandmother's presence in the neighborhood is "some protection to me" (362), by qualifying the level of that protection Brent understands that the grandmother is neither able nor equipped to safeguard her from all dangers. Brent's second young mistress is not only just a child; as a member of the ruling class, she would be no protection to Brent. Mrs. Flint, neglected wife of Dr. Flint, would hardly provide assistance to Brent; their relationship is, inevitably, adversarial. In fact, Mrs. Flint vows, after sending Brent away, that "she would kill me if I came back" (404).

With all avenues apparently closed, Brent retreats into the shadows to protect her children. Most importantly, she can not tolerate the possibility of having children with Flint, which is the crux of the matter — not just the awfulness of sexual assault by him, but the worse circumstance of bearing children that he would treat as mere property. When she learns that he is building her a cottage in which to consummate their liaison, she carves her own mediating space between her grandmother's impossible moral code, the loss of her chosen first love, Mrs. Flint's life-threatening jealousy, and Flint's utter depravity. Her subsequent course shows how her earlier advice to her brother ("We must be good") must be altered when gendered: "Slavewomen cannot expect to stay 'good,' so we must be smart."

> I was determined that the master, whom I so hated and loathed ... should not ... succeed at last in trampling his victim under his feet.... I thought and thought, till I became desperate, and made a plunge in the abyss [384].

Unwilling to be Flint's "victim," she plots another course. Her descent into darkness takes the form of accepting the advances of a prominent white man whose unimpeachable reputation and respectability forestall Flint from challenging him (or Brent). Consenting to a relationship with Sands is clearly a preemptive move on her part, painfully borne — not of a lack of moral values, but of a fierce resolve to distance herself from Flint. While far from ideal, her decision situates her, she feels, with the lesser of two evils. The vulgar (and married) Flint and the less disagreeable Sands are not, however, entirely distinguishable from one another. Both men are highly regarded members of the community, both perceive Brent as an object of sexual desire, and both first proposition her when she is yet a child. But Sands represents for Brent the critical difference between passive resignation and proactive rebellion. Accepting him, in effect, allows her to make a choice, after a fashion.

> It seems less degrading to give one's self, than to submit.... There is something akin to freedom in having a lover who has no control over you.... There may be sophistry in all this; but the condition of a slave confuses all principles of morality [385].

Indeed, there *is* a bit of sophistry in Brent's argument, but not on her main point. Parenthetically, Sands *would* have some "control over" her, simply because he is a White man and she a Black woman in slave culture. That evident truth notwithstanding, Brent has found an alternative of sorts to the "usual fate" of slave girls. Calling upon a terrible energy borne of alienation, injury, fear, and defiance in the face of hopelessness, surrendering all prospect of a virtuous life as her grandmother defines it, Brent becomes, in effect, her own mother. And for her, there is at least some consolation in self-determination. When Flint asks if she loves Sands, a much more worldly Brent, forever past the adolescent stages of innocence and guilelessness, replies coolly, "I am thankful that I do not despise him" (389). But hers is a Pyrrhic victory, one with devastating cost to the victor.

Like the Signifying Monkey, a classic trickster figure in African American lore who, lacking power, uses cunning to outwit the master, Brent's deliberate calculation reveals how she has been forced to move beyond youthful illusions. The trickster serves other important functions besides misdirection and the provision of maneuvering room. Psychologically, Brent's focus on outwitting Flint distracts *her* from the moral issues involved in her action. "I would do anything, every thing, for the sake of defeating him.... It was something to triumph over my tyrant" (352, 385). A defensive tension between anger and shame, and between personal guilt and innocence, runs deep through this section of the narrative, as though the author continues to battle the burdensome weight of her grandmother's moral code. The reader, too, is caught off guard by the narrative trickster's *legerdemain*: Brent's declaration to Flint that "in a few months I shall be a mother" is again subordinated to the exigencies of her battle of wits with Flint (386). Its very placement in the sentence signals her wish to bury, even as she announces, this fact. "As for Dr. Flint, I had a feeling of satisfaction and triumph in the thought of telling *him*" (386).

Despite an often humorous overlay or connotation, "trickeration," or trickery is an art far and above mere gamesmanship. Trickster figures, certainly during slavery, often conduct deadly serious business amidst the precarious power dynamic that they set in motion (and in imbalance). Brent's military language in these passages (e.g., "triumph," "tyrant," "defeat") underlines the gravity of the situation and recalls her earlier statement that this era marks the "war of my life." While her declarations of victory are inconsistent with her metaphor that indicates a fall from grace ("headlong plunge," "plunge into the abyss"), they are perfectly consistent with the delicate balance she maintains on the narrow mediating ledge she has managed to construct between total submission and limited self-determination.

A Plunge into the Abyss

Pregnant, frightened, and alone, Brent rushes to her grandmother for comfort. In a shocking turn, the grandmother's reaction to the girl's first pregnancy precipitates a psychological trauma whose magnitude is perceived only later. Adding to Brent's multiple losses, the normally kind-hearted grandmother rejects Linda, cruelly adding insult to injury when she initially refuses to accept the terrible coming of age that has ensnared her granddaughter.

> "O Linda! has it come to this? I had rather see you dead than to see you as you now are. You are a disgrace to your dead mother." She tore from my fingers my mother's wedding ring and her silver thimble. "Go away!" she exclaimed, "And never come to my house, again" [387].

While the banishment remains in effect for only a few days, it represents a psychological watershed in Brent's life. She has depended, with a child's trust, upon her grandmother for all her needs, including that of reassurance. And now these comforts are shockingly wrested from her by the only living person with whom she has felt completely safe. The literally and figuratively closed door, along with the grandmother's repossession of precious familial artifacts, do incalculable damage to the young girl's sense of self. The reclamation of the mother's ring symbolically tears mother from daughter once again, underlining her motherlessness. And the dispossession of this particular emblem — a wedding ring — marks the pregnant girl as unmarried, therefore immoral. In divesting Brent of her mother's symbol of morality and family and also of the grandmother's thimble — an article traditionally associated with domesticity — the grandmother severs her from the threads of female kinship and the security of domestic asylum. The grandmother's invocation of Brent's dead mother, and her incredible declaration that she would sooner see her granddaughter *dead* than pregnant, betray a mindset that contributes to Brent's later death-wishes for both herself and her children. While Brent's self-described "plunge into the abyss" involves her surrendering her virginity to Sands, I believe that her psychic plunge occurs *here*, at this moment, as her grandmother's home with its "grand, big oven" closes itself off to her at a time of critical need for comfort and sanctuary. This is, arguably, the cruelest of her maternal abandonments, in part because it is so emphatic. While Brent's grandmother is indeed a remarkable and generally loving woman, her devastating response to Brent's pregnancy is totally lacking in empathy. It also strips from Brent the only maternal understanding she could hope to have. Moreover, it aligns the grandmother with a cruel and crippling ideology of impossible virtue for slave women at this crucial moment in her granddaughter's life.

Such an extreme overreaction from Grandmother warrants closer scrutiny than has been accorded in past critical studies, especially on the psychological level. The grandmother's violent rejection and passionate refusal to understand her granddaughter's plight is a classic response to untenable circumstances and, importantly, to loathsome memories.[16] More than denial, it is complicated by the somewhat inconsistent defense of projection as well. Alternately ignoring the slaveholder's power over slave girls on the one hand, and actually, secretly, identifying with her granddaughter's plight on the other, the grandmother's profoundly conflicted mindset drives her to reject Linda out of hand in the heat of first discovery.

It would hardly be incidental to reiterate here that Brent's mother, like her father, was a mulatto. This is an important, generally overlooked point, although Brent relates it on the very first page of her narrative. It would mean

1. Linda Brent: Through a Glass, Darkly

that, by definition, the maternal grandmother's twin daughters—Brent's mother and Aunt Nancy—were fathered by a White man. This biological information, and the widespread practices of the time and of the culture, contribute powerfully to the probability that the grandmother, too, had suffered that hidden, devastating, "usual" fate of slave girls in her own youth. Brent's unfortunate experience arguably forces the grandmother to relive memories she would much rather keep deeply buried. While the grandmother's coping mechanisms protect *her* ego and self-esteem, they seriously undermine those of her granddaughter and do serious damage to the young girl's already traumatized psyche. This temporary banishment from grandmother's shelter—probably Brent's worst nightmare, worse even than the prospect of a liaison with Flint—will resonate loudly and clearly against the sanctuary of Brent's seven years in the garret.

As with her first, Brent relates the fact of her second pregnancy almost parenthetically, and again in connection with Flint's reaction: "When Dr. Flint learned that I was again to be a mother, he was exasperated beyond measure" (404). The insertion of this announcement within a subordinate clause—and the consequent shifting of focus away from her pregnancy and toward Flint's reaction—suggests that again Brent wants to suppress, even as she reveals, the fact of her condition. Though she certainly becomes a mother, her maternity does not initially reflect a desire in itself, but rather the inevitable result of her liaison with Sands. Even when she had hoped to marry her true love, Brent expressed no desire whatever to have children: "If we had children, I knew they must 'follow the condition of the mother.' What a terrible blight that would be...!" (374). Brent's pregnancies evoke deep feelings of shame, exacerbated by society's displacement of blame from the patriarch onto the slave woman. She relates, for example, that ministers who have White children outside of wedlock are typically dismissed from their position, but if the mother of such children is Black, no action is taken upon him, no stain is attached to him, and he is free to continue his spiritual work. Slavery created an economic subject whose profit rested in being *outside* the kinship system; all slave family ties and social processes were mediated by the owner.[17] Such rupture is most graphically seen in the relationships between mothers and their children.

D.W. Winnicott coined the term "good-enough mother" to characterize adequate maternal nurturing—the yardstick by which he defines acceptable and healthy behavior on the part of the mother in raising her children. Broadly stated, the good-enough mother fulfills her child's basic physical and emotional needs.[18] The problem with Winnicott's maternal ideal, as with his naïve assumption that social institutions are created by "psychiatrically healthy" individuals,[19] is that it posits a sane world and a benign external universe. And this, in a nutshell, reflects the limitations with traditional psychoanalytic theory in general with regard to any study that requires sensitivity to issues of race, gender, and other Othernesses that are impacted by societal bias. Its neglect of the crucial element of external world realities at particular moments in historical time, and the impact of those realities upon affected groups, result in a limited ability to perceive and to articulate the all-important cause-and-effect relationship at work in such situations, and, therefore, an inevitable distortion of actual psychic events.

Meillassoux's important point — that kinship ties are controlled by the slaves' external environment — invalidates virtually all the notions that define the so-called "good-enough mother." The institution of slavery, and its less devastating but severely discriminatory permutations in subsequent eras (e.g., Black Laws, Jim Crow, contemporary racial discrimination), are totally incongruous with theoretical propositions that assume the hegemony of individual will and of the family. Absent from this picture is the acknowledgment of the powerful impact of the larger society upon disenfranchised groups. In such cases, the theory is much more helpful in defining effect than it is in pinpointing cause. Winnicott situates full responsibility of parenting on the mother, but provides minimal latitude for complications that might constrain her. While he acknowledges that the best care in the world will not shield a child from hereditary disturbances, he fails to make the same claim with regard to the hazards of a prohibitive environment.[20] Notwithstanding these issues, Winnicott's theoretical base provides a conditionally coherent foundation upon which one can study the effect of Brent's limited nurturing of her children.

Keeping in mind that Brent has already established her firm aversion to having children as long as she is enslaved, she also never indicates that she would wish to have children if she were free. The children are an inevitable biological consequence of her relationship with Sands, the reason for which Brent made crystal clear: to avoid Flint. Neither immorality, sexual desire, nor the wish to have children factored into this decision. But children do come.

Brent gives birth to two children — a boy, Benny, and, not long thereafter, a girl, named Ellen. This mother at once deeply loves and sincerely regrets her children. Their existence constitutes visible signs of her degradation, irrefutable marks of her transgression, and the prospect of her children's eventual judgment against her ("My unconscious babe was the ever-present witness of my shame" [404]).

Brent's relationship to her children begins in denial and proceeds to even darker depths. The strain of mothering herself as well as her children depletes her psychic resources; anxiety leads her to indulge in fantasies about the children's deaths:

> I could never forget that [Benny] was a slave. Sometimes I wished that he might die in infancy.... Death is better than slavery [392].

> As I held [Ellen] in my arms, I thought how well it would be for her if she never waked up ... how much easier it would be to see her die [413].

Brent's language indicates that her children's non-existence would be not only easier for them, but for her as well. Her fantasy of her children's peaceful deaths primarily reflects her desire to shield them from slavery's abuses, but underlying this aim is her secret desire to keep them innocent of her shame. After the family is separated, the "death" that threatens Brent's relationship with her children is a symbolic one — and it is hers. Mrs. Flint's vengeful removal of Brent from the Flint plantation is a classic move on the part of slaveholders' jealous wives; it also, most effectively, ruptures family ties. Such separation, as Frederick Douglass declares in his own narrative, serves only to "blunt and destroy" the natural affection between mother and child.[21] When Brent — like Douglass's mother — steals home to visit her own, yet not her own, children, she finds, to her horror, that because of her absence they think her dead. When she comes into their room one night, Benny awakes. Brent whispers, "Mother is here." Benny is happy but surprised: "O mother! You ain't dead, are you?" (414).

Until this point Brent has been psychologically incapable of even considering other alternatives to slavery or death. Now, however, her painful estrangement from her children and her growing inability to accept their slave status, coupled with a rebellious spirit nurtured by Dr. and Mrs. Flint, finally provoke her to redefine her goal. Brent's death wishes give way to a growing determination to live in order to deliver her children from being "owned" by anyone: "Now I did not want to die, unless my child could die too" (391).

Brent's family boasts a proud line of freedom fighters and escapees, including her brother William and her uncle Ben. Here she calls upon her father, channeling his defiant spirit that, she feels, urges her toward freedom. Her uncle's escape, though, teaches her a critical lesson: One must choose between kinship and freedom. "As Benjamin turned away, he said, 'Phil, I part with all my kindred.' And so it proved. We never heard from him again (360). The grandmother worsens the fundamental incompatibility between freedom and kinship by using the children to hinder Brent's escape plan, which involves sending for the children later. Repeatedly declaring that a mother must never "forsake her children," the grandmother blatantly campaigns to displace Brent and insinuate herself as the mother.

> Whenever the children climbed on my knee, or laid their heads on my lap, she would say, 'Poor little souls! What would you do without a mother? She don't love you as I do.' And she would hug them to her own bosom, as if to reproach me ... [418].

Brent's ability to forge her own mediating space serves her again as she resolutely places herself in shadow, on middle ground between her and her grandmother's wishes: she leaves her children in order to stay with them. With Flint in relentless pursuit, Brent hides in plain sight, having calculated correctly that, concentrating his terrible energy on her, he would sell the children to Sands. Before ultimately escaping, Linda Brent becomes smoke, wafting between impossible choices. She lives for almost seven years in a minuscule, almost crypt-like garret at the top of her grandmother's house.

Nowhere: The Garret Years

The narrative describes the garret as nine feet long by seven feet wide, the highest part of which was, at the tip of the slope, just three feet. Before she commandeered the space as her personal hideaway, it was a haven for rats, mice, and other small creatures. Not truly fit for human habitation, it lacks both light and air. The garret is to be a mere stop-gap for Brent until she can escape north. The hazards involved in an escape attempt necessitate extremely deliberate planning. The lengthy process toward freedom in Brent's case, however, is arguably attributable more to her psychological state than to the inherent dangers of such an attempt. While her claustrophobic self-imprisonment seems fantastic on the manifest level, it is completely credible in light of Brent's tortured psychological state.

Brent writes that several escape plans never materialized, but it is also likely that she does not really *want* to leave the garret. Nor does her grandmother want her to go.

"Don't worry yourself, grandmother.... I shall get out of this dark hole some time or other."

"I hope you will, child ... but whenever you do go, it will break your old grandmother's heart" [452].

The grandmother's dexterity with mixed messages is engendered by a psychological imperative that drives her to hurt her granddaughter even as she protects her. Her concurrent affirmation and repudiation of Brent's intention, as she no doubt understands on some level, only feeds Brent's stasis.

In fact, she acts only when she overhears Flint Jr.'s vow to "break Ellen like a horse" (412), a prospect that echoes her own adolescent abuse at the hands of Flint Sr., and also one that holds an implicit sexual threat. Brent recalls the devastating experience of being psychologically "broke in" and the hopelessness that ensues. She is painfully aware that, even as the child is being beaten, the powerless mother is also being broken — on a psychological level. "The spirit of the mothers was so crushed by the lash, that they stood by, without courage to remonstrate. How much more must I suffer, before I should be 'broke in' to that degree?" (413).

Brent's loss of her biological mother, and of her other surrogate mothers, in childhood have resulted in a severe narcissistic wound and, consequently, a perpetual search for nurturing. The brief, yet traumatic, banishment from her grandmother's home has only intensified her feelings of abandonment and childlike need. Although her children's welfare and freedom are extremely important, her severely battered psyche drives personal impulses to the forefront as she seeks to return to the safety of a mother's protection. Needless to say, this protection ideally extends to calm her deep fear against further vulnerability to sexual predators. In Brent's world, an enslaved female of adolescent years or older is at constant risk. She has already profoundly compromised her moral code and sense of self, and she is afraid that even her own children will view her as an immoral woman. Is it any wonder that she would subconsciously attempt to turn back time, to try to recapture the innocence and sanctuary that once was hers?

Brent's tomblike shelter, a sphere that exists, for all practical purposes, outside of life — in essence, *nowhere* — enables Brent to mediate between a number of oppositions at the same time. The garret is unencumbered space between motherlessness and maternal nurturing. In a larger sense, it serves Brent as a sphere between freedom and slavery; childhood and adulthood; childlessness and motherhood; maternal presence and maternal absence; knowing and not-knowing; presence and absence; even life and death.

This crucial interval enables Brent to return to the security of early childhood and to remain with her children at the same time. Like the "grand big" oven, the garret represents her unconditional reinstatement in the home as beloved daughter to her (grand)mother. Significantly, although the garret is exceedingly cramped and uncomfortable, Brent characterizes her stay there as "the first time since my childhood that I had experienced any real happiness" (437). Her reference to childhood is precisely the point: The garret shelters her from adult dangers, and leaving would be tantamount to abandoning the safety of the womb. Brent regresses to a pre-sexual, infantile—even, arguably, a prenatal state, sheltered in a mother's internal embrace. Her confinement and chronic illnesses require that she be cared for, so the grandmother feeds, washes, and nurtures her as she would an infant. Brent's loss of speech, regression, and refuge into a passive position during this period suggest hysterical reaction, likely generated by deeply repressed mourning for her biological mother.[22]

Brent's relationship to her children during the garret interval is profoundly compromised but not nonexistent; it is like the perspective afforded by looking through one-way glass. A tiny gimlet, which admits a trifle of light and air, allows Brent to see and hear the children when they come into view. But between mother and children there is no sharing, no touching, no apparent knowledge on the children's part that she is there. More to the point, Brent observes, rather than participates in, their lives. She is conscious of her children but, as she had earlier wished during death-fantasies, they are unconscious of her.

This lack of reciprocity means that she cannot provide positive mirroring to her children. Even more hazardous are the psychic implications of their lack of preparation for the outside world. Winnicott posits that primarily through early nurturing and teaching, a child begins to build up a "continuity of being," or a secure sense of self. "If maternal care is not good enough," he warns, "then the infant *does not really come into existence*"[23] [emphasis mine]. The rupture of the all-important "continuity of care," like the continuity of being, that establishes and affirms the parent/child bond is highly significant in shaping Brent's children's development and relationship to their mother.[24] Brent and her children represent a transgenerational cycle of virtually self-perpetuating maternal inadequacy. In a sense, because of deficient nurturing extended to Brent when she was herself a child, a part of her has not yet come into existence. This theory is played out by Brent as she remains in the garret, giving, in essence, birth to her own self.

But the maternal consequences of her continued concealment and absence are considerable. For one, her children's memories of her are waning. On one occasion, when her grandmother brings the children within hearing distance for Brent's benefit, she hears her daughter and son express the desire to go find her mother and live with her. But the situation has been complicated by the passage of time. Ellen wonders aloud just how this might be accomplished, when "I don't remember how mother looked — do you, Benny?" (454). Unseen and almost unremembered, Brent is becoming a stranger to her children. As long as she remains a child, she cannot mother them. By relinquishing her maternal role, Brent requires her children to grow up without her.

The grossly inadequate nurturing that Brent has been able to provide (painstakingly sewing Christmas presents for them, for example) compromises crucial elements of her children's upbringing, including a dependable and affirming maternal presence, freedom from the fear of abandonment, positive mirroring, the construction of a sound racial identity, and a secure sense of self. Benny's expressed but unwitting confusion about his maternity, as he shares his fears with Aunt Nancy, mirrors some of this deficiency: "The speculator is going to take me and Ellen away. He's a bad man. It's wrong for him to take grandmother's children. I want to go to my mother" (430). Benny's poignant misstatement ("grandmother's children") effectively neutralizes Brent's status as his mother.

Similarly, his unformed racial identity — the silence, confusion, and mystery surrounding his heritage, prefigured in childhood — inflicts a narcissistic injury which will torment him in later life.[25] An unforgettable experience ironically involves his biological, but unacknowledged, father when Mr. Sands and his wife encounter Benny while walking along the road. Mrs. Sands sees the boy and comments, "What a pretty little negro!" Brent does not disclose whether Mrs. Sands is being disingenuous, or whether she is merely asking an innocent question when she follows up with, "Whom does he belong to?" (457). Benny comes home very upset at having been called a "negro." Whether or not by design, Brent fails to educate her children about matters of race. She gives no indication, for example, that she ever explained to Benny what it means to be a Negro or why the lady had called him one. Her reticence, compounded — and no doubt, triggered — by society's prejudices, gives Brent's children no means of building a sense of respect for, or pride in, their African ancestry.

After coming to live with Brent in the North, both Benny and Ellen are perceived as white in their respective spheres of work and school. Brent relates that their parentage, "never before suspected," is discovered inadvertently, confirming that she is complicit in her children's passing as White. Brent supports her children's deception simply because being perceived as White offers so much more opportunity and is a much less risky proposition than being seen as Black. Of her uncle Benjamin's escape attempt years before, Brent notes:

> For once his white face did him a kindly service. [The whites] had no suspicion that it belonged to a slave; otherwise, the law would have been followed out to the letter, and the *thing* rendered back to slavery [359].

Brent does not want her children to be *things*. Unlike her, visibly "tinged with the blood of Africa" (491), they can live secure lives as white people. But more than this, Brent's silence to her children on this issue suggests that she might be paying some sort of penance, or compensation, in allowing them to deny their Africanness and, by extension, their mother, in order to live as free people.

The effect of Brent's exposure as a fugitive slave is quite different for Benny than for Ellen. While Ellen's boarding school friends sympathize with her and the administration supports her continuing education there both financially and socially, Benny's co-workers on the dock do not respond with such kindness. Benny had initially been popular among his apprentice peers, but when they stumble upon the well-kept secret of his ancestry, their behavior toward him immediately becomes mocking and persecutory, driving him to ship out to sea. "This at once transformed him into a different being.... He was too spirited a boy to stand that" (499). Benny's "transformation" is both internal and external. His peers' derision deals a serious blow to his sense of self. Willful suppression of his heritage reflects an unrealistic self-perception, as when he had bristled at being called a Negro as a boy. Denial of his Negro blood is tantamount to a denial of his mother, and his abrupt departure from New York, once exposed, suggests a bitter response to his environment and a need to distance himself from her.[26]

"Weary of Flying"

Despite his promise, Sands does not free his and Brent's children while Brent is in the garret. His behavior is not so much malicious as it is the result

1. Linda Brent: Through a Glass, Darkly

of the corruption and incredible sense of entitlement that slavery promotes among the ruling class to the extent that the condition of slaves — even of his own children — is simply not a very important issue. When, for example, Brent's brother William seizes the opportunity to escape from him, Sands's surprise and irritation reveal an astounding disregard for William's (or any slave's) humanity, the cutting irony of his own words completely lost on him: "I trusted him as if he were my own brother, and treated him as kindly.... I intended to give him his freedom in five years. He might have trusted me" (456).

Sands's failure to act on behalf of the children forces Brent to accept that she alone will have to secure their freedom. Clearly, this struggle cannot take place in her grandmother's garret, nor any place else in the South. Meanwhile, Benny and Ellen have assumed a very adult — not to say parental — role toward her throughout her concealment. Having eventually become aware of her presence, they have protected her secret despite continued pressure to reveal her whereabouts. Their pretense of being unaware of her whereabouts suggests phenomenal equanimity and poise. It also indicates that the children have learned to live without their mother. An unexpectedly selfless act on the part of her grandmother finally evicts Brent from the garret. Even as the grandmother begs Linda not to carry out her escape plan, she actively propels her granddaughter out of the nest.

> I found her in a nervous, excited state ... she had forgotten to lock the door behind her.... In her agitation [she] opened the door, without thinking of me. In stepped Jenny, the mischievous housemaid.... "Poor child!" [grandmother] exclaimed, "My carelessness has ruined you. The boat ain't gone yet. Get ready immediately, and go" [471].

In fact, the grandmother *is* "thinking of" Brent: escape from slavery cannot be accomplished until Brent leaves her hiding-place. Operative words such as "nervous," "excited," "forgotten," "without thinking," and "careless" imply that a deliberate act is taking place in the guise of a blunder. Exposing Brent's hiding-place is hardly believable behavior from a woman who has so conscientiously guarded Brent all those years. With this loving deceit, the grandmother's parapraxis ultimately puts to rest her conflicting impulses and redeems her earlier possessiveness.

Brent's narrative resonates with Ralph Ellison's in the imagery, and intent, of her "dismal hole," characterized as a "dark hole" in *The Invisible Man*. Ellison's hero refers to his underground period as hibernation, "a covert preparation for a more overt action."[27] By the epilogue, the narrator has decided that "The hibernation is over. I must shake off the old skin and come up for breath.... In going underground, I whipped it all except the mind, the mind."[28] Similarly, it is time for Brent to emerge. She, too, has "whipped it all except the mind." But the psychological forces that have kept her immobile have yet to be reconciled. Brent's shame, fears, and sense of loss must be confronted even after she leaves her secure hiding-place.

Epilogue: "Mother Is Here"

Following her escape north, Brent secures employment with the Bruce family. After Mrs. Bruce dies, Mr. Bruce remarries. The Mrs. Bruces are the first White women Brent has known who actually embody *her* ideal of True Womanhood. Both are gentle yet strong, noble women, fiercely opposed to the oppression of any human being. The first Mrs. Bruce actually "gives" Brent her baby to take into hiding with her, as insurance against Brent's deportation without a hearing, through the Fugitive Slave Law. The second Mrs. Bruce also speaks and acts directly against her husband's less enlightened point of view. When he argues against harboring a fugitive slave, Mrs. Bruce forcefully replies, "Shame on my country.... I will go to the state's prison, rather than have any poor victim torn from my house, to be carried back to slavery" (506). Brent maintains throughout that the reunion of her family is her strongest desire. Her fervent prayers are centered on having her children back home with her; her life is "bound up in my children" (426). Yet when the first Mrs. Bruce dies, Brent leaves her children, whom she has succeeded in bringing north, to accompany Mr. Bruce and baby Mary to England for several months. After all her efforts to establish a home for her children, her return to baby Mary Bruce seems, at first glance, incongruous with her stated desires:

> The little motherless one was accustomed to me, and attached to me, and I thought she would be happier in my care than in that of a stranger.... So I put Benny to a trade, and left Ellen to remain in the house with my friend [496].

What emerges on closer examination is a picture of a woman who embraces the attachment of another woman's child because she is already estranged from her own children. Whatever the depth of their understanding, neither Benny nor Ellen could have escaped some feeling of abandonment during

1. Linda Brent: Through a Glass, Darkly

Brent's lengthy absence when they were children. Though Brent has "longed to be entirely free to act a mother's part towards my children," the dream of a united family has eluded them. Even with physical freedom, the psychological damage to the family structure is too deep to allow her wish.

Brent retains a bond — perhaps more sisterly than parental — with her daughter Ellen that she has been unable to sustain with her son. The mother relates her profound need for absolution from the individual in whose image she sees her younger self. In fact, the only forgiveness that Brent ever personally seeks is Ellen's. Her fears evaporate when Ellen responds to Brent's tortured confession of her earlier years. "O don't mother! ... I know all about it.... I never think any thing about my father. All my love is for you" (500).

With her daughter's approbation, and her son's subsequent move to California with his uncle William, Brent attempts to reconcile herself to the disconnected state of her family. She communicates with Ellen, but Benny seems indisposed to maintain family (or at least racial) ties with his mother. Because his mixed racial heritage was never affirmed within the family, his perception of Blackness has been formed by the external world. Consequently, his mother is a part of the racial world that he rejects. Further, her earlier disappearance from his life has apparently transformed his youthful equanimity into feelings of betrayal and resentment in adulthood. At the end of the narrative Brent considers her maternal loss: "The dream of my life is not yet realized. I do not sit with my children in a home of my own" [513].

Brent's mothering, like her life, is circumscribed by an insupportable social system. In spite of this, Brent never truly abandons her children. Rather, her absent mothering, regression to childhood, and complicity with her children's denial of their African blood all point to a denial of her own self and body. Baby Mary symbolizes Brent's immaculate conception — untainted by sexuality, immorality, or mixed blood — so that Brent is free to love her with no sense of shame.

> I loved Mrs. Bruce's babe.... It made me think of the time when Benny and Ellen were babies [486].
>
> I was very desirous that my dear Mary should steer straight [497].

The possessive shift from "Mrs. Bruce's baby" to "my dear Mary" reveals Brent's desire to assume the role of mother to Mary Bruce. The distant dream of Benny and Ellen in her arms is actualized by the reality of Mary in her embrace. The death of the first Mrs. Bruce allows her to *be* Mary's mother. In England, where, for the first time Brent feels free from racial discrimination, with baby Mary in her arms and Mr. Bruce by her side, Brent stands inside a portrait that represents the familial ideal that she has been denied throughout life: mother and wife with child and husband, accorded all the freedom, legitimacy, and respectability that accompanies Whiteness. Brent's final space is not the dream she wished for, but it is an enclosed situation that provides security and comfort, unencumbered by racial prejudice or sexual danger. She shares her space at the end of the novel not with her children, but with a decent man who makes no demands upon her, a female employer she can trust, and, most importantly, a beloved child who gives her guileless, uncomplicated love.

It is surely by design that Brent reserves her final thoughts for her grandmother. Just as she has received redemption from daughter Ellen, Brent in turn absolves her grandmother, honoring the unstinting love and devotion that overwhelm her grandmother's shortcomings which must be considered within the framework of the external world in which she lived. In these final paragraphs Brent exhibits both a deeper understanding of the older woman's heroic nature and an integrated, restored vision of "her" grandmother, no longer distanced by the impersonal "the" that she had used to characterize the older woman earlier in the narrative. Brent's last lines express a benediction of sorts — both to, and from, her grandmother. Amid more weighty recollections are "tender memories of my good old grandmother, like light, fleecy clouds floating over a dark and troubled sea" (513).

Brent's wish to live with her children will likely remain unfulfilled. But despite a life circumscribed by an unconscionable social system, she never truly succumbs to its imperatives. Time and again she conjures up avenues of possibility from impossible circumstances: without a mother, she locates maternal figures; forced to relinquish her chastity, she reconstructs virtue on her own terms; torn between heaven and hell, she secures a place in purgatory. Most importantly, she has kept her children protected and nurtured, even when she herself was psychologically unable to tend to their needs.

Although she always insured that they were protected, Brent's maternal method had been suffused with "middle ground": she had neither nurtured her children with dependable consistency, taught them moral values, nor instilled in them racial knowledge or pride. Her determination, however, to liberate Benny and Ellen from slavery was unequivocal. This single, momentous accomplishment, due solely to Brent's perseverance and profound maternal love, is an extraordinary achievement. Winnicott theorizes that a devoted mother is a good-enough mother,[29] and Brent's devotion has never been in question. Notwithstanding all the other preconditions of adequate mothering that Brent has not met, if her efforts are not good enough, then what *is*? A mother whose children are born into slavery can give them nothing more precious than freedom.

Chapter 2

Sappho Clark: Double Exposure

Sappho Clark has two separate identities: she is a proper single young woman who lives a quiet life; she is also the severely traumatized Mabelle Beaubean. Mabelle no longer exists, and Sappho is adamant about keeping her past buried; her greatest fear is that it will be exposed. Consequently, neither woman is in any position to raise the child that was created in the wake of Mabelle's ordeal. Melanie Klein's theories on a divided self help structure the form and contours of this portrait.

Pauline Hopkins's *Contending Forces*[1] explores both the inexorable reality of racial oppression in the post–Reconstruction era and the restrictive gender roles that, particularly for Black women, inhibit personal fulfillment. A careful reading of central female figures—Grace Montfort, Mrs. ("Ma") Smith, and, especially, Sappho Clark—uncovers Hopkins's perspective on models of behavior ("how to" and "how *not* to"), especially in the areas of marriage and motherhood. Together, these women convey the author's vision of female empowerment in turn-of-the-century America. While critics have criticized Hopkins for promoting traditional (and restrictive) "True Womanhood" values,[2] I suggest that Hopkins wrote with her 1900 audience clearly in mind and was careful not to alienate that audience. Thus, her gender critiques are often subtle and muted. The important point, however, is that they are there.

Besides harsh critical judgment for its alleged equivocation on matters of gender and race, there is also the matter of the novel's unlikely and melodramatic plot twists.[3] *Contending Forces* provides its share of damsels in distress, tearful separations, and fortuitous reunions, but it is, after all, a romance, as its subtitle (*A Romance Illustrative of Negro Life North and South*) notes. My sense of the novel is that despite odd, awkward, and contradictory moments, its passionate insights, deliberate characterizations, and rhetorical technique compel the reader's interest in both its private sphere and also the larger sociopolitical perspective through which Hopkins intended her novel to be read.

The contending forces to which the title alludes are the broad cultural patterns that impede Black liberation, particularly Black female self-determination. Briefly, the novel recounts the story of Sappho Clark, a Southern mulatto, who comes to Boston and takes a room in a boarding-house run by Mrs. Smith and her children, Dora and Will. Having attracted the attentions of both Will Smith and Dora's fiancé, John Pollock Langley, Sappho represses feelings for Will because she hides a shameful secret: The child she conceived through a vicious rape by her White uncle and his accomplices. Langley discovers Sappho's past and threatens to expose her unless she submits to his sexual advances. Sappho flees with her son Alphonse to the New Orleans convent where he had been born nine years earlier and obtains a position as governess in the home of Monsieur Louis, a kindly older gentleman. After three years, she hesitantly considers M. Louis's proposal of marriage. Meanwhile, Dora and her childhood friend, Dr. Arthur Lewis, marry and move to New Orleans. Will, who has never stopped searching for Sappho, encounters her in the New Orleans convent. He affirms his love for her and her child, and they are happily married.

The Mothers: Grace, Ma Smith, and Sapppho

The three pivotal maternal characters in the novel depict three distinct approaches to mothering, all complicated by issues of race and gender. Two of the mothers are separated from their progeny through circumstances rooted in racial and sexual abuse. At least two (and possibly all three) are of mixed racial heritage. The first and second mothers, Grace Montfort and Mrs. Smith, appear, at first glance, to epitomize good-enough mothering, but closer analysis uncovers important mothering issues. The third woman's maternal story is rooted in trauma, absence, and denial. The psychic structure and development of this central figure, Sappho Clark, is informed in large part by Melanie Klein's psychoanalytic theories.

The history of the first mother frames the central narrative. Situated outside the central plot, Grace Montfort is a fragile, ethereal figure who functions mainly on the level of allegory. Beautiful, refined, and elegant, as her name implies, she is a loving and attentive wife to Charles, a Bermudan slave owner, and mother to the two Montfort sons, Charles and Jesse. Although island life is idyllic, the acquisitive, pro-slavery Charles, Sr. relocates his family and estate to the southern United States to avoid the "gradual emancipation" movement that threatens British slave policy in Bermuda.

Removed from her neighbors by her newcomer status and European education, Grace fails to develop close acquaintances during the Montforts' three-year stay in North Carolina. She claims one true friend, her "foster sister" Lucy, but her idealization of this relationship underlines the myth of the extended "family" in slave culture. "Their relations had always been those of inseparable friends rather than of mistress and slave.... To Lucy her mistress was always 'Miss Grace'" (46). Lifelong exposure to a system based upon racial hegemony has blinded Grace to the inherent inequality embodied in her friendship with Lucy. Even the narrative refers to the Black woman by her first name only, but to Grace by her surname. Grace does not note the lack of reciprocity involved in their roles — Lucy does "Miss Grace's" bidding; Grace does *not* do Lucy's — or that such imbalance is anathema to true friendship. And although her marriage is apparently solid, Grace is very much a woman of her time. She epitomizes True Womanhood values, deferring to her husband in all matters, including the family's relocation, which she bitterly regrets. Mistress of her home, she has little contact with the outside world. She mothers her boys with deep affection in tranquil times, but when tragedy strikes she is unable to function on their (or on her own) behalf.

Ironically, although Charles has come to the United States in order to keep his slaves, his British roots label him a traitor to the institution of slavery in his more conservative new country. Montfort's neighbor Anson Pollock spreads the rumor that Grace Montfort is tainted with Negro blood, and Pollock's personal agenda — to acquire Montfort's wealth and wife — is advanced by other White Southerners who embrace the rumor because of Charles's perceived liberalism, blurring their identities in the process. *Charles*, not Grace, is referred to as "a d— West Injy half–White nigger" (61). One of Pollock's hired men supports suspicions about Grace with what he considers incontrovertible political, as well as physical, "evidence":

> "That's too much cream color in the face and too little blud seen under the skin fer a genooine White 'ooman. You can't tell nothin' 'bout these Britishers; they're allers squeamish 'bout thar nigger brats.... I've hern tell that they think nuthin of ejcatin' thar Black brats, and freein' 'em, an' makin' 'em rich" [41].

Grace's isolation renders her ignorant of negative forces breeding around her. Unsupported by friends or community, she is unprepared to withstand the conflict when it erupts. In the end, Pollock kills Charles, plunders and destroys his estate, then tries to force Grace into submission by whipping her with the lash he usually reserves for his slaves.

Grace's abuse illustrates how race functions as a sociopolitical construct and symbolizes the rape of Black women as a terrorist political device in the service of racial dominance, and the distinctly gendered counterpart to lynching.[4] The fact that none of the visible signs of Grace's breeding — or, for that matter, of her Whiteness — protect her once she is suspected of having mixed blood, underlines the intense racial paranoia of American slave culture. The reader never learns the truth about Grace's racial heritage, because the truth is irrelevant. Once Grace is reduced, by perception alone, from the ruling to the slave class, the Montfort family is easily ruined. Pollock kills Charles, burns their home, and abducts Grace along with her two children and Lucy. Grace Montfort is never seen again, but "the waters of Pamlico Sound tell of sweet oblivion for the brokenhearted found within their soft embrace" (70–71). Under threat of sexual, physical, and psychological violence, Grace commits suicide. By this desperate act, she also abandons her children, obliterates their past, and compromises their future. Through mere whispers that she is Black, the Montforts succinctly represent the very real threat to the African American family during slavery: the father is violently killed, the mother is sexually abused, and the children are forsaken.

Lucy, Grace's so-called foster sister and slave, is forced into surrogacy on Grace's behalf from this moment on — not only as unwilling mistress to Pollock, but also as mother to Grace's children. The pattern of estrangement, privation, and sorrow caused by the loss of "grace" inflicts narcissistic injuries that the Montfort sons never overcome. Charles is "a helpless invalid until his death," and Jesse's life is "but a path of sorrow to the grave" (378, 384). The Montfort sons, with no actual proof of their racial heritage, eventually choose their respective racial affiliations — one White, one Black — an act that, certainly in Jesse's case, ultimately cements the (White?) Montfort ties to the (Black) Smith family of a later era: Mrs. Smith is Jesse's child.

Ma Smith

Two generations and a thousand miles hence, Mrs. Smith runs the family boarding-house in 1896 Boston. The Montfort history intersects with the

Smiths' at the end of the novel, but even now, the full names of Mrs. Smith's children — Dora Grace Montfort Smith and William Jesse Montfort Smith — signal a connection between the two families. Throughout the novel Mrs. Smith relates her sketchy family history to the children in almost ritualistic fashion. Sparse as it is, this retelling captures two themes that resonate through African American literature: the inescapable weight of the past upon the present, and the necessary self-knowledge and grounding that storytelling and history — especially, personal and family history — provide.

A widow, Mrs. Smith lives an active and apparently fulfilling life based upon family and community. Affectionately called "Ma" Smith by most because of her warm and nurturing nature, she is active in church and women's groups. Ma Smith is a much more socially integrated individual and successful parent than Grace Montfort. Yet her character — despite (or perhaps, *because* of) otherwise sterling qualities — emphasizes that uncritical acceptance of traditional White societal values is neither necessarily healthy nor conducive to equally good mothering to her two children. Specifically, Mrs. Smith's values profoundly diminish her daughter Dora's sense of self and life options.

Curiously, although Mrs. Smith is friendly with a great many people, she does not appear to have personal friends. Mrs. Smith is characterized by Claudia Tate as "the ideal maternal figure."[5] Together, the Smiths present a picture of a loving, close-knit clan: "The little family always managed to have an inviting tea and to pass a cheerful evening together.... Even in palatial homes a more inviting nest could not be found" (88). The extent of that closeness, however — particularly with Dora — is problematic. Her relationship with her children is, on the one hand, commendable, but on the other hand, carried to the extreme and combined with the exclusion of other adult friendships, it threatens to intensify Mrs. Smith's dependence upon them and her need to hold onto them. Before Sappho appears, Mrs. Smith is apparently her daughter's only confidant. Dora is oddly distant with the other "girls in [her] set," finding a perverse pleasure in having "stolen" the devilishly handsome John Pollock Langley from under their noses:

> "I must say that I feel real *comfortable* to spoil sport by walking off with him just when they think they've got things running as they wish. Yes, it's real *comfortable* to know that they're all as jealous as can be" [122].

Narrative repetition and italicization of the word "comfortable" underscore the notion that true friendship is compromised when one party is comfortable with the other's discomfort. Schooled *by* her mother, Dora seems to feel that she needs no friend other *than* her mother. Privately, Dora is mildly unhappy with her engagement and deeply frustrated by an undefined restlessness. Placid outside, on the inside Dora is beginning to discern the restrictions of her circumscribed existence. While Will is presented as a remarkably self-assured young man, similar initial impressions of Dora gradually give way to the more accurate picture of an insecure young woman plagued with internal conflict.

Another family scene indicates that Mrs. Smith is extremely comfortable with Will's single, live-at-home status: "Mother and son settled down to the enjoyment of a quiet evening together" (96). Though hardly the stuff of Oedipal fantasies, this cozy image *does* suggest the possibility that Mrs. Smith might feel that her son's rightful place is by her side. Dora shares a room with her mother, and is thus ironically deprived of her small sphere of privacy in an establishment — their boarding-house — designed to provide just that. Certainly, most parents would wish to keep their children close to hearth and home; but it could be argued that Mrs. Smith keeps her son and daughter a little *too* close.

Mrs. Smith has apparently raised her children in an abundance of love, security, and enduring values. But deft turns of phrase and brief illuminating sketches tacitly critique the accepted practice of gendered child-rearing. The daughter's upbringing has been defined by traditional gender roles that restrict Dora to the realm of passive domesticity and conjugality, while the son enjoys a great deal of mobility in the public sphere. Will works outside the home and is preparing for graduate studies abroad, but Dora's formal education ended after high school and her work is conducted inside the home. Although she has developed management skills under her mother's guidance in the running of the boarding-house, one could say that while Will is a man of the world, Dora is a lady of the house. Dora's limited options might account in some way for her dispassionate feelings about marriage and her undefined restlessness.

Mrs. Smith has been an unwitting conspirator in Dora's feelings of inadequacy. Her subtle deployment of the verb "to lose" offers a veiled but pointed comment on her conventional and distinctly gendered thoughts about marriage:

> Could it be possible that she was about to *lose* her son? ... She ... tried to imagine what it would be to have another share the love and reverence of the idolized son. At first it seemed that she could not endure the thought [175, 177, italics mine].

> The only cause for a mother to grieve in the idea of marriage for her daughter was the awful chance of that daughter's remaining single. The girl's life should be *lost* in that of the wife and mother. Such an end to maidenhood was a happy achievement for the girl and a glory to her family. But with her boy it was different [176, italics mine].

The profound disparity in Mrs. Smith's words is lost on her. A son is idolized in and of himself, but a daughter is regarded as having come into her own only if and when she marries. Mrs. Smith's belief that "the girl's life should be *lost* in that of the wife and mother" while "with her boy it was different" underlines the fluidity of the perception, as well as the object, of "loss" by traditional standards: A woman should subsume her identity within marriage for the universal good, but the marriage of a son constitutes a painful loss to his mother. Dora's demonstrably inadequate sense of self invites an exploration of what there might be in Mrs. Smith's maternal nature that has *not* been good enough to provide her daughter, as opposed to her son, with a healthy ego.

Will is subject to his mother's gender-role imposition in only one particular area where he is not encouraged to flourish, i.e., his love of another woman.

> "Your boy is very happy. Will you have Sappho for a second daughter?"
> "Gladly, my son," replied his mother; and then she sank upon a chair, overcome as she comprehended the full meaning of his words.... "Oh, Will, my boy, you will not let this new love cause you to forget the love of your old mother?" [325].

Her melodramatic collapse upon the chair and verbal response to his news could hardly be the gracious, motherly response he would wish for. "Your boy," "my son," "my boy," terms used by both Will and Mrs. Smith, belie Will's maturity and his imminent defection from his mother's home, and falsely convey the idea that he is but an adolescent, too young to marry. Most importantly, Mrs. Smith's mixed message sets up a conflict that need not exist, i.e., the presumption that a man's love for his wife and love for his mother might be mutually exclusive emotions. The mother's artful characterization of Sappho as the "new" love, and herself ("your old mother") as the giver of eternal, permanent love, reduces the fiancée even as it elevates the mother, with the apparent intent to undermine his decision to marry.

The discrepancy between Mrs. Smith's views on her son's, as opposed to her daughter's, impending marriage reveals a distinct partiality and def-

2. Sappho Clark: Double Exposure

erence to men. Her passion places Will's marriage almost on par with his death. Her initial inability to "endure" the thought of her son's marriage indicates an excessive, even smothering maternal devotion that, for better or for worse, does not extend to Dora. Mrs. Smith's contradictory behavior toward her male, as opposed to her female, child exposes her valuation of men and, by extension, her unconscious devaluation of women. Although Dora is certainly well loved, there is no evidence that she is idolized or revered by her mother; nor does Mrs. Smith agonize over Dora's marriage as she does her son's. Langley is known to be something of a scoundrel, and even Will is concerned about Dora's engagement ("Dora and John worry me ... I fear that there is trouble ahead for my little sister if she marries him" (208).) Yet Mrs. Smith is simply content that her daughter will soon "lose" herself in marriage. Worse, Dora *understands* this disparity. She knows that "her mother had always felt that no woman could be good enough for Will's wife" (178), even though Mrs. Smith is satisfied that the somewhat disreputable Langley is apparently good enough for Dora. Small wonder that every now and again, under the guise of daughterly concern, Dora deliberately stokes her mother's anxiety about "losing" her son: "Mummy, dear," she said, "you have made up your mind to give him up to Sappho if things turn out that way?" (178). Her clever wording does not completely mask a bitterness that Mrs. Smith does not even begin to perceive. Mrs. Smith's portrayal of Dora ("It was not like Dora to be petulant and have moods. She was a happy, healthy, active girl, with a kindly disposition" [179]) indicates that, protestations to the contrary, she does not truly know her daughter's inner self.

Mrs. Smith's partiality to Will contributes to Dora's feelings of insecurity and envy that eventually draw Dora to Sappho Clark. Her fascination with and idealization of Sappho are arguably based upon the perception that Sappho lives the life that Dora *wants* to live — outside of tradition, her own woman, in control. In this sense, both Will and Sappho serve as exemplars for Dora: neither is tied to the passive, domestic role to which Dora sees herself bound. While racial prejudice is a visible challenge in Mrs. Smith's life, she seems completely unaware of the gender bias that defines her society, or the fact that she participates in its perpetuation. A nearly ideal mother, her uncritical acceptance of society's gender-based parenting practices are especially stultifying for her already racially-disempowered girl-child.

Sappho Clark, née Mabelle Beaubean

> Evening star, you bring all things
> Which the bright dawn has scattered:
> You bring the sheep, you bring the goat,
> You bring the child back to its mother.—Sappho, *Fragment 120*

The last line of this poem by the sixth-century poet Sappho mirrors the greatest challenge facing her namesake, Sappho Clark, in the novel: to be reunited with her child—not physically, but on the emotional and psychological levels. The most broadly drawn character in Hopkins's novel, Sappho is also the most impenetrable, representing internal "contending forces" more dramatically than any other character; the narrative alternately characterizes her as "sad," "lonely [and] self-suppressed" (89, 114), and "naturally buoyant and bright" (111). Neither her true identity, nor her maternity, are disclosed until the latter half of the novel.

Sappho's life intersects with the Smith family when she takes a room in their Boston boarding-house. A stenographer, she chooses to bring work home rather than "pass" for White in the segregated office that supplies her assignments. In view of her classic Anglo-American features, only Sappho's proud affirmation of her African American heritage proclaims her mixed racial profile:

> Tall and fair, with hair of a golden cast, aquiline nose, rosebud mouth, soft brown eyes veiled by long, dark lashes which swept her cheek ... covered with a delicate rose flush [107)].

"That's somethin' God made, honey; thar ain't nothin' like that growed outside o' Loosyannie," Sarah Ann Davis says to Ophelia White, alluding to the preponderance of race-mixing that characterizes the citizenry of New Orleans. When Sappho acknowledges that her mother was born there, Mrs. White responds, "I knowed it. Ol' New Orleans blood will tell on itself anywhere" (108). Indeed, Sappho's blood—or rather, the secret *issue* of her blood—does eventually "tell on itself," despite her most rigorous efforts to conceal her unwanted maternity.

The most crucial aspect of Sappho's psychic organization is that she possesses two entirely distinct identities. The story of Mabelle Beaubean, Sappho's former self, eventually is unfolded to readers (and to an audience of townspeople) by Luke Sawyer, a man who loved her and presumes her dead.

2. Sappho Clark: Double Exposure

According to Sawyer, Sappho was fourteen when Monsieur Beaubean's White half-brother killed her father, burned their home, abducted and sexually abused her, and abandoned her in a New Orleans brothel. Luke relates that he found her three weeks later—"a poor, ruined, half-crazed creature" (260)—and hid her in the colored convent in New Orleans, where she later gave birth to a child before dying.

In a sense, Luke Sawyer is right: The devastating assault that Mabelle's ego sustained through the multiple rapes and the birth of her child brought about Mabelle's psychological death and Sappho Clark's genesis. In her Aunt Sally's words, Mabelle Beaubean was a pitiable, victimized adolescent. Conversely, Sappho Clark, *no* one's victim, projects only exceptional self-possession, physical and spiritual purity, and—with men—unapproachability. Apparently indifferent to romance and family life, she maintains absolute control over her emotions, and as much control over her environment as possible.

In classic psychological response to her ordeal as young Mabelle, Sappho has unconsciously translated the tragedy of her past, over which she had no control, into guilt and self-loathing. These impulses stand at odds with the conviction, which she desperately wants to embrace, that she did nothing wrong. "'Why,' she asks herself, 'why should I always walk in the shadow of a crime for which I am in no way to blame?'" (205). Despite an intellectual understanding of her innocence, Sappho is only able to divorce herself from Mabelle's shame by divorcing herself from Mabelle—and, consequently, from Mabelle's child.

The key to Sappho's dual personality is articulated through the Kleinian phenomenon known as "splitting." Melanie Klein's groundbreaking psychological theories, largely developed between the 1920s and 1950s, focus primarily on early childhood development, but provide a sound basis for exploration into the psychic life of adults as well. Grounded in Freudian theory, but moving beyond its confines, Klein developed new insights. Freud's "stages" (oral, Oedipal, etc.) are "positions" to Klein; they are less rigid and are at work within the individual much earlier than Freud's formations, being more structural than developmental. Klein overcomes the Freudian bias of "envy" as a gendered function (i.e., women's so-called "penis envy") and appropriately elevates it to the universal realm. For Klein, envy is simply the result, in both males and females, of a lack of good "splitting." Splitting is an ego defense mechanism against severe trauma in a child or an adult from either the internal or the external realm.[6] Specifically, Klein defines splitting as "the process by which a deeply hated and despised part of the personality is split off."[7] It is typically characterized by an individual's privileging desired attributes and rejecting undesired ones. Splitting can perform invaluable short-term service for the devalued and/or threatened ego. Ultimately, however, healthy psychic development depends upon the ego's ability to reconcile its split selves in order to achieve ego integration and reparation. Klein's splitting theory describes precisely the transformation of Mabelle Beaubean into Sappho Clark.

The divided self, a classic trope in African American culture, is eloquently described as double consciousness by W.E.B. DuBois in *The Souls of Black Folk*:

> The Negro is a sort of seventh son, born with a veil, and gifted with second-sight in this American world,—a world which yields him no true self-consciousness, but only lets him see himself through the revelation of the other world. It is a peculiar sensation, this double-consciousness....[8]

Although DuBois's expression refers to the consequence of being viewed negatively by others and is not precisely parallel to Klein's "splitting," the latter is a corollary to the former. Thomas Otten's analysis of the aspect of double-consciousness bridges the distance between the sociology of double consciousness and the psychology of splitting:

> The split [in double consciousness] is both physiological and psychological; the task ... is to point the way toward a cure for this withering divide, a cure in which double selves will 'merge' into a better and truer self.[9]

It is certainly true that the chaste, childless, aloof Sappho Clark emerges as a direct result of Mabelle's sure knowledge that Black single motherhood is an acutely unacceptable state in both her internal (psychic) and her external (societal) world.

It is one thing to deny a part of oneself; quite another to obliterate an entire persona. As such, Sappho's divided self is even more literal than the psychic split that Klein describes. Sappho buries the trauma that Mabelle suffered by splitting to the ultimate degree: "killing off" her former self and assuming a new identity.[10] Sappho "never spoke of her early life" (127), not only because of her secretive nature, but because she *has* no early life of which to speak. Mabelle's "death" and Sappho's "birth" present an obvious dilemma with regard to Mabelle's child: Since Mabelle is dead, and Sappho does not have a child, then *who* is Alphonse's mother?

This question further presses the maternal issues that are introduced with Grace Montfort's abandonment of her children when she committed suicide. Even dire circumstances must not prevent care and nurturing of children; also, African American children must be allowed access to their familial pasts — including the tragedies — if they are to come to terms with their present. Further, they must develop a secure sense of self in order to realize their full potential. As these and other tools are generally provided by a nurturing parent, it follows that the psychological health of the mother is crucial to the subsequent development of the child.

Sappho's maternal course over a period of a few years is traceable, in Kleinian terms, along a classic developmental path. Klein identifies two "positions" that develop early in individual life — the *paranoid-schizoid* and the *depressive* positions.[11] Because they both remain an ongoing part of the personality to varying degrees, it is the extent to which an individual adopts these postures that determines whether or not pathology is present. The paranoid-schizoid position is a defensive response to persecution anxiety, and it is in this position that splitting occurs. Sappho "begins" her life in a state of almost complete dissociation from her past — and from her child. Her rigid control, her wariness of men, and her lack of spontaneity are all symptomatic of the resoluteness of Sappho's denial of Mabelle.[12] Her need to disclaim the traumatized part of herself is an understandable but ultimately damaging mindset that forestalls healthy psychic development and negates a very important part of her reality.

When, years later, Sappho is spurred primarily by guilt to do something about her neglect of Alphonse, this evolution signifies her progression to the depressive position.[13] Just as persecution anxiety characterizes the paranoid-schizoid position, depression is the major anxiety identified with the depressive position. The "depression" involved is broadly analogous to the emotional pain of mourning, and may be compared to the physical pain of, say, an injury that is on the mend. The most imminent threat during healing is the possibility of relapse and failure. The presence of this threat promotes anxieties — specifically, that the "bad" part of the self will overwhelm the "good" part, rather than the converse, and that the carefully constructed inner world will be disrupted.

While Kleinian theory effectively illuminates Sappho's psychic processes, it does not address the all-important sphere of her external world and its impact upon her psyche. The internal/external dialectic informs the manner in which Sappho's external reality complicates Klein's theory. Klein does write at more than one point that "external experiences are, of course, of great importance" in the attempt to unify one's ego.[14] But the examples that she invariably gives — consistent with those of most theorists — refer to the nuclear family, and particularly, to the mother.[15] Klein's description of the love and sense of fulfillment and gratification the expectant mother feels hardly provides for an understanding of the conception of a child through brutal assault. Similarly, her assumption that the family's protective environment will make a daughter a better mother does not take into account Sappho's reality, wherein her entire family was not only unable to protect her, but was itself constantly at risk, and eventually destroyed, by societal forces. Finally, discussions about "imagined" sources of persecution, and of ego reparation equipping the individual to face the external world — psychoanalytic viewpoints by no means unique to Klein — do not even conceive of, much less allow for, a truly persecutory external environment in which even the most integrated ego would inevitably be damaged. Klein's elaboration of defenses necessary to cope with the inner world must be extended to acknowledge the understanding that Sappho must defend against real threats, and that her persecution anxieties are grounded in actual experience — an actively hostile racial environment and a society comprised of strictly formatted gender roles and boundaries.

The first indication of Sappho's maternity is not even murmured until the midpoint of the novel, well after her celibate character has been firmly established. Alphonse, who first appears at the church fair, is identified only as great-nephew of Aunt Sally, aka Madam Frances, the fortune-teller. White fairgoers, emblemizing America's cavalier dismissal of slavery's ravages upon the Black family, are incredulous that such a "beautiful boy ... with golden curls and dark blue eyes" is related to someone "cut from purest ebony" (200–1). Unlike Grace Montfort and her "foster sister" and slave Lucy, Sappho and Madame Frances actually share a bloodline. Yet, the present continues to mirror the past in altered form as Sappho repeats Grace Montfort's abandonment of her child, placing Aunt Sally in the role of surrogate mother, much as Grace used Lucy. Costumed as Mercury for his role of carrying messages between fairgoers, Alphonse's kinship to Aunt Sally just as clearly carries the message of his mixed bloodline. The boy, though only about nine years old, "looked out on life ... with a glance all too melancholy for one of his tender years" (201). His sober, unchildlike demeanor suggests a heaviness of spirit, some void in his life. "Mercury wanted to find you, Miss Clark," Langley informs Sappho, initially oblivious at the time both to the literal truth of that statement, and to the profound effect of his unwitting remark upon the boy's true biological mother (208).

During most of the fair scene, Sappho determinedly ignores her child; Langley, his suspicious nature aroused, later recollects that she behaved as though she had never seen the child before. Her indifference signifies profound disassociation from her son.[16] Only one brief incident interrupts this pattern, when Sappho impulsively cradles Alphonse in her arms. Such maternal demeanor, however, quickly collapses under too-close scrutiny. With the sly perception of a born troublemaker, Langley makes a point of noting, for Sappho's benefit, Alphonse's handsome features, not incidentally adding, "I fancy he resembles you" (210). Unsettled by this observation, Sappho unceremoniously ejects poor Alphonse from her lap and leaves the fair, repositioning herself firmly into the role of disowning mother.

The novel relates only one visit by Sappho to Aunt Sally's, where Alphonse lives. Even then, Sappho comes only to provide for her child's material welfare, not to see, or interact with, him. Sappho's extraordinary emotional distance from her son is implicit in her reference to him as "the boy," as well as by her rather detached remark that it is Aunt Sally, not she, who wishes to secure some particulars for him: "That money will do what you wish for the boy, Aunt Sally.... There is no need for him to know — let him continue to think —" (278–9). This scrap of dialogue, gleaned from Langley's eavesdropping, suffices to indicate that Alphonse is unaware that Sappho is his mother. It also suggests that Sappho has instructed Aunt Sally to tell Alphonse that his mother is dead. Sappho's willful refusal to communicate to the child his true history is inextricably linked to her unwillingness to confront her own past.

Meanwhile, at the boarding-house, there is the complication of Sappho's growing affection for Will Smith, concealed only by her demeanor of cool indifference. Will's adoration of Sappho is, on the other hand, obvious and therefore threatening to her. When Sappho finds him making a fire in her room one morning, her reaction is disproportionate to the ill-mannered, yet well-intentioned nature of his trespass: "'How horrid you are.... You mustn't make my fire again.... No,'" came firmly from Sappho's lips; "no more fires" (173). Sappho's extreme portrayal of Will as "horrid" for his misdemeanor reflects the extent of the threat that she feels from men in general. Sappho does not want Will to "light her fire," literally or figuratively. Because of her past, she unconsciously conflates "fire," which she wants "no more" of, to connote both desire and undesired assault, thereby associating even innocent affection toward a man with threat and injury.

Later, Sappho's searching questions to the chairwoman at a church meeting suggest a desperate anxiety about the "fires" that physical passion represents:

> Do you think that God will hold [Negro women] responsible for the *illegitimacy* with which our race has been obliged, as it were, to flood the world? ... In a moment of passion, or ... circumstances which we cannot control, we commit some horrid sin, and the taint of it sticks and will not leave us, and we grow to loathe ourselves ... [149, 154].

Because Sappho equates "a moment of passion" with a circumstance out of her control, or one in which she has *lost* control — the result of which would be the commission of "some horrid sin" — she resolutely avoids intimacy with men. The "horrid sin" echoes Sappho's indictment of Will ("How horrid you are"), explaining her suppression of tender feelings for him. Sappho verges on loss of control as her church meeting monologue continues, taking on the character of private musings inadvertently spoken aloud, then spiraling downward and inward from the general to the specific. Perilously close to personal revelation, Sappho's compulsive, confessional tone marks once again the relentless pressure that her past exerts upon her present and the vast amount of continual energy required to suppress it. In the meantime, Sappho's son is growing up without a mother.

Sappho and Dora

Given her reticent nature, Sappho would seem an unlikely companion to Dora, but in fact, the two women establish a close bond. Their relationship is highlighted by one particular scene related in the chapter entitled "Friendship." While this segment might seem digressive from the central topic of mothering, it is in fact directly related to issues of maternity. It sheds unique light upon Sappho's child-disowning character, and connects Mrs. Smith's gender-based mothering to Dora's deflated self-esteem and her consequent feelings about men.

On this particular day, Sappho has "beg[ged] Dora to pass the day with her in her room..." (117). In contrast to Mary Helen Washington's view that Hopkins "diminish[es] the stature of women's friendship by describing [this scene] as 'playing company, like children,'"[17] I find that this particular interlude reflects high regard for female friendships. Further, the women's "play" might very well mask a very adult venture. Though couched in ambiguity, the language in this passage is imbued with undeniably homoerotic overtones.

The veil of secrecy that Sappho adopts for this rendezvous is echoed by Dora, who tells Mrs. Smith that "she [is] going visiting and [will] not be at home until tea time" (117). Stealth and deceit — extraordinary behavior for Dora, especially in interactions with her mother — cue the reader to the gravity, and the discretion, surrounding this engagement.

> By eleven o'clock they had locked the door of Sappho's room ... had mended the fire ... and had drawn the window curtains close.... Sappho lay back among her cushions.... She folded her arms above her head and turned an admiring gaze on the brown face of her friend, who swayed gently back and forth in her rocking-chair [118–9].

Only Dora is invited into this private space. Sappho's sharing in the fire-lighting with her (which she refused to do with Will), the locked room, and the women's relaxed positions establish a level of trust and intimacy that Sappho has accorded no one else. The women's conversation during this lazy afternoon revolves primarily around relationships with men — love, sex, and marriage. Sappho's womanist views contrast graphically with Dora's True Womanly deference to men: "[Dr.] Arthur [Lewis] thinks that women should be seen and not heard, where politics is under discussion.... I generally accept whatever the men tell me as right" (126, 125). Sappho bristles ("Insufferable prig!") at Lewis's presumption and Dora's passivity; she also criticizes Lewis's accommodationist racial philosophy.

Politics aside, Dora and Sappho share deep reservations about men. Dora admits to a lack of passion toward her fiancé, confiding that she feels "*unsexed*, so to speak.... When one is terribly in love one is supposed to want the dear object always near," insinuating that she feels just the opposite about Langley (121–2). "I get tired of a man so soon! I dread to think of being tied to John for good and all; I know I'll be sick of him inside of a week" (122). Sappho appears to agree, regretting "the necessary man" to form "a harmonious whole." This is a curious statement, especially when coupled with Sappho's next words, after a thoughtful pause, that "all things are possible if love is the foundation stone" (118). Sappho's meaning gains significance in light of her fierce distrust of men and, certainly, in view of the name she has chosen for herself. Both Dora and Sappho use the term "man" generically, Dora implying that *any* man would bore her within a week, Sappho that *all* men are depraved and untrustworthy. In fact, for Dora, it is "Sappho Clark [who] seemed to fill a long-felt want in her life" (98). The inference that men are unsuitable companions for women raises the possibility that both women might be considering the alternative — another woman — as a partner. ("All things are possible.")

During this interlude, Sappho teases Dora about her sweet tooth, which has become a subject of gentle amusement around the boarding-house. The dialogue, on the manifest level, reads like a playful precaution against eating fattening sweet. Its subtext, however, suggests the tempting, delicious lure of forbidden fruit:

> "Well, here are John's chocolate bonbons.... I suppose you won't want me to touch them, for fear of getting fat."
> Sappho shook her head in mock despair.... "Think of your fate, Dora!..."
> "I'll eat all the bonbons I want ... I'll eat your slice of cream pie, too." At this dire threat there ensued a scramble for the pie, mingled with peals of merry laughter, until all rosy and sparkling, Sappho emerged from the fray.
> Presently lunch was over, and they resumed their old positions [120].

Dora perceives that Sappho doesn't want her to eat her fiancé's candy "for fear of getting fat" (becoming pregnant?), conceivably projecting onto Sappho her own reluctance to accept "favors" from him. When Dora appears to favor Sappho's sweets over John's, the subtle word-and-action play begins to assume a cast of sensual enjoyment. Physical contact ensues, and the "play" ends on an exuberant note, with Sappho "rosy and sparkling" and both parties "emerg[inig]" obviously stimulated. The two women then "resume their old positions" (120).

Two immediate observations support this segment's possible homoerotic content: First, Dora's concealment of her plans with Sappho is bizarre; the two young women had often spent time together on outings. Why should this afternoon at home be clothed in such secrecy, with Dora actually lying to her mother, her closest confidant? Second and more pointedly, I think that Hopkins's deliberate naming merits serious consideration. The choice of "Sappho" is overdetermined in the sense that not only does the author choose this name for her character, but also within the storyline itself, Mabelle Beaubean intentionally re-christens *herself* Sappho. This is a clear allusion to the original Sappho of circa 600 B.C. who wrote erotic love poetry to and for her female disciples. Claudia Tate, the most attentive Hopkins critic, acknowledges that Mabelle's new name references "the famous classical poet — Sappho — who wrote gynocentric verse" and who was homosexual, but makes no comment on the possible significance of Mabelle's (and Hopkins's) choice of a name.[18] The term "lesbian," etymologically derived from the island of Lesbos on which Sappho lived, was not recorded in the

English language until 1908.[19] However, the connotation of "Sappho" had long been established when *Contending Forces* was written and would be known to even casual students of Greek history at the turn of the century. Sappho Clark, an educated young woman, would undoubtedly have been aware of the name's inference.

While I have gone to some pains to point out the viability of a homoerotic interpretation of this "Friendship" interlude, I actually find that a more compelling reading involves both female bonding and female dread of men. Even though Dora's experiences with men have been much less traumatic than Sappho's, both women, to varying extents, have been exposed to a sense of gendered powerlessness in a male-dominated society. Nancy Cott's study of nineteenth-century American women notes that diaries from this era show that women found "truly reciprocal interpersonal relationships only with other women," resulting in a "newly self-conscious and idealized concept of female friendship."[20] Carroll Smith-Rosenberg amplifies this notion, stressing that nineteenth-century female friendships were not restricted to the simple, dichotomous categories of either platonic or sexual love, but were "part of a continuum or spectrum of affect gradations strongly affected by cultural norms and arrangements."

> To interpret such friendships more fully, one must relate them to the structure of the family and to the nature of sex-role divisions and of male-female relations, both within the family and in society generally.... At one end of [this] continuum lies committed heterosexuality, at the other uncompromising homosexuality; between, a wide latitude of emotions and sexual feelings.[21]

Given this broad perspective, Dora and Sappho's afternoon venture could reflect not only their genuine affection toward and ease with one another and their respective anxieties about men, but also their resistance to the traditional female role. Dora's engagement to Langley, based upon *his* stated love for *her* and upon the understanding that "in due course of time they would marry" (88), reflects a rather bland acceptance of her fate. In fact the "long-felt" want that Sappho appeases might primarily reflect Dora's need for true intimacy on the one hand, and a sort of Sappho-like self-possession that she lacks on the other.

Conversely, Dora's appeal is a manifestation of Sappho's need to locate safe and comfortable emotional closeness while her ego is strengthening itself. It is hardly incidental that Dora is Will's sister, perfectly plausible that, as a kinder, gentler, *female*—ergo, *safe*—version of Will, she is the ideal object:

a sort of temporary security blanket — a transitional object of Sappho's displaced feelings for Will.[22] Her room affords Sappho a sense of security that she can not access in the company of men or in the larger world. Dora's temperate manner lends itself to Sappho's needs — a companion who will allow Sappho the control she needs within her restricted sphere, and also one who provides warmth and affection.[23]

My sense is that Hopkins is acutely aware of her reading audience and of the conventions of her time. In this passage, and elsewhere throughout the novel, generally more progressive views are couched within conventional forms and language, attempting a delicate balance between acceptable, traditional content and perspectives that simultaneously critique the status quo. It is feasible that Hopkins names her character "Sappho" not so much to define her heroine's sexuality as to call the reader's attention to *issues* of sexuality. The name certainly does provoke the reader to ask why, of all the names at her disposal, she would choose one that connotes female intimacy. One answer might be that Hopkins wished to stress the profoundly gendered imbalance of power — the stifling oppression of women under patriarchy and the subtle aspects of True Womanhood that perpetuate gender oppression. This dynamic made female friendships especially important as they constituted, in Cott's words, "the only equal, non-subordinate relationships available to women."[24] Sappho's history especially argues for a supportive and non-threatening female community, given that the core of her secret self rests upon that traumatic moment of repeated sexual assault in her (Mabelle's) life — when her self-image becomes, in an instant, irreconcilable with her life experience. Mabelle's ordeal at age fourteen, and her deliverance into the safety of the sympathetic sisterhood at the convent, must certainly have crystallized specific attitudes and expectations about gender in her mind: men signify greed, danger, and perversion; women provide comfort, understanding, and safety.

Sappho and Dora are both in search of an unnamed something, and they each project this vague desire onto the other. Dora's compulsive eating points to the acting-out of some compulsive need to fill an internal emptiness ("long-felt want") — frustration, perhaps, that her life, unlike Sappho's, is circumscribed and uninteresting. Thus, at the root of Dora's admiration of Sappho lies envy. Her confidences to her mother express complex feelings about her friend — the desire to *be* her, or at least to be *like* her. Failing that, there remains, despite Dora's protests, her intense anxiety about Sappho as a rival:

2. Sappho Clark: Double Exposure

> Oh, I do wish I was handsome like Sappho Clark! ... Sappho is the best and dearest girl on earth, and I only hope that Will may be so lucky as to marry her.... There won't be a blessed man left to us girls if she remains single long [180–1].

At some generally unacknowledged level, negligible smatterings of envy and minute acts of displacement are common enough elements in successful relationships, so this passage is relatively unremarkable. However, the depth of Dora's (mostly silent) envy goes to a level too deep to be healthy in a true friendship.

When an individual reaches a certain level of psychic health and expands his/her range of interests and ego capabilities, the transitional object is no longer needed. Circuitous a route as it may seem, Dora as Sappho's transitional object intersects with the path that enables Sappho to confront her terrible fear of intimacy and ultimately to embrace her motherhood. She knows that Will loves her, but that knowledge has heretofore only saddened and unnerved her. Here she makes an intermediate step — the transition from detachment to closeness with Will. "I love this man; I know it now! I want his love, his care, his protection. I want him through life and beyond the grave, we two as one — my husband. Oh, my God, help me, help me!" (181–2).

Dora constantly betrays her desire to identify more closely with Sappho. When Will tells Dora about his engagement to Sappho, his sister appropriates the news as though it were *hers:* "Mother! Mother! come quickly, I have something to tell you" (324). Her clearest expression of envy occurs later, when the Smiths find Sappho's poignant letter revealing her child and Langley's unconscionable proposal, which prompts her flight from Boston. Dora initially responds with compassion ("Oh, that poor, miserable girl!"), but barely pauses before adding, "I do not wonder that she turned a coward and fled" (331). Of course Dora has been forced to process in quick succession Sappho's fall from idealized grace and the shock of her own fiancé's betrayal. Either of these considerations alone could account for her transformation of Sappho, the former "best and dearest girl on earth," into "a coward." But the grudging tone and subtle dig suggest that her words are triggered by envy.[25]

"I Am Your Mother"

Meanwhile, Sappho plans to accept Will's proposal after sharing with him the truth about her child. Her new resolve indicates that she has begun the painful process of reconciling herself with her past. But circumstances intervene as Langley, having stumbled onto Sappho's secret, tries to press his advantage by proposing a sexual relationship in exchange for his silence. His intrusion into her private room at the boarding-house violates the secure universe she has established after banning Will, rendering it henceforth uninhabitable. Langley's threat throws Sappho's past in her face with an immediacy that startles her, triggering the flight impulse. Like a thief in the night, she creeps from the boarding-house "and was swallowed up"—physically and psychologically (322). Simply put, Mabelle is back.

Sappho's departure from Boston is not simply aimless, terrified flight. Given her gradually healing psyche, this trip is a deliberate, although tentative, confrontation with the past and her damaged alter ego Mabelle. But achieving wellness is a lengthy process, and its accompanying anxieties impede straightforward advancement. Sappho's return to New Orleans corresponds with her earlier decision to tell Will the truth, to marry him, and to acknowledge her child. These actions all anticipate a gradual, progressive movement from inner persecution and denial toward acceptance of her whole, reintegrated self.[26]

Just before leaving Boston, Sappho begins to take control of a situation that had controlled her for so long by disclosing everything to Will in a letter, thereby effectively removing the threat that Langley held over her. Most significantly, she finally embraces her maternity by transferring guardianship and primary care of Alphonse from Aunt Sally to herself and taking him to New Orleans, where she brings him into her life:

"I am your mother, Alphonse."
The child put up one slender hand and smoothed her cheek. "You're the pretty lady I saw at the fair. I didn't know you were my mamma" [346].

The process of reparation unfolds as Sappho consciously advances from feelings of guilt brought on by past neglect of Alphonse to an honest acceptance of the reasons for her past treatment of her child. Hating that part of herself that unwillingly conceived Alphonse, she admits to having hated, by extension, Alphonse himself ("She had felt nothing for the poor waif but repugnance" [342].) Such awareness represents a crucial step in the psychological recovery of her maternity and of her child. What she lacks in feeling for Alphonse she resolves to offset with commitment. This resolution effects a great unburdening and ironically calls forth, unbidden, the love that she had been heretofore unable to experience for Alphonse. When she holds him, "something holy" passes between them. Sappho is transformed by "the sweet contact of the soft, warm body into the cold chilliness of her broken heart. The mother-love chased out all the anguish that she had felt over his birth" (346). Sappho's love is intensified by Alphonse's guileless dependence on her and by the constancy of his unconditional love.[27]

However cathartic, this breakthrough represents only partial progress toward psychic wholeness. Once in New Orleans, she finds herself stumbling, rather than gliding, toward her goal. The old colored convent, the "safe house" where Mabelle Beaubean had been brought to have her baby, is now also a refuge for Sappho, another sign of impending symbiosis between her two selves. She tells the Mother Superior of her decision to publicly acknowledge her child.

> "My child," [the Mother Superior] said "...are you still determined to pass as the boy's mother?"
> "Yes, Mother, I am."
> "Well, then, you must be Madame Clark."
> "No," replied Sappho hastily; "no more deception" [351–2].

The Mother Superior's striking use of the verb "to pass" holds dual implications. First, because this term is typically used to describe the act of masquerading on a *racial* level, it reminds the reader of Sappho's racial integrity, i.e., of the fact that she has always had the prerogative of living a less subjugated life as a White woman because of her physical features but has always rejected this option. Secondly, it maintains the tension surrounding Sappho's efforts to truly mother Alphonse: If Sappho is planning merely to "pass" as Alphonse's mother, the inference, then, is that she is only masquerading, rather than living, this maternal role. As such, the women's exchange challenges the degree to which Sappho has actually internalized the fact that Alphonse is indeed her child.

She soon assumes another alias, but "Madame Clark," widow, is not deceiving herself; she claims this status in order to secure employment. On the maternal front, she replaces one self-deception with another, guiltily overcompensating for her former neglect by virtually overwhelming Alphonse with attention. Alphonse is "her anchor.... She would devote her life to him" (347, 342). Her language, more indicative of a romantic attachment, might reflect Sappho's unconscious substitution of motherlove for romantic passion, which she has forbidden herself to experience. This love might feel "right" to her because, although profound, it is not sexual, and therefore not threatening. But her expectation of the all-encompassing role that she has Alphonse play in her life leaves no room for anyone else. Most importantly, the healthy development of the child simply cannot be accomplished by years of maternal neglect followed by a sudden period of intensely smothering mothering.

Still, Sappho's revelation to Alphonse about their kinship enhances their relationship: "It was a rare sight to see the two together—the lovely girl who held the child in such a passionate embrace, and the delight of the child in his 'beautiful mamma'" (350). Curiously—particularly in the face of her pledge that she and her son would "nevermore be separated"—although Alphonse frequently visits Sappho, he does not *live* with her, but instead, at the convent. Monsieur (M.) Louis is Sappho's employer and grandfather to the two young charges Sappho cares for. As their governess, she lives on the estate. M. Louis is an elegant gentleman with a spacious home, dotes on Alphonse, and is extremely fond of Sappho. Since he would presumably have no objection to Sappho's child staying on the premises, it would seem that Alphonse's unusual living arrangements have been determined solely by Sappho. She soon became the spiritual center of the Louis home, loved by all. "It was a happy, restful life; it suited her" (353). The inference, then, is that Alphonse's constant presence would *not* be "happy and restful," would *not* "suit" her. In uncanny mirroring of Linda Brent's status at the end of her narrative, Sappho substitutes real family life and nurturing of her own child for the maintenance of a ready-made surrogate family and home, standing in as wife and mother without fear of scandal and, most critically, romantic or sexual involvement.

This mother's need to have her son close by, yet still apart from her, points to Sappho's continuing inability to define his place in her life. While her id and ego defenses play tug-of-war, Alphonse remains a casualty. Her mixed signals confuse and distress the typically stoic man-boy, whose new status as non-orphan provokes him to overtly agitated, childlike behavior for the first time in his young life:

> "Have I said anything wrong, mamma?" he asked anxiously.
> "Not wrong, my child, but mamma prefers that you never speak of the past to anyone."
> "I will do just as you say, Mamma Sappho!" [356].

Alphonse most assuredly does not know his mother's birth name. He addresses her by her assumed name. His poignant reference to her as

"Mamma Sappho" compromises the endearment "mamma" and implies kinship distance — such as one would use to refer to an aunt, rather than a mother. Sappho's continuing injunction against speaking of the past hinders their development into an intimate, informed family unit.

While Sappho continues to struggle with maternal issues, three years of a stable and uncomplicated life in the secure environment of M. Louis's guarded walls effect a great deal of healing. The refuge of Sappho's immediate world allows her the freedom to rebuild her inner self gradually and without external pressures, to reduce the anxiety, guilt, and self-persecution that has for so long been a part of her psychic baggage.[28] M. Louis's feelings for Sappho follow a predictable course, and the elder gentleman proposes marriage.

It is here that Dora's ongoing story intersects thematically with Sappho's. At last sighting, Dora, enraged with John Langley after discovering his attempt to blackmail Sappho, has broken her engagement to him. Her childhood friend, Dr. Arthur Lewis of New Orleans, shrewdly takes advantage of this turn of events, courting her circumspectly by mail. Acutely aware of her single status, she agrees to his proposal. By various narrative devices, not the least of which are the somewhat disparaging portrayal of the groom and the awesome solemnity of the wedding ceremony, the reader is drawn to the conclusion that Dora's decision is a fundamentally flawed one — a not necessarily unhappy, but certainly not fulfilling, capitulation to her expected role. This is exactly the kind of decision that Mrs. Smith raised her to make and precisely the compromise that Sappho would be making if she were to marry M. Louis.

The Dora/Sappho suitor parallel is most pointedly drawn with the use of homonymous names — Dr. *Lewis* the educator, and Monsieur *Louis*, grandfather of Sappho's two young charges. Again, such deliberate naming, with an infinite number of choices at the author's disposal, certainly invites comparison of some sort. I'd suggest that these two men are intended to perform a similar function in the novel. Both are respectable, sexually nonthreatening (and nondesirable), fatherly types who offer safety, security, and marriage to Dora and Sappho, respectively. The women's differing responses to Lewis/Louis (Dora accepts, Sappho doesn't) offer alternate readings of how a woman might "lose" or "gain" herself, in or out of marriage.

Dora's ego damage has been sustained by a number of factors: in the external world, by society's devaluation of Black people and of women; closer to home, by her mother's favoritism toward her brother, the loss of her idol

Sappho, and humiliation by her former fiancé Langley. Her diminished sense of self leaves her particularly vulnerable to Dr. Lewis's judicious courtship. In spite of a degree of pomposity and narrow-mindedness, he is a "good" man. But Dora does not so much accept Lewis as she rejects passion and its attendant risks.

The wedding ceremony is as grim as a funeral, in part because of Dora's insistence on a minimalist service on this, the most important day of her life:

> Dora would have no bridesmaids.... They were a striking couple: she serious, he so grave and steadfast.... An unusual solemnity enfolded this couple as they took their vows upon them ... [382].

That their vows are a burden they "took upon" themselves lends an even more ponderous note to an already cheerless affair. And however much Dora once minimized her feelings for Langley, the emotional bond that still exists between them is insinuated at her wedding. "As the bride came down the aisle...she caught for one instant the full gaze of John Langley. She never forgot that look; so full of despair and unhappiness.... It haunted her..." (382).

The narrative later refers to Dora as "a contented young matron ... *her own individuality swallowed up* in love for her husband and child" (389–90, italics mine). Dora's behavioral history belies her apparent contentment. Her demeanor masks unexpressed needs and frustrations, with which she copes by suppressing them and/or projecting them onto others. When Will, back from philosophy studies in Heidelberg, despairs over losing Sappho and repeats his determination to find her, Dora argues against his plan. If Will truly does not expect to see Sappho ever again, then why waste any more time pining for her? She presses her argument: "Why not, then, seek to solace yourself for her loss by marrying some good girl who will make you happy? ... It would please me, and mother would die happy" (390). Like her mother, Dora's use of "loss" is ambiguous. Here, "her loss" implies that Sappho, not Will, has forfeited something of value. Her attempt to persuade Will to abandon his search for "real" love and settle for a safe haven, as she did, suggests a residual bitterness. The blatant emotional blackmail of her last remark also expresses, I think, that Will should for once try to please others before himself, as she, the girl-child, has always been expected to do.

While Dora has married Dr. Lewis, Sappho also considers marrying *her* M. Louis, having grown, also like Dora, "resigned to her life" (355). But the "swallowed-up" state in which Dora now lives as wife and mother resonates uncannily with the "strange feeling of suffocation" (358) that Sappho experiences when M. Louis proposes. The difference is that Dora embraces this swallowed-up life, choosing to share with Lewis the "dull monotony of his methodical existence" (304), while a more resilient Sappho resists suffocation. When, at novel's end, Sappho announces her engagement to Will, M. Louis himself acknowledges the rightness of her decision by graciously (and appropriately) assuming a fatherly role, insisting that he should handle the wedding details and even give the bride away.

This matrimonial climax is set in motion when, after three years, Sappho finally decides to bring Alphonse "home" with her. As a narrative reward for having reached this maternal plateau, Sappho is reunited with the ever-faithful Will who, having searched the country for her for three years, finally arrives in New Orleans. The success of Sappho's psychic battle with herself and with motherhood, as well as the sanctity of her union with Will, is highlighted by religious language and motifs, especially those of Easter, with its powerful theme of rebirth and redemption. Will has fortuitously sought a place in which to worship at the same moment that Sappho has come to the women's convent to recover her child. Their paths converge on the same holy ground where Mabelle had last been seen. Thus, Mabelle and Sappho finally meet on common ground. Will and Sappho, blissfully reunited, are happily married.

By Dora's and Sappho's examples, the narrative privileges the latter's decision to seek fulfillment by directly confronting her demons. Sappho's personal story ends with the joyful establishment of a complete family. Importantly, Sappho and Will's characters challenge the patriarchal demand for premarital virginity in light of the racial climate, where sexual atrocities against Black women are commonplace.[29] Will's integrity is manifested in his refusal to blame the victim. His compassionate understanding of Sappho's past and his steadfast devotion to Sappho and her child, and Sappho's acceptance of her past as well as her present, allow the three members of this newly formed family to establish their own course. While her society has not fundamentally changed, Sappho has grown tremendously. Buttressed by the healthiest sense of self she has ever had, she is ready to face the world.

> Sappho was happy in contemplating the life of promise which was before her. Will was the noblest of men. Alphonse was to him as his own child. United by love, chastened by sorrow and self-sacrifice, he and she planned to work together to bring joy to hearts crushed by despair [401].

But what of Alphonse? For the first time, he is fully integrated into Sappho's world. But this happy resolution does not overshadow the fact that the boy, now about twelve years of age, has spent most of his young life lacking both a personal history and dependable maternal care. Reborn in mid-life, so to speak — like Sappho/Mabelle — with a lifetime's worth of missed childhood experiences, Alphonse is more like a child now than he has ever been, and his subsequent development and adjustment will not be effortless.

And Dora? Perhaps, in spite of — or more to the point, *because* of — her repressed emotions, missed opportunities, and unfulfilled life, she is determined to have the last word after all. No more limits, she seems to be saying: The future must be boundless for the next generation of little Black girls. When she has a daughter, Dora names her Sappho.

CHAPTER 3

Irene Redfield: Smoke and Mirrors

Can vapor be represented on canvas? If so, this would be the psychological portrait of Irene Redfield: both elusive and illusive, elegant as poetry but, at base, all form and no content. Of all the portraits, hers is the least substantial. The illusion of actual essence, which she painstakingly constructs to make herself seem real, is a stock illusionist's trick, and Irene is a master magician. Sadly, she is a mother of two boys who need real, not feigned, maternal care. This unforgiving portrayal reveals a woman damaged by both her communal and larger society and who, in turn, does major damage to others. Heinz Kohut's theories on narcissism inform this character.

> "I think," [Clare] said at last, "that being a mother is the cruellest thing in the world."
> "Yes," Irene softly agreed. For a moment she was unable to say more, so accurately had Clare put into words that which, not so defined, was so often in her own heart of late [197].

The subject is mothering and, as the above exchange implies, neither Irene Redfield nor Clare Kendry is comfortable in the role. Their conversation, taken from Nella Larsen's 1929 *Passing*,[1] reflects their respective psychological natures as mothers as well as in other areas. Irene personifies the restrictive and censoring super-ego, Clare the uninhibited, pleasure-seeking id. Neither woman is balanced at the level of the ego. Though both Irene and Clare have children, issues of maternity hardly figure in *Passing* at all. But this novel calls for examination of the maternal precisely because of what it does *not* say about mothering, children, or sexuality, because of what is deliberately missing in a text replete with ambiguity, absence, and silence.

Largely unappreciated in its time, *Passing* has traditionally invited critical interpretation as an African American text in the "tragic mulatto" tradition that unsuccessfully attempts to redress the racist American perception of Black women. Alain Locke set the tone for much subsequent criticism of the novel with his judgment that *Passing* "fails, somehow, to overcome a self-conscious effort to convince the reader that the leading characters are really caught between two worlds or two cultures."[2] Even Hoyt Fuller's introduction to *Passing*'s own 1971 Collier edition disparages *Passing* as "deliberate scene-setting" by "a mediocre home magazine story-teller."[3]

Re-viewed and closely read by scholars who today perceive it as a *tour de force*, *Passing* is finally acknowledged for the multi-dimensionality of its text, the deliberate self-consciousness and telling pathology of the narrative voice, its highly subversive issues couched in "light women's reading," and the elaborate impulses that drive the action, and the intrigue, of the plot.[4] Its elegant narrative style ironically veils a richness of form and content, and the layered subtext makes important statements about identity and masquerade, empowerment and disempowerment, desire and devastation.

Passing's uncommon and compelling psychological representation of motherhood is one of a role frustrated by both internal and external conditions. However, the mother in question in *Passing* is not prevented from providing good-enough mothering because of her social status, as was slave woman Linda Brent, or because of sexual trauma, like Sappho Clark. Motherhood, for Irene Redfield, is a virtually irrelevant role on the emotional and psychological levels. Her preoccupation with race, color, class, and gender role-playing — a direct consequence of familial and societal mirroring — develops into a narcissistic pathology that makes good mothering impossible. Irene's relationships with her children, her husband, and especially with Clare Kendry cast her in harsh light. Heinz Kohut's studies on narcissism inform this analysis of Irene and her milieu.

> **Pass,** *v.t.* 2. *To let go without notice, remark, etc; leave unconsidered; disregard ... overlook.... 3. to cause or allow to go through or over a barrier, obstacle, etc. 34. U.S.: to live and be known as a White person although having some Negro ancestry; 49. to die.*[5]

Passing resonates with these disparate connotations, transcending the issue of race to overdetermine the possibility of meaning. Larsen manipulates the illusive transparency of the text to offer a powerful discourse that blends an exceptional economy of language with an extravagance of imagery and texture. While the novel certainly demonstrates the pervasive and debilitating impact of racism upon the African American community, *Passing* merely passes for a book solely about race.

Deborah McDowell's masterful introduction in the 1988 Rutgers edition of *Quicksand and Passing* plumbs, for the first time, the psychological and homoerotic dimensions of Larsen's novel. McDowell notes that Larsen's era was both "the Freudian 1920s" and a time when Black women's novels maintained a strict reticence about sexuality.[6] Larsen accommodates these contending forces by offering a severely repressed heroine within a narrative replete with language that privileges the sexual unconscious to uncover what the character and the plot conceal. Within very proper settings, Larsen explores the theme of female sexuality, illuminating its authenticity as well as the restrictions placed upon its expression by middle-class conventions.[7]

Larsen artfully overturns preconceived notions with a deftness that requires close, careful study to perceive. She upends the classic trope of the "tragic mulatto"—the near-saintly, abused mixed-race female character with whom readers, Black and White, can easily empathize. Cary D. Wintz notes *Passing*'s aberrant rendering of the "tragic" mode, finding *Passing*'s women "negative" and "depressing."[8] William H. Robinson's assessment that Irene is "not all that tragic"[9] reinforces the notion that she is different from the standard most conspicuously in the area of affect: Irene is simply not very likeable. Underneath high polish, she is an unsympathetic, profoundly broken character.

Sharpening this focus of inquiry, the text presents a broader truth: that is, that Irene's pathology emanates not only from her individual inadequacies, but also from societal pathology—manifested primarily by a virulent racist environment—which imprints itself both individually and collectively upon African Americans. While each character is individually responsible for his or her actions, it is demonstrable that those in *Passing* are "tragic" not only because of their personal flaws, but also because they inhabit a universe that despises and persecutes them. In the vicious nature of this cycle of oppression, the internal/external ills are neither clearly nor cleanly divisible. Repudiation by their society exacerbates and, in some cases, even gives rise to, individual defects.

Irene Redfield embodies many of the paradoxes and anxieties that inhabit her devalued community. Born around the turn of the century when lynching was still a popular pastime, Irene and other young Black children of her era could not be shielded by their parents or by their community from the devastating manifestations of ubiquitous American racism. Even with highly positive mirroring within the nuclear family, members of disenfranchised groups are inevitably affected by universally negative societal mirroring.[10] Paradoxically, the existence of an even more ruthless level of racism during their parents' childhood only increases the odds that the parents' egos—and therefore, their ability to positively mirror their children—will also be damaged. Transgenerational oppression virtually assures that, long before a child is born, external forces will have been busily at work to challenge the parent's ability to positively nurture his or her child.

Irene Redfield and her circle represent that segment of the African American community that attempts to defend itself from the indiscriminate discrimination of American society by distancing itself from the masses. They effect this—or attempt to effect this—through a deliberate, determined, even ruthless assumption of things White and a rejection of things Black. Such behavior is most pointedly manifested by intra-racially distinguishing color and class differences, and placing higher value on those differences generally assumed to be closest to White characteristics and modes of living. E. Franklin Frazier's *The Black Bourgeoisie* renders a scathing portrait of this subgroup of the African American community, portraying it as rife with mental and emotional conflicts, existing in a netherworld of make-believe, willfully (but secretly) isolated from the Black world, and barred from complete acceptance in White society.[11] Irene Redfield so sharply defines this role that she virtually parodies it. The height of propriety, yet spiritually bankrupt, she pursues a lifestyle that is, in the end, empty, delusional, and self-defeating. *Passing*'s women appear to thrive, but are in fact trapped, in the roles of wife and mother. Children are lost inside their mother's preoccupations.

The Psychology of Passing

Passing's elusive, dreamy quality, its unexplained lapses and abrupt shifts in scene, as well as an overall attitude of vagueness render it especially accessible to psychological analysis. Irene is exposed as a narcissist, stifled by racism and sexism in her external world and by her own impulses of envy and resentment in her internal world. Preoccupied with color, she is also caught up in gender and class roles in a vain search for fulfillment.

Heinz Kohut's principles are more progressive than traditional psychoanalytic theory.[12] Specifically, his concept of narcissism is infinitely more coherent and objective than, for example, Sigmund Freud's; he reads narcissism as simply "an investment of the self," an inevitable aspect of the human condition; some degree of narcissism is present in any ego, and the degree to which object love functions as an independent emotion, rather than as a function of one's own narcissism, is the measure of a healthy, mature, outer-directed relationship. In other words, only an excessive level of narcissism defines it as a pathology, or narcissistic personality disorder.[13]

Kohut has written widely on the pathology of cultures, but he does not address adequately the impact of external environmental dynamics upon certain oppressed groups.[14] Indeed, his work illustrates two major limitations of psychoanalytic theory in general: that it ignores significant cultural factors that figure in the development of the psyche, and that it presents severely uninformed cultural biases as scientific, empirical data. Specifically, he reads African American culture as intellectually deficient and conveys a blatant disregard for social and historical reality.[15] In a 1978 essay, Kohut addresses the changing face of contemporary American culture: "One need call to mind only the rapid emancipation of the American Negro and his impetuous tendency to use militant means."[16] His dismissive tone and disingenuous characterization of African Americans as "impetuous" and "militant" in their struggle for civil rights is deeply at odds with his understanding of other oppressed groups.[17] However restrictively one defines "emancipation," Kohut's notion that Black America's attainment of freedom has been "rapid" is not only bizarre, but historically indefensible. His contribution to this study, then, while considerable, is in the area of the internal, rather than the external, realm.

Irene

Wife, mother, socialite, "race woman," model of middle-class conventionality, Irene Redfield says that she has "everything I want" (160). The difficulty rests with what it is that she wants, and with the fact that, in any event, her statement is a lie. Just as the novel passes as a book primarily about race, Irene merely passes as a loving, happy, successful woman. The major presence in the novel, Irene Redfield is continually marked by absence. Her tenuous and fragile self-concept is entirely dependent on the way she is perceived by others. A telling self-insight, that "alone she was nothing" (224), explains why she attempts to manufacture an identity. Frantz Fanon notes that such an individual is incapable of true, authentic love, and that, saddled with internal conflicts, "her resentment feeds on her artificiality."[18]

From the opening of the novel Larsen relentlessly peels away the multi-layered façade that Irene has so painstakingly constructed. The unreliability of the narrative voice that reflects her consciousness is immediately established: "This is what Irene remembered" (146), suggests a broad disparity between what Irene "remembers" and what "is." The untrustworthiness of the narrative voice continually resurfaces through memory lapses, inconsistencies, inappropriate silences, confusion, repressions, narcissistic preoccupations, and lies. By the end of the novel, the blatant absence of a fundamental self highlights the tragedy of Irene's life: that is, as Gertrude Stein once said, when you get there, there's no there there. Frighteningly shallow, Irene demonstrates at every turn total self-absorption, or classic narcissistic pathology.

Psychoanalysis locates the root of narcissistic disorders in a severe lack of early positive mirroring from the environment during one's early years. But while Kohut, like most psychoanalysts, uses the term "environment" in this context to refer narrowly, i.e., to the nuclear family and particularly to the mother,[19] *Passing* shows that the term is best applied literally, and broadly. The narcissistic injury that results from environmental deprivation interrupts ego maturation, so that unless sufficient healing occurs, the individual remains fixed at an early developmental stage throughout life. The disturbance signals chronic anxiety about self-esteem, fear of losing one's cohesive self, and an intense desire for the nurturing and confirmation that was not experienced earlier in life. It typically manifests itself in behaviors that express "lacks"—of vitality, humor, a sense of proportion, empathy for others, interest in sex; in feelings of emptiness and depression; an inability to sustain relationships; pathological lying; and, importantly, attacks of uncontrollable rage. The substitute nurturing and validation missed in earlier life assumes the exaggerated form of an idealized object (person), in search of which the narcissistic ego turns inward, looking for an ideal that does not exist, as well as outward, to locate such an ideal.[20]

Piqued when even the weather fails to conform to expected patterns, Irene pursues a life of order, stability, predictability, and convention: "She didn't like it to be warm and springy when it should have been cold and crisp.... The weather, like people, ought to enter into the spirit of the season" [213]. Her obsessive need for security as an adult is a reaction to the lack of security she experienced in both her internal and external worlds as a child. Within the bounds of predictability, Irene — who doesn't "like changes" — has carved an existence, a social structure, and a pattern of activity that rigorously defines who she is (188, 235). Her conscious and unconscious thought processes are compellingly mirrored by the narrative through language, syntax, and texture. What Robert Bone calls the "force of inertia"[21] in Larsen's texts might well apply to *Passing*, but not in the undisciplined manner that Bone presumes. *Passing* appears torpid in sections because Irene's chronic lethargy drives the text — with language that not only creates, but mimetically echoes, Irene's sensibilities. "[Irene] was weary and depressed.... she couldn't be free of that dull, indefinite misery which with increasing tenaciousness had laid hold of her..." (213–14). Her lack of vitality, symptomatic of emotional emptiness and repressed thoughts seeking expression, threads through the novel to dispute her earlier statement that she has "everything she wants." Rather, her hypochondriacal preoccupations signal a deep-seated fear of ego-fragmentation.[22] The state of her marriage is perceptible in a telling remark she makes about her husband: "Brian doesn't care for ladies, especially sick ones" (173). In view of her chronic illnesses, Irene is essentially describing herself.

Conventions substitute for actual substance and emotion in Irene's life. Her speech is clichéd, as though, like her life, she's had to resort to mechanical methods: "Idlewild, you know. It's quite the thing now. And you'll see absolutely everybody" (156). While her "friend" Clare mocks Irene's predictable conventionality ("You're married? Yes, you would be" [155]), even subtle nuances are serious matters to Irene; they guide her rigid social mores. Class consciousness is the basis upon which she has always felt superior to Clare, daughter of a janitor, who had never fit in with Irene and her group: Clare's smile at lunch is "too provocative for a waiter," and her familiarity with Irene's servants shows "an exasperating lack of perception" (149, 208). Similarly, her old classmate Gertrude, in an ill-fitting, non-designer dress, looks "like the wife of a butcher" (167).

Irene's standards of correctness, which she extends to mystifying proportions, are often thinly-disguised defenses against threatening issues, especially race and sex. When Clare's husband jokingly calls Clare "Nig" in reference to her dusky ivory skin, Irene thinks only: "How rude, how insulting, to address her in that way in the presence of guests!" (171). Brian's attempt to explain racial violence to their sons nets a reprimand: "I do wish, Brian, that you wouldn't talk about lynching before Ted and Junior. It was really inexcusable for you to bring up a thing like that at dinner" (231).

While political correctness is *de rigueur* in Irene's world, serious talk about race and sex is taboo, certainly at dinnertime.

Irene knows everyone of, she feels, major or minor importance in both the Black and White communities, but apparently is unable to make a real connection with anyone. Her one acknowledged friend, Felice Freeland, responds to Irene's genuine distress at one point by offhandedly advising her to "buy yourself an expensive new frock.... It always helps" (219). Apparently without malice, Felice's reaction typifies the response Irene elicits from everyone. Detached by a defensive air of aloofness and control, unable to extend concern or understanding to others, Irene gets as much as she gives — no compassionate responses from anyone. What Kohut perceives as the "most crucial emotional experience for human psychological survival and growth" — an empathic human environment — is totally absent in Irene's arid universe.[23] Even more profound than the remoteness that separates Irene from others is her remoteness from her own flesh and spirit. While she repeatedly details Clare Kendry's appearance and dress, not one single descriptive word emerges from Irene on Irene herself. Such profound lack of awareness about her physicality is a significant aspect of the deliberate not-knowing that she so fervently embraces throughout the novel.

Irene's biggest fear, "the fear for the future" (193), does not reflect a fear of the unknown but rather an anxiety about her ability to control events. Her narcissism demands that she exercise absolute control over her familial and social environment, and ignore or destroy what she cannot control. When confronted with the undesirable, Irene resorts to her most fundamental defense — denial through repression of knowledge and memory: "Desperately she tried to shut out the knowledge from which had risen this turmoil.... She wanted to feel nothing, to think nothing" (223–4).

As a child, Irene had learned from her father that knowledge can be dangerous. Once, her brother had asked how Clare Kendry's father, a college man, had come to be a janitor. Her father had replied, "That doesn't concern you," then advised his son to avoid such an end as "poor Bob" (154) — an empty lesson, since the father neglects to explain exactly *how* Bob Kendry had become a failure. Her father's silence about Bob Kendry's interracial marriage signals to Irene that sensitive topics, like race, are best avoided. As a mother she adopts her father's myopic view of child-rearing out of fear of knowledge, telling Brian: "You're not to talk to [the boys] about the race problem. I won't have it." When Brian argues that they need to know, Irene's passionate reaction, including raised voice, anger, and tears, is clearly disproportionate to the discussion. The couple's arguments about the boys' sex education follow precisely the same pattern. Brian's insistence that the boys need basic sexual information assaults Irene with "a piercing agony of misery" and "extreme resentment" toward Brian's attitude, which "drove her to fury" (189). Such extravagant emotion locates Irene in the thrall of narcissistic rage, provoked by a diminution of control, Brian's presumption in challenging her, and an almost elemental fear of knowledge about race and sex.

Irene is so out of touch with her inner self that she does even not know she hates being Black. An indication of the racial oppression that burdens Irene emerges at the novel's opening when, visiting her father in Chicago, she is drawn to the Drayton Hotel by a fear of fainting on the hot, crowded sidewalk. This same fear of fainting, a sensation that mirrors her lethargy and detachment from events through much of the novel, presages her unconscious state at the novel's end: "Her smarting eyes ... the scorching cement ... the increasing crowd ... disagreeably damp and sticky and soiled ... her moist face ... about to faint ... need for immediate safety" (146–7). Irene gains entry into the Drayton by passing. The narrative locates her own personal paradise in that "Whites Only" universe where the cool atmosphere is "all that she had desired" (148) as imagery of heat, physical contact, and danger conflate into "Blackness," and that of coolness, remoteness, and safety into "Whiteness." Irene's escape to the Drayton roof represents an ascendance from the depths of a specifically racial claustrophobia. Her conviction that she passes for White only "for the sake of convenience" (227) obscures the truth, and the depth, of her desire to not be Black under any circumstances.

In fact, Irene discards her darker racial identity both publicly and privately by consciously denying her devalued (Black) self and privileging her valued (White) self in the service of ego protection and a heightened sense of self.[24] From her elevated vantage point of the Drayton rooftop, where African Americans are not allowed and poor people cannot afford entry, Irene gazes down "at the specks of ... people creeping about in streets, and thinking how silly they looked" (148). Her contempt for the crowd below exposes at once a narcissistic grandiosity, an aversion to the mass of humanity—especially Black and/or underprivileged humanity—and her self-hatred. This lofty position mirrors Irene's selected work on behalf of Black people—work that aligns her with White and wealthy patrons and insures her detachment from the very people she professes to represent. Her benevolent activities cloak a hidden loathing of them. At a society dance that Irene has organized to benefit "racial uplift," she again assumes a privileged position in the balcony as she dispassionately surveys the crowd below, diminishing them all to one-dimensional, fictional, nursery-rhyme characters. "Young men, old men, White men, Black men; youthful women, older women, pink women, golden women ... rich man, poor man..." (204). Irene diminishes her own household servants by objectifying and disembodying them: Liza is just an "ebony face," Zulena "a small, mahogany-coloured creature" (164, 184).

More pointedly, Irene's decision not to be a party to Clare's reassimilation into the Black community — a desire she finds foolish in the extreme — leaves unclear whether Clare's idea is foolish because she is being unrealistic, or because Irene cannot conceive of returning to, once having escaped from, Blackness. In the Chicago hotel room, Bellew, unaware that Irene and Gertrude are Black, interrupts the women's conversation to comment upon the loathsomeness of Negroes. When he ends by telling a "nigger" joke, Irene cries out, "That's good!" and succumbs to an irrepressible fit of hilarity: "She laughed and laughed and laughed. Tears ran down her cheeks. Her sides ached. Her throat hurt. She laughed on and on and on, long after the others had subsided" (171). Irene's hysterical outburst, coupled with the suggestion of her attraction to Bellew, registers as an indication of her rapport with Bellew's mental state, which she displaces onto the physical, as he transforms before her eyes from unremarkable to attractive because he dares to say what she secretly feels. Before Bellew speaks, Irene notes only his plainness and a pasty, sickly pallor to his complexion. Only after he declares his hatred for "the black scrimy devils" who "give [him] the creeps" does Irene concede that "under other conditions she might have liked him. A fairly good-looking man" (172–3). Bellew naïvely boasts that there are "no niggers in my family. Never have been and never will be." Though he knows no "niggers," he adds, he does know some people who actually have been acquainted with people of color, "people who've known them, better than they know their black selves" (171–2). The resonance between Bellew's words and Irene's statement that she knows her husband Brian "as well as he knew himself, or better" (187), suggests a sympathetic connection between Bellew and Irene: like him, she does not know her spouse at all; also like him, she loathes and fears Black people.

Before Bellew's entrance, when Clare and Gertrude openly share their fear of having a dark child, Irene defensively responds that "one of my boys is dark" (168). But after the tea party, to close off an argument with Brian about the boys, Irene concedes, "I'm sure you wouldn't make a mistake about *your* own boy.... As you please, Brian. He's *your* son, you know" tacitly disowning Junior, the "dark" one (188–9, emphasis mine). Irene's feelings about race and color alone place her in an impossible position with regard to mothering and positively mirroring her own sons, especially the "dark" one. She cannot possibly teach them to love themselves when she doesn't love herself or, at least, that part of her — her blackness — which she has bequeathed to them.

Mother Is __Not__ *Here*

Passing's mothers are uncompromisingly shallow, self-indulgent, and self-absorbed. Both Irene and Clare, for the most part absent mothers, largely distracted by their own search for fulfillment, exhibit a marked disregard for their children's welfare.[25] Irene's upbringing contributes to her damaged ego and subsequent maternal deficiencies. The text offers little information about her early life, but it is precisely this lack of information — the absences and silences — that invites the intuition that Irene's childhood was a disappointing experience. Her feeling of being neglected is arguably a significant factor in her adult decision to pay a great deal of attention to herself— to the exclusion of all others, including her children.

"Most men want sons," Irene advises Clare and Gertrude at Clare's tea party. "Egotism, I suppose" (167). As the only daughter in a family with two sons, Irene's perception is conceivably a lesson from her direct experience. She no doubt felt devalued in her father's, and by extension her own, eyes. Irene's mother was apparently alive until Irene was at least eighteen years old, yet Irene gives the announcement of her mother's death no special placement or emphasis. She reels off that information almost parenthetically and every bit as impersonally as the other developments she catalogues when she and Clare are reunited. "[Irene] told Clare about her marriage and removal to New York, about her husband, and about her two sons ... about her mother's death, about the marriages of her two brothers" (155). Irene refers to Bob Kendry, Clare's father, by the generic term "parent" ("the pasty-White face of her parent," "the day [neighborhood boys] had hooted her parent" (144–5). This odd turn of phrase is perhaps explained by the fact that her father was her only living parent. On the other hand, Irene's use of the impersonal term "parent" rather than "father" could express her emotional distance from things maternal, since the term as she employs it patently excludes the concept of "mother." Irene alludes to her own mother on only two other occasions in the novel, and while both times the parents are talking together with concern about a child, the subject under discussion both times is Clare Kendry, not Irene: "She had heard [about Clare's aunts] mentioned before; by her father, or, more likely, her mother.... 'I'm worried about Clare, she seems so unhappy,' Irene remembered her mother saying" (158, 153).

Irene's father, who had always liked Bob Kendry, has made inquiries into the matter of his friend's death after Bob had been killed. He returns home with no further information. It seems that Clare, he tells his wife as Irene struggles to hear, has disappeared into thin air. "What else he had confided to her mother, in the privacy of their own room, Irene didn't know" (152). Even though a tragic circumstance — Clare's father's death — is the cause of this particular concern, Irene's parents clearly share an ongoing general interest in Clare as well. That Irene deduces, in her first memory, that her mother was "more likely" than her father to worry about Clare suggests that Irene especially resents her mother's concern about Clare. Irene's second memory of her mother conjures a classic but distorted oedipal triangle and primal scene: the parents' private discourse is consummated by Clare's pervasive "presence" in the room with them, while Irene, the "real" child, is shut out from their intimate trio. Both memories bitterly reinforce the notion of Clare supplanting Irene even in her own childhood home. And the mere fact that Irene, who forgets almost everything, recalls these long-ago events with such clarity, testifies to their importance and their threat to her sense of self.

If, as a child, Irene had felt that her father was primarily interested in his sons, and that her parents neglected her in favor of Clare Kendry, she might well have sustained significant psychic damage. This would account in part for her narcissistic vulnerability as an adult. Specifically, if Irene's parents provided inadequate mirroring — or, worse, mirroring that reflected back *Clare*'s vivid likeness, not hers, as the desired daughter — then her incomplete ego development and resultant anxiety, her inability to give self-approval, and her intense resentment of Clare Kendry would be inevitable. These considerations account in part for Irene's profound insecurity as an adult, but they are only part of her broader pathology. To situate the root of such narcissism exclusively in a lack of positive early mirroring from distant, understimulating parents is to vastly understate the external forces that impact the collective ego of an entire culture.

3. Irene Redfield: Smoke and Mirrors

Psychoanalytic theory does not generally address what Larsen underscores, that is, that her characters are psychically disturbed — not only because of insufficient nurturing, but also through pervasive negative imaging from their external world. No amount of parental care can entirely protect African American children from negative societal mirroring and behavior. Further, as seen primarily through Clare's parents, parental care within an oppressed community might well be deficient to some extent precisely because of societal damage inflicted earlier upon the parents, which results in their reduced sense of self. The effect of racism upon Irene's parents would have been inevitable and considerable, given America's racial climate. Further, although Irene the child reads her parents' concern for Clare as excessive, the fact is that they were presumably anxious about Clare as an individual *and* as an adolescent alone in a forbidding social position. Her parents' interracial marriage had not been tolerated by family or society. White, college-educated Bob Kendry not only severed family ties, but also relegated himself to menial jobs by marrying a Black woman. The marriage, like the parents, had deteriorated under the pressure. Whispers around the neighborhood contend that Clare's mother would have abandoned the family if she hadn't died. In the meantime, Clare — whose mother and father were preoccupied with their own feelings of isolation and depression — obviously did not receive adequate parenting. Irene's parents would be well aware that now, as an orphan of mixed blood, Clare would have no real institutional or familial support and, without her parents, would not "belong" to either the Black or the White community.

The women in *Passing* act out not only a gendered role, but a dramatic one as well. The most distinguished parts they play are as wives and mothers. Irene, Clare, and Gertrude have all married "well," all are mothers, and all place such restrictions upon their availability as marital companions and mothers as to suggest that these roles are required, rather than desired. Given the lack of intimacy in Irene's marriage in particular, her union with Brian has the flavor of a contractual agreement rather than a love match. A successful physician, Brian provides Irene with status and financial security. In return, she is the consummate hostess and perfect mother to their sons. Nonetheless, their marriage rests on fragile ground, sinking at the foundation under the weight of accumulated resentments and unspoken anger, supported primarily by the image of its strength and propriety, or what Irene refers to as its "outer shell" (235).

Outwardly intact, Irene's marriage is strained and rent, merely "passing" for a solid union. Irene feels that Brian does love her, in his own detached manner, but in fact neither expresses the slightest affection toward the other. Until a critical point at the end of the novel, they never touch. Notwithstanding her professed conviction that "the bond of flesh and spirit between [her and Brian] was so strong" (187), they live like strangers, withholding secrets and affection from one another. They have not only separate beds, but separate bedrooms. Brian, disappointed by their lack of intimacy, bitterly refers to sex as "a grand joke, the greatest in the world" (190). Despite Irene's perception that she understands him as no one else does, their relationship lacks even a basic bond of empathy. Her misguided perception she knew him "as well as he knew himself, or better" (187) suggests that Brian's will is, to her mind, merely an extension of hers.

Irene especially despises Brian's expressed desire to go off to Brazil to escape American racism. The thought both angers and frightens her. Her anger is a function of the extreme narcissistic rage that overcomes her whenever she fails to command complete control over her environment. The fear comes from the same need to control; the idea of Brian's obeying his desire rather than her will is unconscionable. "[Brian's idea] would have to be banked, smothered, and something offered in its stead. She would have to make some plan" (188). The idea of "sacrifice"—something destroyed and "something [else] offered in its stead"—is a major resource in Irene's tactical arsenal, one that she will develop to a critical level by the end of the novel. In this case, the "something else" is her children. Irene assumes the role of fretful mother by drawing him into a concern that Junior, eleven, is growing up too fast, in order to divert Brian's thoughts from South America. While openly pandering, Irene's speech does not in the least resemble married people's talk; her dialogue is stilted—and the technique needs work:

> "You know, I'm awfully glad to get this minute alone with you. It does seem that we're always so busy—I do hate that—but what can we do? I've had something on my mind for ever so long.... It's about Junior. I wonder if he isn't going too fast in school? You're better able to judge" [188].

The argument that ensues pushes Brian to comment on their own nonexistent sex life; Irene's fury exposes the raw truth of the loveless marriage underneath the fairy tale.

Deep as it is, Irene's self-deception regarding her marriage pales in comparison to her role as mother. She thinks that she cares for her children and perhaps she does, to the limited extent that she is able to care for anyone but herself. However, her narcissism, by definition, severely distorts her maternal commitment and behavior. Evidence of her maternal claustrophobia is clear from the distance she maintains from her children. Rhetorically, her maternal detachment is artfully represented by the complete absence of Irene's (and, for that matter, Clare's) children within the text. No child-sounds ("Mommy, I'm hurt"; "Mom, come see my toy!") clutter the sterile atmosphere of the household. Ever. Little shadow creatures, Ted and Brian Jr. are insubstantial as ghosts, padding through the pages on little cat's feet, barely registering on the reader's consciousness. The boys are once seen and twice heard in the novel, but *never* in contact with Irene. Mother and children never so much as touch or exchange a word. The children's failure to appear as substantial entities mirrors their extreme marginality in Irene's life. At best, they teeter precariously on the extreme edges of her consciousness.

As the novel opens, the boys are away at summer camp — a circumstance that, while not indicative of parental neglect, does indicate the pattern of familial separation that Irene adopts. Though they supply the only sounds of genuine gaiety in the entire novel, Irene's sons do not appear to bring her, or to receive from her, any spontaneous joy. In the entire novel, she devotes only one memory exclusively to the boys' welfare — "Junior's birth ... [and] the time Ted had passed his pneumonia crisis" (228). Even this poignant remembrance is tainted by self-referentiality as she abruptly but effortlessly switches gears, fretting over Clare's disruption of her (imagined) happy home. While dimly aware of her two sons as individuals, her intense solipsism prevents her from perceiving them as unique, separate beings of true worth in their own regard. Rather, she values them as "selfobjects"— extensions of herself. As their function is to serve her demanding ego, they hold little intrinsic value for her in and of themselves.[26] Her plan to send Brian Jr. to school in Europe reflects not *his* needs, but *hers*: a European education would at once distinguish her, remove her son from the need of her everyday care, and further connect her to Clare, her idealized object, by elevating Brian Jr. to international-boarding-school standing, like Clare's daughter. When Clare first visits Irene's home, Irene presents her two sons like trophies. Freud's extraordinary comment on parental love (below) actually fits Irene, not because it captures the richness of the role, but because its cynicism blinds it from the possibility: "Parental love, which is so moving and at bottom so childish, is nothing but the parents' narcissism born again, which, transformed into object love, unmistakably reveals its former nature."[27] Freud's unilateral devaluation of parental love fails to distinguish between narcissistic pathology and object love. Irene Redfield makes the same mistake.

Irene sees maternity less as a joy than a burden that must be borne in the interest of role-fulfillment. Defending the importance of motherhood against Clare's apparent indifference, Irene self-deprecatingly confesses: "I take being a mother rather seriously. I *am* wrapped up in my boys and the running of my house. I can't help it" (210). Yet she demonstrates constantly that she can, and *does*, help it very well. Her statement presents a false image of maternal enthusiasm superimposed over carefully veiled resentment and cool indifference, tinged with self-pity. Because of her own ego deficiency, Irene is incapable of extending true object love to anyone. Specifically, she cannot provide adequate nurturing or positive mirroring to her own children.[28] Her relationship with her children, like her relationship with everyone else, subordinates the potential for real caring under an insatiable need for self-gratification.

Clare's statement that opens this chapter—that "being a mother is the cruellest thing in the world"—illuminates the relentless selfishness of both Irene and Clare. Mothering doesn't concern their children; it concerns the women and their needs. Motherhood is cruel because it interferes with their self-absorption. What Clare specifically means by her statement in its context is that her daughter is the only consideration that prevents her from returning to the black community. Yet Irene, who has no such problem, agrees with Clare that motherhood is "cruel"—mostly because, for her, it distracts her from herself. Having fulfilled her biological duty by giving birth to sons, she now doesn't know what to do with them. Just as she fails to mirror them, she is not even mirrored *by* her children; instead, she sees them as reproductions of her husband. Shopping for a present for her son Ted, irritated because she cannot locate the book he has specified, Irene's bitter mood, excessive to the occasion, also reveals anger displaced from her husband Brian onto her son: "Why was it that almost invariably he wanted something that was difficult or impossible to get? Like his father. For ever wanting something that he couldn't have" (148).

Above all, the children represent the glue that keeps Irene's marriage bonded. Irene might well be correct in perceiving that her indifferent marriage is secure only because it complements her role as mother of Brian's children: "She didn't count. She was, to him, only the mother of his sons. That was all" (221). The irony is that she accuses Brian of objectifying her without realizing that she does the same to him and her children.

Irene's essential lack of even maternal empathy is nowhere more evident than in her proficiency at manipulating others by using her own, and even other people's, children to protect her sense of security. She constantly throws up the notion of What Is Good For The Boys to quell Brian's wanderlust and to maintain control on the home front. She tries to restrict Clare's visits to Harlem by imposing parental (and marital) guilt, warning, "Think of what it would mean to your Margery if Mr. Bellew should find out. You'd probably lose her.... She'd never forgive you" [197]. Later, a more desperate Irene condemns Clare's desire to live in Harlem on the same grounds: "And what about Margery?" she asks her, "cold and tense" (234). Irene's absolute ruthlessness in the interest of her own needs reaches appalling heights when she callously wishes for "something to happen" to Clare's daughter to speed Clare's exit from New York: "Anything. She didn't care what. Not even if it were that Clare's Margery were ill, or dying" (225). The bald depravity of her wish underlines her sincerity when she says that "she didn't care what" happens to others, as long as her needs are met. Even the life of Clare's child—and by extension, perhaps, of any child—is expendable in Irene's larger design.

By her actions, Irene inverts the sense of her earlier statement that mothers are responsible for their children's happiness and sense of security. In her belief that children exist to elevate the standing and the image of their parents, she does not know how to truly value children for themselves. Her children are lovable, yes, but only to the extent that they reflect the desired image. Gertrude's fixed conviction, that "of course, nobody wants a dark child" (167), universalizes a self-loathing traceable back to slavery. This skewed perspective articulates the often transgenerational nature of internalized cultural intolerance cultivated within both the internal and external spheres. How *could* Gertrude love a dark-skinned child, and how *can* this child learn self-love, in the face of such unqualified parental bias? Irene, Clare, and Gertrude each reflect back to their children a damaged sense of self, consistent with the impact of their environment's view of them. As such, motherlove is a challenge of herculean proportions.

Although Irene is typically unsympathetic to everyone, her conduct toward her children is a behavior that puts ego development of others at greatest risk. The adults with whom Irene interacts, including her husband, can fend for themselves. But her children's self-esteem and potential for psychic growth are highly dependent on the parenting she and her husband provide for them. Irene's boys *do* enjoy a sort-of maternal figure for a moment, though: Their eager responsiveness to her sporadic visits and fairy-godmotherlike interest in them engenders "an admiration that verged on adoration" for Clare Kendry (208).

Irene and Clare

> Dark, almost Black eyes ... peculiar eyes, so dark and deep and unfathomable ... strange, languorous eyes ... slanting Black eyes ... dark eyes; Black [eyes] ... dark eyes ... Black eyes ... arresting eyes, slow and mesmeric ... withdrawn and secret ... Negro eyes! mysterious and concealing ... eyes of some creature utterly strange and apart ... eyes sparkling like dark jewels ... hypnotic eyes ... shining eyes ... dreaming eyes [144, 148, 149, 150, 157, 161, 171, 172, 203, 209, 238, 239].

This is obsession, nothing less; the repetitive thoughts come from deep inside the hidden soul of Irene. For an individual as dedicatedly self-absorbed as she, it is a curious lapse. Moreover, the object of her obsession is not her husband Brian, but rather, a woman — one she professes to loathe: Clare Kendry. While maternal issues are merely peripheral to *Passing*, the complex and profoundly layered relationship between these two women is the major storyline. Because it contributes so significantly to Irene's psychological profile, it deserves attention.

No one — not even Irene — is immune to Clare's extraordinary emotional and physical appeal. In a rare sincere moment, Irene allows that Clare has "a strange capacity of transforming warmth and passion" (161); Clare's beauty, she thinks, is amazing, extraordinary — impossible. The cool dispassion with which Irene appraises her husband contrasts sharply with her thoughts of Clare:

> Brian, she was thinking, was extremely good-looking.... in a pleasant masculine way, rather handsome [183–4].
> [Clare's] lips ... sweet and sensitive and a little obstinate. A tempting mouth.... The seduction of Clare Kendry's smile ... disturbing [161–2, 202].

Notwithstanding an undeniable homoerotic aspect of Irene and Clare's relationship which is, at points, so blatant and at others so brilliantly veiled that it escaped critical notice for decades, something else is going on between the two women. Their bond is both symbiotic and dysfunctional, as they pursue a quest to access, from the other, that undefined something that they both want and do not want. Irene's own rigid, implacable superego keeps her much-valued life secure, but prevents her from having any fun. For impetuous and reckless Clare, the very personification of the uninhibited, amoral id, living on the edge has become a virtual way of life. Both unsatisfied with half-measures, they want, impossibly, to satisfy mutually exclusive impulses within themselves by channeling the other. Clare wants to be Black without having to pay dues, so to speak, and Irene is her conduit. Irene wants to be both audacious and proper, a *femme fatale* like Clare, without losing an ounce of the vaunted security for which she has fought so hard, and Clare is her model. This push/pull conflict of emotions will result in the physical death of Clare, and, perhaps, the definitive spiritual death of Irene, even as she continues to live her empty life to its fullest.

The text's continuous eruptions in the above collection of quotes mirror the development of Irene's fascination with Clare's eyes into a compulsive obsession. The suggestion of a strong emotional attachment between Irene and Clare suggests that Clare has come to represent, in Deborah McDowell's words, "the object of [Irene's] sexual feelings,"[29] in Kohutian terminology the *idealized parent imago*, or the ideal of "perfection, power, and bliss" which Irene has been seeking for much of her life.[30] Both readings underscore the sexual dynamics at work between the two.

Irene and Clare's highly eroticized friendship also reflects, in psychological terms, the relationship between a narcissistic self and the object it idealizes. The bond, from the perspective of the narcissist, is immensely powerful: the object incorporates all the power, nurturing, and approval denied in early life, finally giving the self the validation which it has sought since childhood. In separate scenes, both women are depicted as clear glass. Psychologically, this transparency reflects both a fragile, almost nonexistent sense of a true self, and a dependence on others for validation. Clare tells Irene of a near-encounter with an old classmate years ago: "Once I met Margaret Hammer in Marshall Field's…. From the way she looked through me, even I was uncertain whether I was actually there in the flesh or not" (154). Clare's feeling of "not being there" is shared by Irene, who experiences precisely the same subjective invisibility when Brian comes to wake her one day for tea: "There was in [Brian's gaze] some quality that made her feel that at that moment she was no more to him than a pane of glass through which he stared" (216). In both cases, this "not being seen" extends past a single episode to expose a more general fear, created by profound ego vulnerability and a frightening sense of insubstantiality.

Irene's attachment to Clare, her idealized object, is infinitely deeper than her relationship with her children or husband. Further, her skewed egocentric worldview does not allow her to distinguish Clare as an individual separate from herself. From the beginning Irene blurs their identities, and toward the end she recognizes, without really understanding, that "she could not separate ... herself from Clare Kendry" (227). Her continual need for confirmation manifests itself in an intense hunger. Tragically, the passionate conflict between desire for, and fear of, merger is a recipe for disaster.

The action that begins the novel is Irene's formerly repressed recollection of her last encounter with Clare two years earlier at the Drayton Hotel, precipitated by a needy, pleading, eroticized letter from Clare ("I am lonely, so lonely ... cannot help longing to be with you again, as I have never longed for anything before...." [145]). Having "passed" in order to enter the cool elegance of the Drayton on that sweltering afternoon, Irene remembers being stared at. An initial ability to distinguish only disembodied whiteness ("ivory skin," "white hand") in her onlooker suggests a preoccupation with race and skin-color, as well as a latent anxiety about ego fragmentation. Even before she realizes who Clare is, Irene is unsettled by the woman's unwavering gaze: "She tried to treat the woman and her watching with indifference, but she couldn't.... Still looking. What strange languorous eyes she had!" (150). The obscured, ambiguous subject referent reflects Irene's inability to differentiate, even here, between herself and the other woman, and supports the notion that her ego boundaries are not only disturbingly indistinct but also extremely pliable: "Did that woman know that before *her* very eyes sat a Negro?... Some clue to *her* identity.... Who was *she*? Who could *she* be?" (150–151, emphasis mine). Distracted by the idea that the woman suspects her to be black — and therefore, out of place — Irene assures herself that she has not been found out, unwittingly casting herself in the role of a "stupid" White person in the process: "Absurd! Impossible! White people were so stupid about such things for all that they asserted they were usually able to tell" (150). On a deeper level, below the fear of being "discovered," Irene actively resists recognizing her childhood friend, and unconsciously expresses anxiety before she acknowledges the identity of the woman approaching her table. When Clare teases her memory ("Don't you know me? Not really, 'Rene?"), the first two words of Irene's response ("*I'm afraid* [you're mistaken"]) capture her fear of "knowing" Clare.

Before this encounter, Irene had last seen Clare twelve years earlier when Clare was fifteen, and the police had brought her father's body home from the saloon fight that ended in his death. Clare had stood disdainfully in her homemade red dress, "silent and staring." Then, "She glanced quickly about the bare room, *taking everyone in*.... And in the next instant, she had turned and vanished through the door" (144, italics mine). The moment of her father's death is the definitive moment of Clare's vanishing from her narrow, squalid, Black world as an orphan. She re-emerges to "take everyone in" again, but this time in the sense that she deceives others by passing (144). The incredible resolve of her act is emblematic of the adult Clare's dry-eyed determination to defeat life's odds, whatever the cost. The "pathetic little red frock" that Clare wore the day her father died is replaced with finery and images of passionate rebellion as red and gold become Clare's triumphant banner colors. "Wide mouth like a scarlet flower.... Red arch of her full lips.... Clare, radiant in a shining red gown.... her full red lips ... her disturbing scarlet mouth" (144–239). Clare's red is never again homemade or pathetic, the walls enclosing her no longer bare and dingy. "Gold" refutes her Blackness and inscribes her within a circle of regal stateliness, luster, radiance, and supremacy. "Clare, exquisite, golden, fragrant, flaunting ... her slim golden feet.... Clare fair and golden, like a sunlit day ... little golden bowl of a hat ... a flame of red and gold" (203, 204, 220, 239).

At her most accessible level of consciousness, Irene thinks of Clare as her opposite, a woman who has made (very bad) choices so completely different from hers. As she does in order to enter the Drayton Hotel, Irene again denies the unwanted part of herself by splitting,[31] this time by rejecting that part of her identity represented by Clare, whom she finds flighty and irresponsible. Clare readily, almost defiantly, admits her recklessness, gently mocking Irene for having chosen the safe, secure route. Later she warns her, "Really, 'Rene, I'm not safe" (196, 210): "Can't you realize that I'm not like you a bit? Why, to get the things I want badly enough, I'd do anything, hurt anybody, throw anything away" (210).

Even if perceived distinctions between Irene and Clare were real, this would not be enough psychic ammunition to neutralize Irene's repressed idealization of Clare. But the contrasts between the two women blur as they increasingly come to mirror one another. Irene and Clare's similarities, including a certain surface resemblance, vastly overpower their differences: Although emotionally estranged from their husbands, both are firmly attached to their marriages for status and security; both are distant mothers, oppressed by their children's need for them when they have so little to give; both depend entirely upon external perceptions for their identity; and both are deeply burdened by their racial heritage, which Clare deflects by passing and Irene by simply denying it. Both women are both deceitful, selfish, and determined to live the lives, and the lies, that they have created. More alike than either wants to be, the essential difference between them is that Clare deceives others, while Irene essentially deceives herself.

Clare and Irene *do* differ on the issue of race, but ironically so, as each would rather embrace the other's racial identity. Irene acknowledges neither her own discomfort with Blackness nor Clare's love of it. "Clare cared nothing for the race. She only belonged to it," Irene concludes (182), ignoring both Clare's having been forced by her aunts to pass as an adolescent and Clare's often-stated desire to return to her roots. "You don't know, you can't realize how I want to see Negroes, to be with them again, to talk with them, to hear them laugh" (200). This over-the-top dialogue would be laughable if it were not so pathetic. In repeating her earlier life — passing for White, but stealing back to the old neighborhood to be with Irene and other Black people — Clare represents the return of the repressed, forcing Irene to confront her own conflicted racial identity.

The women's renewed relationship in Chicago is characterized by an intense ambivalence that springs from several sources. In the first place, Irene's narcissistic idealization of Clare is inherently conflicted, as she continually struggles with the tension between the desire to maintain continuous union with Clare and a fear of losing herself through too-close identification with her. Also, Irene's long-standing resentment of Clare, in part territorial, re-surfaces as Clare threatens to replace Irene on the domestic front as she had done when they were children, and also on the social front, now that they are adults. Irene's resentment is counterbalanced, however, by a secret admiration, even envy, for Clare's beauty, style, and reckless disregard for danger. Finally, Irene's powerful attraction to Clare holds threatening sexual implications that conflict absolutely with her profound need for conventionality. Hortense Spillers describes the two women as at a dangerous impasse, given the push/pull, love/hate nature of their relationship ("Irene Redfield and Clare Kendry ... [are] stranded in some region of terrible ambiguity"[32]). Accordingly, Clare's death at novel's end is not entirely unanticipated: given two such egoistic and imposing personalities, the life span of any impasse between them is, predictably, severely limited.

Before her death, however, and conflicts between them notwithstanding, no other person in the life of either Irene or Clare perceives or authenticates the other as each woman does. The women use the language of desire, not friendship, with one another. When Clare asks, "You mean you don't want me, 'Rene?" Irene, always careful to avoid physical contact, cannot restrain herself: "Reaching out, she grasped Clare's two hands in her own and cried out with something like awe in her own voice: 'Dear God! But aren't you lovely, Clare!'" (194). Excepting her rages, this is Irene's most expressive passage in the novel. Such ecstatic response to another individual does not produce contentment, however, but rather, the central anxiety in narcissistic personality disorder: the fear of merger with the other and consequent loss of the self.

Such continued influence and domination on the part of the idealized object is intolerable to the narcissistic imperative, whose most emphatic need is to exercise absolute control of its environment and to maintain unconditional approval and compliance of its selfobject(s).[33] While Clare extends sympathy and confirmation to Irene, she also opposes, ridicules, and manipulates her, confusing Irene with mixed signals that further compromise Irene's sense of control. This, along with Clare's intrusion into Irene's realm, her increasing attachment to Harlem, and the sensual desire that she excites in Irene, is unforgivable behavior. Any action short of total acquiescence is the deepest form of betrayal in Irene's mind, and the feeling of having been betrayed would explain the intensity of her subsequent rage. Clare incalculably compounds her offenses, and seals her fate, by a stubborn refusal to leave New York once a desperate Irene determines that she must go. Callously neglectful of her own children, even more than usual during this period of preoccupation over Clare, Irene shamelessly drags out her already overworked refrain on maternal responsibility in order to manipulate Clare.

> "I imagine you'll be happy enough, once you get away.... Remember, there's Margery. Think how glad you'll be to see her after all this time."
> "Children aren't everything," was Clare Kendry's answer [210].

Indeed. "Children aren't everything" is an understatement for these two women for whom children are barely *anything*. But Clare has chosen the wrong time for such insouciance. Her disinterested, reckless refusal to be manipulated by Irene sets the stage for her own destruction.

The tragic climactic scene—fittingly set, given the pervasive irony of the novel, at an upscale Harlem party—anticipates the fateful intersection of several plotlines. Irene, Clare, and Brian are among the revelers, but their personal breathing space is a far cry from the general light-hearted atmosphere. Brian is, as usual, clueless, while Irene's murderous thoughts of his and Clare's alleged affair render her literally mad enough to kill. Clare's enigmatic smile suggests that she has accepted whatever the night might bring, even as her husband rushes to the scene, almost insane with the new information that his wife might be tainted with what he most dreads — Blackness. Indeed, bell hooks characterizes Clare as the *only* character in the entire novel who truly desires Blackness and sees Clare's murder as a direct consequence of this desire.[34]

While the elegant, elusive prose of the narrative leaves in question the nature of Clare's death (i.e., suicide, accident, homicide?), no one even begins to suspect Irene. Yet with the manifestation of her true self comes compelling circumstantial evidence of her crime: all those barely suppressed death-wishes for Clare; the frightening build-up of what ultimately becomes uncontrolled rage as Clare infiltrates her world and refuses to leave; Irene's quicksilver, almost invisible rush at Clare by the window; her hand on Clare's arm; and, finally, her convenient fall into unconsciousness and subsequent memory lapse as Clare falls from the window invite the conclusion that, with consummate motive and golden opportunity, she is the agent of Clare's demise.

Psychologically, Irene's killing of Clare harkens back to Sappho Clark's killing of Mabelle Beaubean in *Contending Forces*, with the crucial difference that Irene does not merely perform a symbolic murder of an unwanted alter ego; she actually *kills* another human being, acting out Klein's "splitting" concept to the ultimate degree. Were she pressed, Irene would explain away this crime as tidily as she would a bothersome hangnail or a gangrenous limb. In psychological terms, she would not be far off the mark: Inasmuch as Clare is, to Irene, no more than an extension of herself, the solution is simply to kill off her "bad," undesired part in order to retain, unthreatened, her essential "good" self. Regrettably, there is little of moral value in either of her two selves. Unmasked, Irene's tragic flaws are all too evident. Irene's children are destined to be, at best, neglected. They, too, are extensions of the narcissistic self, virtually ignored in the turmoil of Irene's psychoses. How ironic that Irene, who insists that she never passes, practices deception in every role she plays. Nowhere is this more evident, and more tragic, than when she plays at being a mother.

Chapter 4

Maud Martha:
Gray, Lined in Silver

Maud Martha: at first glance, the essence of grayness. Her world is suffused with shades of gray. Even her Blackness renders her portrait not black, but gray — in an environment where dark skin is common but generally undesired, its very ordinariness only serves to underscore its tendency towards invisibility. Dark-skinned and female in 1950s Chicago, she constantly fights just to be seen, much less appreciated. Maud Martha's inner self alternately accepts and rejects her nondescript life. Like a butterfly encased in a cocoon, she longs to burnish her drab canvas with brilliant color, but is inhibited by both external and internal factors. Only when she becomes a mother does a subtle blush of silver begin to work its magic at the edges of this otherwise unexceptional rendering and frame it with possibility.

The role of the mother is not the central focus of *Maud Martha*.[1] A *bildungsroman*, it traces the title character's maturation from childhood to adulthood. Maud Martha does not even become a mother until two-thirds into the text. Nevertheless, maternity is a crucial theme. Maud Martha's developmental process informs the quality of the nurturing she provides to her daughter, and her maternity, in turn, significantly influences her subsequent development. Just as her waking dreams liberate her from the narrow confines of everyday existence, motherhood stretches her boundaries. Written in a series of brief chapters, *Maud Martha* is largely anecdotal. These *tranches de vie*, or slices of life, are as often disjointed from the previous and following ones as they are chronological. By this expressionistic form of artistry, what emerges is a sketch whose indistinct lines suggest a finely drawn portrait of a girl who evolves into a wife, a mother, and a woman, in that order.

Gwendolyn Brooks' 1983 novel has been characterized by critics as a "celebration of the ordinary." African American women critics in particular appreciate its subtle depiction of an unremarkable protagonist and its attention to daily life.[2] *Maud Martha* emphasizes the critical importance of "ordinary" individuals, rather than designated "leaders," and of private as much as public life, in the quest for social change.[3] In concentrating on the particular, *Maud Martha* complicates and implicates the general state of the novel's larger universe, particularly issues of race, color, class, and gender, and the hovering shadow of World War II. The novel's orientation and largely domestic settings do not diminish its universality, but rather reflect the physical restrictions of urban Black women of its time, i.e., the strict race- and gender-role-conscious, pre–Civil Rights era of the 50s. Frantz Fanon's psychological theories underscore the profound sense of alienation that threatens Black people, both from themselves and from society.

The Psychology of Oppression; or, Born with a Veil

Frantz Fanon is unique among the field of major psychoanalysts in this study in that his work focuses on the impact of the structure of society upon the individual and, especially, the collective psyche of a debased and disenfranchised culture within that society. Fanon's observations led to groundbreaking conclusions in the field of psychoanalysis and race. An Antillean psychiatrist, author of the powerful and revolutionary text *The Wretched of the Earth* and political activist until his death in 1961, Fanon was educated in France and stationed in Algeria during the North African liberation effort. He has not only clinical, but also intimate acquaintance with racism and color bias, having been the darkest of eight children in a family afflicted with color consciousness.[4] From this vantage point, he was uniquely situated to study the psychology of colonized peoples. Citations from Fanon are primarily from *Black Skin, White Masks* (©1952), his earliest work. The missing element in traditional psychoanalytic theory — the impact of external factors upon the individual — is of foremost importance in his view.[5]

Fanon reverses Winnicott's assertion that "the structure of society is built up and maintained by its members who are psychiatrically healthy"[6] with his unequivocal contention that the invisible source of "racial illness" resides, in fact, *within* the structure of a given society and its institutions.[7]

An unhealthy society inevitably produces unhealthy individuals; in order for a culture to heal itself, it must first recognize and understand its illness. Further, without reference to historical, cultural, and racial dynamics, "the discoveries of Freud are of no use to us."[8] Although my perspective would argue for a "both/and" rather than an "either/or" point of view, Fanon's observation outlines the fundamental incompatibility between psychoanalytic theory and cultural reality for non–White peoples.

Fanon largely rejects Adler's psychology of the individual, Freud's theory of Oedipal neuroses, the illusory symmetry of Hegel's master/slave paradigm, and the foundation of Jung's "collective unconscious" for oppressed groups because these models stem from an individual and/or Eurocentric frame of reference that cannot, with any scientific integrity, be overlaid upon a fundamentally disparate culture. For the European, he contends, the family is an almost perfect microcosm of the state, so that no fundamental disproportion exists between them. But precisely the opposite occurs with oppressed groups: the broad chasm between the nuclear family and a hostile external world cannot be navigated without trauma. The person of color risks being overcome by a sense of inferiority, and, consequently, of manifesting pathological behavior both within and without the oppressed group.[9] And although Fanon's focus on the psychology of the oppressed parallels *Maud Martha*'s primary focus on intra-communal dynamics, wide cultural differences between Fanon's Martinique and *Maud Martha*'s Chicago setting must be acknowledged. At the same time, the universal oppression of African peoples results in an experiential and psychic kinship.[10]

Fanon recalls the racial self-consciousness that he experienced on the streets of Paris, jarring his sense of self:

"Dirty nigger!" Or simply, "Look, a Negro!"
I came into the world imbued with the will to find a meaning in things, my spirit filled with the desire to attain to the source of the world, and then I found that I was an object in the midst of other objects.[11]

Similarly, Maud Martha's racial anxiety, prompted by an impending visit from Charles, a White schoolmate, reorders her perception of her own familiar living room. The mantel, for instance, that has always seemed beautiful and ornate to her now suddenly becomes, in her imagined projection of White people's more "refined" tastes, "unspeakably vulgar" (158). Her anxiety over her friend's visit is reflected in her thought that "she only hoped she would be equal to being equal" (159). Elegance is reduced to crudeness, and pleasing aroma to offensive odor, by the anticipation of Charles's scrutiny. Maud Martha's behavior suggests the distance between intellectual and psychological "knowledge": she sniffs the air and even then raises the windows in spite of the long-established certainty that her home smells fresh. The same unease erupts when Maud Martha and her husband Paul spend an evening at the theatre. Their hopes of losing themselves in the adventures played out on the silver screen evaporate the moment they realize that they, like Fanon, are being dissected, and not very discreetly or kindly, by the ocean of White eyes surrounding them, the only Black people in the theatre. "'I don't know why you feel you got to whisper,' whispered Paul.... [Maud Martha] hated him a little'" [217–18]. Recognizing that they are mere objects of disdain and curiosity diminishes Paul and Maud Martha's sense of self. When Paul hesitates to approach the cold, closed faces of the candy-counter attendant and the ticket-taker, Maud Martha feels even more anger towards him for what she sees as cowardice on his part, rather than rudeness on the part of the White theater employees, which is the real problem. Resenting each other without even understanding why, they are "two shy Negroes wanting desperately not to seem shy" (217–18). The simultaneous repetition and disavowal of terms in both the living room and the theatre episodes ("equal to being equal," "...why you got to whisper, whispered Paul," "...shy ... not to seem shy") underline a conflicted consciousness. The wide societal gulf that separates Black and White people is explicit. Maud Martha and Paul are interlopers, cheating the other theatre-goers of something indefinable by their very presence. Their self-consciousness, in the face of punitive social mores, dehumanizes and objectifies them; the lights show not who, but rather "what" they are. Paul and Maud Martha's displacement of their resentment from the White stares that diminish them, and their projection of it instead onto one another, demonstrates the profound effect of the external gaze upon interpersonal relationships.

The qualitative difference between the theatre incident and those that Maud Martha experiences in her own community, however, is striking. Despite the psychic damage that racial prejudice inflicts, the hostility that emanates from White society is at least located *outside* her immediate environment. Most importantly, because racism extends universally to Black Americans, it does not evoke the same personal sense of betrayal that Maud Martha experiences when she encounters prejudice within her community and, worse, within her own family.

4. Maud Martha: Gray, Lined in Silver

Black, Get Back

> *If you're white you're all right*
> *If you're yellow you're mellow*
> *If you're brown stick around*
> *If you're black get back.* —Traditional

Maud Martha approaches life with the quiet ferocity of one who is constantly rebuffed from its embrace. An intelligent, sensitive girl, she exists in an external universe whose varied components have in common one bitter element: the responses she evokes from others are overwhelmingly negative, ranging in intensity from indifference to disapproval to downright rejection. The scope of these responses, which are based solely on her physical self, extend from the broad impersonality of the larger white society to the narrow intimacy of her nuclear family. That Maud Martha considers life to be "more comedy than tragedy" (307) communicates a sense of her extraordinary equanimity. In the scheme of personal, unheralded triumphs, her determination to maintain a cohesive self in the face of constant disparagement is nothing short of heroic.

Maud Martha's opening chapter is entitled "Description of Maud Martha," but the only physical description proffered is of her sister Helen, immediately setting up the theme of Maud Martha's invisibility, as well as that of color-consciousness, both of which run relentlessly through the novel. At seven, Maud Martha already perceives that Helen's beauty is "heart-catching," while her own allurements are merely "ordinary" (144). The text's coded language is nonetheless transparent: "Helen's soft little hands ... sweet and fine little feet ... cool and gentle eyes" (177–180). The profusion of adjectives and adverbs describes White, never Black, American womanhood. In *Black Rage*, psychiatrists William Grier and Price Cobbs explicitly frame the standard of American female beauty within its national context:

> In this country, the standard is the blond, blue-eyed, White-skinned girl with regular features.... [The girl who is Black] is, in fact, the antithesis of American beauty. However beautiful she might be in a different setting with different standards, in this country she is ugly.[12]

What Harry B. Shaw calls the "war with beauty" in *Maud Martha*[13] — that unrelenting tension between White standards and Black representations of physical attractiveness — rages through the final chapter of the novel as Maud reads a newspaper: ads promoting the feminine ideal hold center stage, prominently overshadowing tragedies of war. The front-page placement of "enhancement" products, including skin lighteners and hair straighteners, and their bizarre juxtaposition with stories of Southern lynchings, underline the severely misplaced focus of many in the Black press (and community), especially as Black men fight for their lives at home and abroad.

Maud Martha's unease about her dark skin is vague only because of her denial. When revelation finally comes, it is both startling and specific. One afternoon when Maud Martha responds brightly to what she thinks is an invitation to a wagon ride ("Hi, handsome!"), she is humiliated by her classmate Emmanuel's scathing response: "I don't mean you, you old Black gal.... I mean Helen" (176), thereby initiating her early on into the ruthless world of color bias in her own community. The young Maud Martha does not consciously allow herself to know what it is that causes family and friends to favor Helen, because to know would deepen the injury she has already sustained by their indifference. Everyone's champion, she cannot accept that her family fails to champion *her* on the grounds of something as uncomplicated as the hue of her skin. Maud loudly and vocally protects her younger brother Harry from neighborhood bullies and even dresses his wounds, but such consideration is not reciprocated. Harry, who invariably holds doors open for Helen, lets them slam in Maud Martha's face.

The slammed door is metaphoric for the lack of empathy Maud Martha receives, even from her family. Their father's preference for Helen is perhaps most painful because Maud Martha worships him. She alone defends his honest labor as a janitor while Helen disparages his work. Yet Helen is still the favorite, the valued one, not only with Emmanuel and their other friends, "but even with their father — their mother — their brother" (176–7). The mother's position in Maud Martha's reflections above — separate from, yet bracketed between, the father and the brother — highlight her centrality in her daughter's thoughts. Yet although the young girl indicts all her family members for favoring Helen, Maud Martha relates no such incidents specifically involving her mother. The mother's voice is conspicuously silent during incidents of this kind: she is neither seen to noticeably prefer Helen, nor to intervene on Maud Martha's behalf. Her mothering, on the "good-enough" scale, can be characterized as a failure by default to adequately affirm her daughter. This tendency provides the counter-frame of reference from which Maud Martha's own mothering skills later develop. Her mother's silence during her earlier years molds her gradually diminishing voice. Initiated by her family into feelings of relative unworthiness, she suffers what

Kohut calls a "lost childhood experience."[14] Lacking affirming mirroring from her parents, her superego has had neither time nor opportunity to develop in a healthy manner.[15]

As she moves into adolescence, Maud Martha comes into contact with another bias that often operates dynamically with color-consciousness. Within her community, classism is a cutting exclusionary tool used by its practitioners with a zeal that would rival the historically rigid British class system. Maud Martha's high school boyfriend, David McKemster, is imprisoned not within his skin color *per se*, but within his second-class Blackness which, by definition, excludes him from upper-class society. Besides explicit discrimination allowed by law and policy, poverty further prevents him from enjoying life's finer offerings — extensive travel, cultural pursuits, a broad and comprehensive education. He indulges, and at the same time stimulates, his cravings by taking a few courses at the University of Chicago, where, even on the inside, he is an outsider. Although only marginally of that world of privilege and entitlement, David is painfully aware of the extraordinary resources, riches, and possibilities accessible to the average White student. He resents the limited universe available to him in contrast to the timeless tradition of opportunity afforded White society. The more he learns, the more he realizes how deficient, how limited, how racially engineered his own segregated education has been. "Chaps on that campus ... read [Parrington's *Main Currents in American Thought*] years ago.... They've been kicking him around for years, like a *foot*ball!" (185). David's hunger for what he feels the White male students have always taken for granted is unappeasable. Predictably, however, on the psychological level, he directs his resentment *not* primarily at the White world, but at his uneducated, working-class parents and, by extension, his community. His bitterness creates a need to escape the multiple drawbacks that accompany his Blackness.

Gender interacts with color and class to compound the deluge of *-isms* (racism, sexism, classism, etc.) that compromise the health and the integrity of the Black community. Although they factor significantly into Maud Martha's socialization process, issues of gender are, like issues of race, often played out almost invisibly. Her earlier experience with dark-skinned boys who disparaged *her* dark skin illustrates both gender and race pathology: Skin color that might be acceptable for males is unacceptable for females, although at some deeper, unacknowledged level, the boys' and men's derision of dark-skinned girls and women is unquestionably a projection of their own negative sense of self.

The pervasive male preference for light-skinned women also reflects a paucity of role models. References to Black women are conspicuously absent from Maud Martha's female classmates' conversations. They chatter endlessly on about all kinds of subjects — hair styles, boys, activities, food, people, school. But when it comes to female idols, they are limited. Whereas little black boys have Joe Louis and Duke Ellington to look up to, the only female role model mentioned — what Kohut refers to as a "cultural selfobject"[16] — is Bette Davis. Cultural selfobjects are extremely important mirroring and confirming images, universally accessible devices that can help an individual to develop a positive sense of self. But selfobjects that resemble Maud Martha in her culture are virtually nonexistent — all the Black ones are men, and all the women are White. Helen is generally favored over Maud Martha because she more closely resembles the Bette Davises of the world.

Young children who lack grounding cultural material are subject to severe ego deprivation and identity conflicts. Fanon notes that in the Antilles, the consequence of inadequate positive Black images in print, film, or in classrooms is that the Black view of the world is White "because no black voice exists." When a Tarzan film is shown in Martinique, "the young Negro identifies himself *de facto* with Tarzan against the Negroes."[17] The Black female view in the 1950s is even more obscured than the Black male's, because no Black female voice exists. Fanon's Tarzan example is exacerbated for young Black girls because, historically, even fewer women than men of color are privileged with "heroic" status in any sphere.

Then there is the overarching matter of gender restrictions in general. Notwithstanding the ponderous weight of racism poised over their lives, little Black girls of Maud Martha's era are generally raised within their own communities much like little White girls: they are typically socialized to play with dolls, to forego higher education, to "catch" a husband, and to embrace motherhood and management of the home.

"An Order of Constancy"

The classic human response to pervasive negative feedback is eventual capitulation. Instead Maud Martha painstakingly erects, on both the conscious and the unconscious levels, strategic defenses in response to attacks upon her ego. True to the nature of defenses, Maud Martha's choices are inherently imperfect: while extremely useful in protecting her ego in the short term, they are, potentially, profoundly damaging in the long term.

On the external front, Maud Martha arms herself with a deceptively mild, acquiescent demeanor that masks an uncommon resilience and perceptivity, as well as her unacknowledged sensitivity. But most important are the internal defenses that she erects within herself to combat the negative inner voices, and to confirm her intelligence, attractiveness, and fundamental decency. For example, to the extent that she is able, Maud Martha understands the color bias that has overtaken her family. In one of a series of defensive moves, Maud Martha represses conscious rage toward her family by "forgiving" them. "She did not blame the family. It was not their fault. She understood. They could not help it. They were enslaved..." (177). But the curt, chopped sentences and the overrepeated denial "not" intimate that in spite of her words, Maud Martha *does* blame them; she masks her anger under a mantle of virtue she does not truly feel. Even though such understanding could not possibly eradicate all disappointment, the empathic response that she is able to access, on at least this intellectual level, gives her a certain control over the situation. This ability assuages what might otherwise become destructive narcissistic rage.[18] Such efforts are central to Maud Martha's conflicted but burgeoning acceptance of self. Maud Martha's deepest desire is simply "to be cherished" (144). Toward that end, she strives to make herself distinctive and valuable. "What she wanted was to donate to the world a good Maud Martha ... the bit of art that could not come from any other" (164). She successfully negotiates the dialectic between "ordinary" and "unique" by choosing a common image to represent herself while determining that her own special portrayal of that image renders it singular. In a tacit commentary on the lack of Black female role models, she rejects Bette Davis (and Helen) in favor of the dandelion — ordinary, perhaps, but more importantly, attractive. In the dandelion's reflection she "thought she saw a picture of herself," and it is comforting to group herself in such florid company (144).

The world of Maud Martha is defined by the ordinary, and much of this "ordinary" lacks even the subjective perception of a dandelion's prettiness. In tactile prose, multiple allusions to grayness overlay the narrative, from the closed smells in the narrow rooms to the plaintive sounds of lonely children. The "gray, dirty dishwater" (256), the "dirty gray windows" ((187), "the gray house" (160), combine to conjure an image of ubiquitous drabness. She sees the lives of her neighbors, the Lewys, as "not terrifically tossed.

Saltless" (256). At her uncle's funeral, Maud Martha considers, philosophically, that all life "comes down to gray clay" (167).

The persistent theme of ordinariness colors Maud Martha's worldview in general. She considers, for example, that "to most people, nothing at all 'happens'" (291), so she takes care to render the ordinary memorable and precious. Her grandmother, an "ordinary woman" despite all her loving kindness, achieves greatness not in life but in death when, in her casket, she "suddenly became a queen" (155). The young girl's transformation of the commonplace into transcendent moments is driven by her struggle to locate meaning and beauty within the ordinary (and consequently, within herself), to situate the ordinary in the realm of distinction. At the same time, her reverence for "little miracles" is mediated by unspoken resentment that "ordinary" does not seem to be good enough for others. When the family is threatened with loss of their home, Maud Martha's agitation contrasts starkly with her mother's and sister's calm acceptance. "It's just going to kill Papa!" cries Maud Martha dramatically [173]. Reflecting passionately on the "sweet dullness"—practically a contradiction in terms—of the family home, she marvels that other family members can seem so detached. Activities of her seventeen years in that home are microscopically detailed as she remembers specific foods she ate in the kitchen, unexceptional happenings, everyday tasks performed. The one memory that lingers, and that she repeats, is one of her "crying, crying in that pantry, when no one knew" (180–1).

The contrast between Maud Martha's outburst on behalf of the house and her silent, lonely tears in the pantry underlines the terrible isolation and lack of nurturing from which she suffers, even in the family home. The broad division between her inner and outer self has nudged her more into wallflower than dandelion status. Yet she manages to reconfigure even that painful aloneness into a bittersweet memory of the kitchen, making every small moment spent there count for something. In this sense the familiar, the reliable, and the expected become extremely important to Maud Martha. She treasures the traditions and rituals that her family observes, not only for their celebratory aspect, but for the all-important sense of security that she realizes from their predictability. The coherence of Maud Martha's ego is enhanced by the measure and the comfort of reliable persons, institutions, and events that she can depend on in an otherwise insecure and unpredictable world.

Because she observes, more than she participates in, life, Maud Martha's passivity helps her avoid situations that might be harmful to her ego. This silent pastime is not a mindless activity, but rather a deliberate and relatively effective sort of escapism, a device by which she redirects her thoughts onto nonthreatening distractions. She consciously studies, poeticizes, and commits to memory scenes from life that others would ignore. "She was learning to love moments. To love moments for themselves" (220). Even if they are not *her* moments, Maud Martha devotes herself to observing others with voyeuristic alacrity, cherishing any hint of enchantment that they might exhibit. Her interiority is a powerful tool that helps her establish a firmer sense of self. An extremely self-contained individual, Maud Martha virtually soars at the level of interiority. She confirms herself and expands her universe through private, affirming, and often humorous interior conversations. She also creatively designates her own inner self, in addition to other specifically chosen individuals, as one of her idealized selfobjects. Her self-stimulation and -confirmation on the psychic level has a down side, though. Through this device, she closes herself off from other people, so that her social skills are never fully developed.[19] Yet her fecund poetic imagination does free her from the drabness and inadequacy of her surroundings, and allows the realist in her to coexist with the dreamer. Maud Martha's vivid conception of fellow classmates as "little promises"—the unlimited potential in young Black children that others cannot see—reverses the gray tones of the sky and landscape. "Mixed in the wind ... bits of pink, of blue, white, yellow, green, purple, brown, black ... blew by the unhandsome gray and decay.... Past the tiny lives the children blew" (147). Maud Martha sees the children as outdistancing the drab confines of their immediate environment. She transforms them into dynamic, multi-colored, airborne leaves, soaring above the drab reality of their earthbound lives.

Yet there is something almost too pat, too determinedly upbeat, about her professed worldview; optimistic as it insists on being, it does not ring entirely true. Because Maud Martha's spirited ego sustained significant damage over and over again early in life, it remains fragile at core. This fact is definitively established by her choice of selfobjects. In reference to the ego imperative—or object hunger—that compels her to seek external figures to help shape her sense of self, a youthful Maud Martha's choice of beaux is instructive: She describes her first boyfriend, Russell, as fun and flashy, "a flourish," but he "lacked—what?" (183). The undefined something that he "lacks" is depth. In contrast to Russell's flamboyance, Maud Martha's second boyfriend David McKemster, the would-be participant in the university world, cultivates understatement and affects unnatural airs in an attempt to project an image of an English country gentleman. That she rather indifferently aligns herself with these two young men, in spite of their superficiality, says both that she is aware of their shortcomings and that they fill a need in her. Apparently Russell's flash and David's sophistication supply what she feels is missing in herself. More importantly, the fact that she has chosen two young men who can only consider themselves superior to her is a graphic indication of her own damaged sense of self.

While these adolescent attractions are fairly typical and not necessarily indicative of low self-esteem, the issue becomes much more serious with regard to the lifelong mate Maud Martha chooses as an adult. The psychic injury that Maud Martha sustained in childhood inevitably influences her choice of selfobjects. These subsequent relationships, in turn, work in a vicious cycle to deepen her sense of inadequacy. Maud Martha's desire to marry Paul Phillips, and the subtle but hurtful accommodations that she makes in order to do so, reflect a damaged psyche deeply at odds with her determination to value herself. Dark-skinned Maud Martha willfully marries a man who, she knows, has a problem with dark skin.

Her decision is inherently self-defeating, as it virtually ensures that the devaluation that damaged her in childhood will accompany her into her new family. Because her skin is darker than his, she will again be mistreated by someone who should love her. It is a case of exterior eyes wide open, interior eyes deliberately shuttered — shuttered as in practically closed, yet somehow, intuitively, knowing. Maud Martha's choice of a husband is a classic example of a psychological impulse, born of early psychic damage, characterized by inviting guaranteed anguish into one's life because deep down, there exists the secret conviction that one is somehow deserving of the pain and the disparagement that is sure to come.

"Stand Off, Daughter of the Dusk"

"I am certainly not what he would call pretty.... Pretty would be a little cream-colored thing with curly hair ... [while] I am the color of cocoa straight" (195). Not all members of a devalued society have low self-esteem. The health of one's ego corresponds closely to the degree to which the individual is able to counteract negative images and internalize positive ones. This ability varies from person to person, depending on one's developmental experiences. One of the things they all have in common is the fact that the ubiquitous images of beauty projected by the larger world differ dramatically from the typical features of their group. People of color who posses a strong and positive sense of self do not aspire to be, or to look, White. Yet Maud Martha quite knowingly marries a man who does not value his racial self, and who, consequently, will be constitutionally incapable of loving her.

Unselfconscious about his partiality to White standards of beauty, Paul is concerned enough about the "grade" of Maud Martha's hair to ask if her curls are natural and to be disappointed when she assures him that they are not. When he and Maud Martha imagine the children they will have, his candid self-assessment confirms that Paul directly associates light skin and curly (i.e., naturally wavy, *not* kinky) hair with beauty: "I'm light, or at least I can claim to be a sort of low-toned yellow, and my hair has a teeny crimp. But even so I'm not handsome" (196). During this important discussion on children, Maud Martha's fiancé does not pause to consider how well equipped he and Maud Martha are to parent these future beings, or what dreams his progeny might have; his concerns center solely on how his (and her) physical attributes will affect their offsprings' appearance. His telling use of the verb "claim" lays bare his deep conviction that light skin and straight hair are both commodities and attributes of significant value. Obviously, then, for the Pauls of the world, dark skin is a distinct mark of inadequacy and inferiority. Maryginia Washington, an elderly neighbor, echoes his sentiments, matter-of-factly advising Maud Martha to use skin lighteners on "the horror of [her] flesh"—because "they ain't no sense in lookin' any worser'n you have to, is they, dearie?" (264)—drawing a literal correlation between ugliness ("horror," "looking worse") and darkness that is both absolute and devastating.

At the Foxy Cats Ball, Paul leaves Maud Martha alone while he saunters off to dance with a woman who is as "white as a White" (227). Fanon briefly sketches the pathology of color consciousness, or fixation on light skin, in communities of color in a simple progressive formula that attempts to synthesize the dialectic between *having* and *being*:[20]

> By loving me the White woman proves I am worthy of White love. I am loved like a White man.... Her love takes me onto the noble road that leads to total realization.... I marry White culture, White beauty, white whiteness. When my restless hands caress those white breasts, they grasp White civilization and dignity and make them mine.[21]

The compulsive, repetitive, overdetermined eruption of whiteness in Paul's "white as a White" and Fanon's "white whiteness" resonates uncannily with the Black narrator's awe upon first encountering his future wife in *Auto-*

biography of an Ex-Colored Man: "She was White as a lily, and she was dressed in white. Indeed, she seemed to me the most dazzlingly white thing I had ever seen."[22] And indeed, it is through the act of matrimony to this translucent flower that the narrator in *Ex-Colored Man* transforms — no, *elevates* — himself to the status of *ex*-colored man. Although (or, perhaps, *because*) Maella, Paul's dancing partner, is not White, but rather only *appears* to be so, Fanon's formula applies here to the extent that Maella's lightness is significantly closer to Paul's ideal than is Maud Martha's off-putting duskiness. In this way Paul receives the added bonus of appearing to be "loyal" to his race, even as he is publicly disloyal to his wife. Indeed, Paul's distorted way of thinking serves to exemplify how broad the permutations, and how illogical the basis, of color consciousness.

In light of Paul's clear preference for women of lighter hue, then, why *does* he marry Maud Martha? Were Paul the subject of this study, I would develop the idea that he, too, is laboring under a damaged sense of self and that he sees in Maud Martha a woman who is essentially undesirable to him and, therefore, one over whom he can exert supremacy as well as one whom he can easily control. But this isn't about Paul; it's about Maud Martha. So the more pertinent question is, why does *she* marry *him*? "It's my color that makes him mad. I try to shut my eyes to that but it's no good.... He keeps looking at my color, which is like a wall" (229). Maud Martha actually commiserates with Paul for having to "jump" so high over his skin-bias barrier in order to reach her true self. But what of Maud Martha? Does she not tire of all the jumping *she* has to do in this relationship? Why would a woman willfully place herself in this situation?

Maud Martha actively capitulates to color bias by marrying Paul. At the same time she passively refutes it by acknowledging that she has been as blind as he by overlooking his obsession ("I try to shut my eyes to that" [229]). Her empathy for Paul — as though she, not he, is the cause of his labored efforts — masks anger and frustration. The emotions she attributes to him are in fact a projection of her own: *She* is mad, and she is sick and tired of his infatuation with light skin. But the proud, sure knowledge that Blackness is imbued with beauty and riches, boldly asserted in the 1960s and '70s, is missing in Maud Martha's 1950s society. Consequently, despite half-hearted efforts to affirm herself, hers is a conflicted psyche.

Paul is not only fixated on lighter skin; he also harbors social ambitions that Maud Martha does not share. His excitement over the invitation to the Foxy Cats Annual Ball exposes his dream to be a part of high society, one of the "swells." Trapped in a demeaning grocery-clerk job, supporting a pregnant wife, Paul imagines the Foxy Cats as the realization of unfulfilled desire in a realm far removed from the gray tedium of work and home. The Foxy Cats Club is itself a classic representation of intra-communal gender, class, and color élitism. Members of the exclusive brotherhood are middle-class Black men devoted not to moral, civic, or cultural pursuits, but to seeing and being seen, to being recognized and envied for Living the High Life. Echoing the flamboyant Russell of Maud Martha's youth, Paul believes that he "had been born to *occur*" (289, italics mine), while Maud Martha simply "is." She knows that he loves and aspires to what he considers the finer things in life, especially material possessions, prestige, and, to his mind, beautiful (i.e., light-skinned, straight-or wavy-haired) women. Maud Martha sees, but does not see, that his exalted opinion of himself is the means by which he masks and compensates for deep-seated insecurities. She knowingly accepts from the outset an inequitable love-match, a union handicapped by Paul's devaluation of her: "He is thinking that I am all right.... That I will do ... my whole body is singing..." (194).

She comes into marriage as a supplicant rather than as a treasure. Her tone mirrors Fanon's comment that "one must apologize for daring to offer Black love to a White soul"[23]; although this marriage is not interracial, the dynamics resonate. Maud Martha understands that the chasm between Paul's feelings for her and hers for him is as broad as the difference between "occurring" and "being." Paul's attitude fails to diminish his powerful appeal to her; it is actually *part* of his appeal, given her compromised self-regard. The conspicuous disparity between Paul's and Maud Martha's sentiments toward one another — by her own account, she is merely adequate in his eyes while he is wondrous in hers — signal that, in her secret fear that others do not value her, Maud Martha has ensnared herself in a self-fulfilling prophecy by choosing a mate who cannot possibly validate her.

Yet Mary Helen Washington's assessment that Maud Martha "now sees herself entirely through Paul's eyes"[24] does not paint a complete picture of a situation that is more gray than black and white. Although Maud Martha enables Paul to undervalue her, she does not quite fully internalize his view. She distinctly qualifies her language to identify Paul's outlook ("what he would call," "his idea of...") without affirming it. "I am not a pretty woman.... If you married a pretty woman, you could be the father of pretty children" (196): As Maud Martha articulates what she knows Paul is thinking, it is unclear whether she is deliberately expressing his thoughts out of deference to him, testing his commitment to her, or merely seeking a compliment. In point of fact, there is something of a forced nature to her statement; Maud Martha's previous assessments of herself discourage the view that she truly believes herself unattractive. Paul's failure to contradict his wife cannot possibly be the response that she expects or desires.

When Paul callously abandons her at the Foxy Cats Ball to dance with Maella, Maud Martha holds her own under the intensely critical gazes of other revelers. She adopts a posture of cool nonchalance, "trying not to show the inferiority she did not feel" (227). Deft narrative transposition of the word "inferiority" shows that she is aware of, but not completely bound to, others' assessment of her. Although often ambivalent about her own self-image, she struggles throughout the novel to reserve a space, through imagination and language, in which to define herself. "I am ... sweet, and I am good, and he will marry me.... In the end I'll hook him, even while he's wondering how this marriage will cramp him" (197). Maud Martha's understanding of Paul's "White soul" and of her female role as "hooker"—that is to say, captor—of a husband ("I'll hook him") accounts for only part of the deference and humility she brings to the marriage table. A general, yet crucial, factor in romantic relationships of this era was the playing-out of restrictive gender roles and sexual politics. Young women, Black and White, were taught—at home, in social situations, and at school—strategies for "catching" a man. The inadvertent irony of Maud Martha's reference to herself as a "hooker," given its colloquial meaning, is that she does not sell herself to Paul; she sells herself to her*self*, convincing not him, but her persistent disparaging inner voice, that she will ultimately prove to be acceptable to him. In the meantime, she romanticizes the union: "She thought of herself, dying for her man. It was a beautiful thought" (201). This melodramatic, self-effacing (and societally sanctioned) idea does have perhaps one dubious benefit in the short run: It temporarily staves off anger and humiliation.

As early as the honeymoon stage, a scene that lacks all subtlety shows husband and wife in bed, physically close but emotionally worlds apart. Paul is studying *Sex in the Married Life* while Maud Martha concentrates on *Of Human Bondage*, a choice that blatantly suggests that *she* is the one who has been "hooked" into the marriage. Their attempts to establish a connection with one another constitute wasted effort. Maud Martha ignores Paul's urging that she read his book. He, in turn, is unaware that Maud Martha is already disenchanted with his indelicate lovemaking. Paul is equally immune to her attempts at gentle persuasion in other areas. On a library outing that she has convinced him to take, she is pleasantly surprised to see him engrossed in the library cards. When she comments on his apparent interest in literature, he quickly disabuses her of that idea: "No-o. I'm just curious about something. I wondered if there could be a man in the world named Bastard. Sure enough, there is" (210). And sure enough, Paul's mindless search ends in revelation, just as does Maud Martha's failed library experiment. His interest in the inane defeats her ever-diminishing hope that they will ever share a bit of grace. Their increasing incompatibility, and the resultant monotony into which their life together is falling, are signaled by recurrent strokes of dull gray. Grayish sensory allusions — sights, sounds, smells — insinuate themselves into her home, becoming stronger by the day. There was "a whole lot of grayness" surrounding the Browns (206).

Maud Martha believes that even an unexciting marriage should, like a tradition, represent some "order of constancy" — some secure element on which one can depend (242–3). In short, she defers to a stable marriage rather than a happy one. But Paul refuses to accommodate Maud Martha's need for tradition even from the outset: For her birthday he typically unceremoniously gives her drugstore candy — that is, on years when he remembers her special day. The marriage soon degrades to the point where it is no longer reliable, so that even her pregnancy fails to unify the family. The sensation that Maud Martha feels of "something softly separate in her" manifestly applies to the baby's approach, but it also refers, subtextually, to her marriage. Even as his wife struggles to bring their child into the world, Paul, nauseated by the experience, callously transports himself light years away from the maternity ward. At this crucial hour, he deserts Maud Martha for his *true* feminine ideal — the docile, pale beauty of his fantasies: "His thoughts traveled to the girl he had met at the Dawn Ball several months before. Cool. Sweet. Well-groomed. Fair" (233–4).

Mother's Little Helper

Although parenthood does little to enhance the marriage, motherhood certainly brings out the best in Maud Martha. The act of creation buffers her ego as nothing else in her life had done. The day before her baby is born she spares the life of a mouse. Sensing a maternal camaraderie with the unremarkable little creature, she springs the trap, urging the mouse to "go home to your children." In this instance Maud Martha equates saving a life with creating one, and the sensation is "wonderful" (213). Her simple act is founded on the empathy that she has always been capable of, despite having seldom received it herself. For Maud Martha it represents a moment of triumph and presages the protective instincts that will sustain and strengthen her as a mother, and the seriousness with which she treats any life that, as she self-deprecatingly puts it, "blunder[s] its way into her power" (213).

While even before marriage Paul had admitted to his wife that he was not exactly cut out for fatherhood, Maud Martha is immediately comfortable in the maternal role. Her initial response is governed by the conventions of the times by which a woman was validated — marriage and motherhood. Having lived under Helen's shadow all her life, Maud Martha once uses this status to demonstrate to her mother that she has, at long last, eclipsed her sister. Enumerating the facts of her marriage, her motherhood, and her home, she asserts: "I have more than [Helen] has" (309). But Maud Martha never again uses such questionable leverage to elevate her sense of self. Instead, her maternity evolves to become a liberatory role in and of itself, eliciting from her heretofore untapped psychic and emotional strength.

The baby's helplessness provokes the emergence of long-suppressed affection and protective feelings in Maud Martha.[25] Her child's love triggers emotions that she had learned so well to bury, and her defensive walls crumble when the tiny creature, more in need of protection than she, enters her life. The unconditional love that a child gives (and demands) prompts the new mother to respond in an entirely unprecedented manner. Paulette becomes the embodiment of Maud Martha's lost childhood experience, an opportunity for her to be a little girl again. And, through this process, she comes into her own as the woman she would wish to be. *This* time, she will be embraced in all her dark beauty. "Hello, Mrs. Barksdale!" she hailed. "Did you hear the news? I just had a baby, and I feel strong enough to go out and shovel coal! Having a baby is *nothing*, Mrs. Barksdale. Nothing at all" (240).

The baby's birth gives the new mother uncharacteristic vitality — and, importantly, a voice. This brief communication to Mrs. Barksdale constitutes the longest string of consecutive sentences that Maud Martha has uttered thus far.[26] Despite her imagined plea to Maella at the Foxy Cats Ball to leave Paul alone because she was "making a baby for [him]," and despite the baby's name, which designates her as her father's daughter, Paulette is really Maud Martha's gift to herself. That "part of Maud Martha Brown

Phillips expressing itself with a voice of its own" (241) refers both to the newborn's cries and to Maud Martha's own fledgling ability to speak for herself, in her developing roles as a mature adult and mother.

Maud Martha's evolution from voicelessness to voice, from powerlessness to empowerment, occurs gradually, and in direct correlation with Paulette's development. At first, her voice resonates only inside her own consciousness. On their first Christmas, Paul, thoughtless by nature, dismisses the well-established Brown tradition of purchasing a tree on the 21st of December, waiting instead until Christmas morning in order to get one on sale. He further insists that Maud Martha put Paulette to bed rather than spend the evening as a family while he hosts, in effect, a stag party on Christmas night, with Maud Martha as reluctant waitress: "She passed round Blatz [beer], and ... removed from her waist the arm of Chuno Jones, Paul's best friend" (249). While she silently goes through the motions, her body language eloquently conveys a stultifying rage. Contemptuous incredulity about her situation colors her posture as she only pretends to be with Paul and his guests in their living room. The mechanized air of her movements underlines the artificial, perfunctory level to which her wifely role has descended. At the level of interiority, her desire for that sense of tradition which bound all her holidays before her marriage remains strong. "What she had wanted was a solid ... hard as stone and as difficult to break. She had wanted to found—tradition. She had wanted to shape ... a set of falterless customs (244). This quote is striking for several reasons. First, the verb tense reflects disappointment more than determination to reinstate tradition, but the insistent repetition of "she had wanted," like the compulsive resurgence of an idea that she is unwilling to renounce, undercuts the more passive interpretation of that thought. Next, her nominalization of the word "solid" elicits images of firm grounding, unbreachable tradition, substantial memories. Finally, the unmistakable resonance between "falterless" and "fatherless" cleverly suggests an erasure of the father from the family portrait, gently echoing Maud Martha's resolve to establish a life and memorable traditions for her daughter, with or without Paul.

The idea of a fatherless Phillips family is more than a notion: Paul's jealousy toward his child — he refers to Paulette as Maud Martha's, not *his*, "precious princess daughter"— suggests his growing perception that the Phillips family would, indeed, be complete without him. Even his daughter's name allows for a reconfigured familial arrangement, with Paulette representing a kinder, gentler, *female* version of Paul. Add to these points author

Gwendolyn Brooks's own words in a 1977 interview, and we have, in no uncertain terms, one fatherless family:

> Well, [Maud Martha] has that child, and she has another child and then her husband dies in the bus fire that happened in Chicago in the fifties.... I had taken him as far as I could. He certainly wasn't going to change. I could see that.[27]

Notwithstanding the deep, slow-burning anger that has characterized Maud Martha's emotional response to Paul's chronic insensitivity, her definitive emotional break from her husband occurs only when his hurtful behavior extends to their child — specifically, when life begins to repeat itself around issues of Paulette's skin color. Paul seems unhappy that "the baby was getting darker all the time" (289).

"A Voice of Its Own"

Though Maud Martha does not respond directly to Paul's comment about their child's skin color, his remark is doubtless the catalyst for her first expression of anything even close to an objection over this issue. When Maud Martha's mother first comes to see Paulette, she seems surprised at the baby's comeliness. "Well, she's a little beauty, isn't she!" (240). Suddenly realizing that her mother did not expected the baby to be attractive, Maud Martha begins, at this moment, to accept the ego damage she sustained in childhood by her family's preference for Helen. Her own lost childhood helps her to understand how desperately a daughter would need approval from her mother; the desire to be such a mother drives her need to validate her own child.

Maud Martha undoes some of her own negative mirroring by protecting her daughter from Paul's (and the world's) indifference with the enveloping shield of her own unconditional love.[28] Still, her declarations — silenced in adolescence — are tentative, inexpert. The once-strong voice that had boldly protected her brother Harry, had cried out in defense of the old homestead, and had flirted saucily with Emmanuel, has gradually muted in response to the by-now-predictable pain of rejection. While her silence suggests feelings of insignificance and low self-esteem, powerlessness and rage, these negative emotions are somewhat mitigated by Maud Martha's powerful inner voice, which is seldom silent. Her interiority is the level on which she acknowledges and expresses negative emotions, and serves the important function of diffusing some of their potency. The humor and reasoning power of her inner voice, coupled with a fruitful imagination, signal a core, however fragile, of self-worth.

A series of four racial incidents traces Maud Martha's gradual evolution from silence to speech after she becomes a mother. The first scene takes place in Mrs. Johnson's beauty shop, when Miss Ingram, a white saleswoman, arrives at the salon to take an order. At the conclusion of their business, the woman confides to Mrs. Johnson, not too quietly, that hers is hard work indeed: "I work like a nigger to make a few pennies." Maud Martha hears the saleswoman but does nothing. She relies instead on the stunned shop proprietor to correct the situation. Her behavior is passive, even taking into account the forbidding gaze that she directs at Mrs. Johnson, as if to force the other woman to protest this outrage. When Mrs. Johnson fails to react, Maud Martha, out of options, simply wills the incident to have not happened. She turns away from real life and immerses herself in *Vogue*, the preeminent arbiter of American (and European, for that matter) images of beauty, while her interior voice halfheartedly denies what she explicitly heard: "I must have been mistaken. I was afraid I heard that woman say 'nigger.' Apparently not" (282). When the saleswoman leaves, Mrs. Johnson's feeble excuse to her customers for failing to challenge the insult ("What would be the point?" [284]) angers Maud Martha but fails to rouse her voice. Her renewed stare at Mrs. Johnson is rendered ineffectual by her silence.

In the next incident Maud Martha actually uses her voice, but still does not directly confront the issue at hand, i.e., a sales clerk who has no wish to wait on "nigger women" (297). Sensing the woman's disdain, Maud Martha pretends to be merely undecided, then leaves without making a purchase, thereby depriving the saleswoman of a commission:

"I've decided against the hat."
"What? Why, you told — But, you said —"
Maud Martha went out, tenderly closed the door [298].

Maud Martha's well-mannered body language mirrors her verbal posture. She does not slam the door; she closes it softly, repressing anger and sound, but not, this time, intent.

The third instance occurs at Maud Martha's new housekeeping job, which she has taken in order to augment the family income and provide more fully for her daughter. From the moment she enters the house she is reprimanded for using the front entrance and told in no uncertain terms to come to the back door in the future. Mrs. Burns-Cooper's attitude enlightens Maud Martha on an important issue, directly related to tensions between Black women and men of the era. The difference between working at home and working in a racist workplace is measurable in degrees of stress, low self-esteem, frustration, anger, and, often, the mindless impulse to vent these feelings once one returns home. "For the first time, she understood what Paul endured daily" (304). By the end of the day Maud Martha has decided to quit. Her inner voice frames a speech she wishes she *could* make aloud to Mrs. Burns-Cooper, but even this internal argument is circuitous: She uses the impersonal third person ("Why, one was a human being" [305]) to distance herself from her humiliation. Also, she argues an indirect point — the fact of her normalcy, her humanity — rather than the direct issue of Mrs. Burns-Cooper's racism. But this time she at least questions the appropriateness of her silence and constructs, in her head, an argument she *should* have made. After that first, humiliating day, she decides not to return again, and leaves without a word. Hers is a silent rebellion, a somewhat hollow victory that leaves her with a sense of incompleteness. That she "couldn't explain [her] explanation" for quitting her job (305) signals that Maud Martha is aware of her inability to articulate her own feelings. This defiant behavior, so different from her generally compliant nature, is a mystery even to Maud Martha, who has not yet analyzed the reason for her altered response to external antagonism. Her oblique reference to Paulette in her internal argument to Mrs. Burns-Cooper ("One loved one's baby"), however, suggests that, at least on a subconscious level, she is beginning to derive a more resolute sense of being and a new inner strength in direct connection with her maternal self.

In the final episode, set in a department store at Christmastime, Maud Martha's voice bounds dramatically from its earlier passivity. Crucially, this time Paulette is physically with her. The store's requisite Santa is friendly and attentive to the White children, but pointedly ignores Paulette. When Paulette finally approaches him, he looks everywhere but at the young girl, clearly intending to brush her off. Without forethought, Maud Martha confronts the ersatz Santa:

> "Mister, my little girl is talking to you."
> Santa Claus's neck turned with hard slowness....
> "Mister," said Maud Martha.
> "And what — do you want for Christmas." No question mark [315].

In calling him "Mister," Maud Martha reduces the jolly, red-cheeked, larger-than-life figure to manageable dimensions, exposing him as just a man — and a bigoted one, at that — in a Santa suit. The possessive reference to Paulette ("*my* little girl") ties together the mother/child unit and underlines the not-insignificant power of the two, as opposed to the absolute powerlessness of an easily overlooked little Black girl. When Santa's attention is slow in coming around to Paulette, Maud Martha's repetition of the word "Mister"— neither question nor plea, but clear warning— signals the seriousness of her intent. Maud Martha's voice not only serves to amplify Paulette's; it also represents a moment of self-discovery — the re-location of the voice that she had lost.

Despite this epiphany, the adventure does not end happily. Pressured into compliance, Santa only grudgingly goes through the motions. Maud Martha cuts the visit short, and finds herself unable to explain to her bewildered child why Santa, lover of all children, did not seem even to like her. The incident, and Paulette's poignant questions afterward, illuminate for Maud Martha how inadequate her words have been, how underdeveloped her outer voice still is. Finally she acknowledges the existence of "scraps of baffled hate" within herself. This recognition is a major revelation, for it connects her long-repressed hate and anger to what she now sees as her "hungriest lack — *not much voice*" (318, emphasis mine).

Mary Helen Washington calls Maud Martha's story incomplete because she has not yet found "a language powerful enough to confront life's abuses."[29] This is precisely the point of *Maud Martha*: not completion, but fruitful evolution and the promise of possibility. Hélène Cixous's theory, that women find their "lost voice" through their mothers,[30] has not been the case for Maud Martha, but it will certainly be so for Paulette. An unremarkable woman, perhaps, she develops remarkable inner strength through the power of intense motivation — the welfare of her child. Although a work in progress, Maud Martha is unmistakably evolving, developing options for herself and for Paulette, protecting her daughter against the kind of injury she herself had suffered.

At novel's end, an exuberant Maud Martha poses to the sky one final question: "What, *what*, am I to do with all of this life?" Particularly in view of the crucial part that motherhood has played in her revitalization, her question seems an awe-filled response to her second pregnancy. "The sun was shining.... And, in the meantime, she was going to have another baby" (321–22). But the question has to do with more than the life growing inside;

it is also about the *life* growing inside her, the psychological blossoming that she is experiencing. The woman who found her voice on behalf of her daughter at Christmastime emerges in the spring to smile at the sun, and to welcome the future, although she does not know exactly what it holds. This Maud Martha reflects a new resilience. While she had earlier sought solid, permanent, predictable things, she is now confident about a future that she cannot possibly predict, unhesitant in the face of unrestrained possibility.

Maud Martha's internal musings are fundamentally different here. Her earlier imaginings reveal an escapist attitude, a posture of isolation, distancing her from other people. These final thoughts put her in contact with the world, suggesting the emergence of a more assured, more socially connected, more articulate Maud Martha. That she continues to represent herself as that "commonest flower," the quirky, resilient dandelion, confirms that her sense of self remains firmly grounded. She is brimming with confidence in the wake of her pregnancy, and the dandelion metaphor communicates a new resolve: Even if she stumbles, she will reemerge intact in the spring.

This unbridled sense of possibility and potential establishes a clear thematic. The gradual maturity of Maud Martha allows her to replace despair with determination, and bewilderment with self-assurance, in the raising of her children. As drab gradually gives way to bright, there is less gray, more finely textured silver in the portrait, and the promise of Maud Martha who, at novel's end, is still becoming.

Chapter 5

Celie: Emergent Light

In this remarkable work, the outer frame features bold and uncompromising slashes of oppositional color to position the women and the men. As for the maternal portrait, the artist's brush never touches the canvas. Rather, Celie emerges, stroke by stroke, from inside out, with only gradual consciousness of becoming, until, finally, her essence suffuses the surface with such vitality that its presence can not ignored. The picture of this mother is a virtual tabula rasa, the palest of images, as the story begins. It will take a lifetime's worth of lessons and development to render her most dramatically colorful and fully realized self at novel's end. Celie's completed psychic portrait is one of strong definition and vibrant defiance, a well (although untraditionally) nurtured "child" grown to be a strong woman and mother, capable herself of generous nurturing. Karen Horney's theories inform this study.

The Color Purple was greeted with a firestorm of protest from the moment of its publication in 1984.[1] Calvin Hernton notes without irony that "more than with any other Black-authored work so far, *The Color Purple* seemed to have driven some of its critics literally *crazy*." He cites, in the main, Black male criticism, particularly against the novel's portrayal of Black men, and offers Tony Brown's ravings as the most blatant example.[2] Hernton finds that the "clang of fury" leveled against the novel is a telling aspect of Black America's denial, homophobia, and guilt that must be addressed — but not by killing the messenger. The thunderous silence of these same critics on the subject of woman battering that pervades American culture, he asserts, is more telling than we might wish to acknowledge. "Does all of this silence," he asks, "say something about the humanity of not only [*The Color Purple*'s] critics but about the humanity of us all?"[3] If healing is to occur, must we not first confront our ugliest, our basest, truths? This, I think, is a large part of what Walker wished to accomplish in penning this story. Comparing the writerly "uplift" work of nineteenth-century activist Frances Harper to Alice Walker's *The Color Purple*, Deborah McDowell acknowledges their important distinction and similarity:

> Walker sacrifices the impulse to uplift the race, although hers is no less than Harper's a project who[se] aim is cultural transformation. She envisions a new world ... in which power relations between men and women, between colonizers and the colonized, are reconfigured to eliminate domination and promote cooperation.[4]

Walker is keenly interested in the emotional and psychological impact of these power relationships upon women. Her focus is on Black women's devaluation, which, as Mary Helen Washington notes, "far more than the external facts and figures of oppression, is the true terror within; the mutilation of the spirit and the body."[5]

Notwithstanding some critical judgments that Black men are unilaterally portrayed as utterly depraved women-haters in *The Color Purple*, there are, in fact, notable exceptions to domineering and bullying male figures. The Rev. Samuel, Corrine's (and, later, Nettie's) husband, is respectful and loving; Sofia's brother-in-law Jack, married to Odessa, is a kind, supportive husband and father. Grady dotes on Shug and seems content to follow her lead. But I mention these characters — all of whom are peripheral to the main action — not to challenge the critics; barring these few marginal characters, men generally *do* behave badly in *The Color Purple*, and that is the point: Walker wishes to illuminate cultural, gendered pathology that demeans and dehumanizes an entire community in profound ways. She does so in the main by illuminating binary parallels that *should* be oppositional, or, at least, not comparable: in *The Color Purple* a man examines a possible wife like a slaveholder considering a purchase at a slave auction; wives are treated like children; marriage is like prison; and, importantly, gender discrimination is like racial discrimination: Black women are to Black men as Black people are to White society — demeaned, disenfranchised, there to serve. Within Walker's frame of reference, it is more important to focus on the reasons for such behavior and to explore the possibility of changed, positive, even redemptive behavior of both men and women.

Set at an indeterminate point in time, narrative indicators pointing to the earlier part of the twentieth century — say, the 1920s — the world of *The Color Purple* is devoid of renaissance of any kind. The Jazz Age, carefree living, love, or gaiety are not even a notion. It is a stark world that delineates Celie's position in the communal scheme of things as less tolerable even than that of the slave women in this study. Malevolent and miserable as is slavery, for Linda Brent (Chapter 1) and Sethe (Chapter 6) it is at least a construct of their external world. They both have close ties with family and/or friends that assist them in coping with the absurdity of slave culture. And they both understand, at least to a point, that the misfortune that has entrapped them and their children is a function of that culture and not a circumstance for which they are directly responsible. Celie, on the other hand, is blamed by those closest to her for even *being*, no explanation given. Consequently, the enslaved women have a personal sense of self and even a level of self-esteem that Celie is unable to access within herself.

While slavery had been officially abolished some decades before the time in which *The Color Purple* is set, the *culture* of slavery refused to cede its position. Racism permeated every institution in the country. African Americans were victimized by the brutal Black Codes and Jim Crow laws. The power of racism was such that it dictated policy and practice to all other American institutions, bar none. The three most likely challengers with the authority, and the ethical imperative, to counter its sweeping inhumanity — that is, education, the law, and religion — bowed, instead, to its will. And they bowed low. The laws of the land sanctioned racial discrimination and allowed it free reign to press its commanding hand into every aspect of life, including housing, employment, education, health. And instead of promoting human dignity and equality, church dogma as well as school systems preached and practiced White supremacy and inhumane treatment of Black people. The two nations of America were rigidly delineated along the color line. The helplessness, frustration, and psychological castration that this system imposed upon Black males — especially the man of the family whose traditional role of protecting his wife and children could not, under the circumstances, possibly be met — was psychologically manifested in ways that were devastating to the Black female. As a result, it is Celie's *gender* that most directly circumscribes her life within its cold, colorless walls.

Karen Horney distinguishes herself in the field of classic psychoanalysis by a crucial recognition of the impact of cultural thought and practices upon the psychological development of individuals.[6] A generally universally acknowledged point of view today, in the earlier 1900s it was a rare enough insight within the psychoanalytic community. Her understanding of group dynamics informs the gendered construct of Celie's world. "People whose need is to be always right feel entitled never to be criticized, doubted, or questioned."[7] This gleaning from Horney's extensive work on neurosis may be equally applied to the White, racist population and to the male, misogynist population of Celie's world. In other words, it is her *world*— not Celie — that is neurotic. It, not she, defines its existence by feelings and behaviors of entitlement and superiority. Those neuroses, institutionalized by White society — e.g., Jim Crow Laws of segregation, judicial injustice, etc.— impact her in an impersonal, detached way. The fact that her country defines her Blackness in negative terms certainly affects her psyche directly, but is not generally an obvious force in her everyday life because she lives in an all-Black community. Male domination, on the other hand, affects her every move. Both oppressors stultify her dreams and her existence.

~~I am~~

In both literal and symbolic reflection of the profoundly debased status of women in the culture, the mother role is highly compromised in *The Color Purple*. The most compelling aspect of the mother/child relationship in this novel is, in fact, its absence. A great deal of displaced mothering goes on by women who either cannot or will not nurture their own children. Even when the biological mother *is* present, she is not — not for long, not in a truly nurturing or protective way. A sense of pervasive motherlessness underlies the text — mothers losing their children, children torn from their mothers, mothers dying and leaving children behind, surrogate mothers, barely-there mothers.

This maternal study is fundamentally different from the others here, in that this woman has no interaction with her children until the last pages of the novel, when they are finally returned to her as fully grown adults. Because of circumstances far removed from her meager control, in maternal terms Celie is a blatant contradiction — a mother without children. The mothering in this novel is therefore not about how Celie mothers her children. The child raised in this novel — certainly, from a psychological point of view — is Celie herself. With the exception of her sister Nettie, she is nurtured by those with whom she shares no bloodline. In addition to this series of surrogates, the maternal care that contributes to Celie's emotional development predominately comes from herself.

The conflicts presented are, at least on the manifest level, less about race than gender. The Southern, rural, hardscrabble, agrarian setting of *The Color Purple* is, with rare exception, completely Black. The fierce racism that burden its African American community is clear from their segregated, circumscribed lives, the baldly subservient manner that they don like a suit of clothes in preparation for a trip "to town," their generally beaten, resigned natures, the sullenness of their lives. But while its fearsome, ruthless power overarches the lives of the Black inhabitants, the larger, oppressive White world is seldom actually seen as an active character in this story.

What is crystal clear is the pathology of gender oppression that spirals throughout the story, manifesting itself like a palpable presence. The victimization of Black women at the hands of Black men — especially fathers and husbands — is an issue more starkly felt than even the blatantly racist society in which they live. In this country the future of "a dark girl is dark indeed."

> ...depreciated by her own kind, judged grotesque by her society, and valued only as a sexually convenient laboring animal, the black girl has the disheartening prospect of a life in which the cards are stacked against her and the achievement of a healthy, mature womanhood seems a very long shot.[8]

Within the Black community, other psychological forces are at work to exacerbate an already difficult situation between men and women aside from straightforward racism and sexism.

From beginning to end, *The Color Purple* is an epistolary novel — a series of letters, the majority of which are written by a painfully unworldly, uneducated adolescent female over a period of decades. There is no mediating element to intervene between the character's inner thoughts and the reader's perception. The narrative is informed by the heroine's deceptively guileless voice whose unworldliness is immediately apparent. Yet out of this very simplicity of format, language, and style emerges an incredibly layered portrait, its disparate elements — love, hatred, joy, pain, cruelty, sin, redemption — fairly bursting with vitality. More importantly for Celie, the act of writing has cathartic value, allowing her to actually write herself into being, establishing a continuous sense of identity.[9] Over the course of the novel Celie constantly wills herself to be recognized, despite a community and a larger society that typically do not bother to acknowledge her existence. Initially addressed to God, Celie's letters are at once confession, prayer, memoir. The nature of the narrative promotes a sense of constant immediacy of events, and the poignancy of Celie's interpretations is striking in its simplicity and straightforwardness. When Celie shifts her salutations to Nettie, this move enables the all-important matter of her continuing connection to her most crucial lifeline.

The Color Purple opens on a dramatic scene of maternal neglect, cruelty, and abandonment. Celie's mother, gone by page three, dies screaming profanities at her daughter. Celie is pregnant by her mother's husband — whom she believes is her biological father — through repeated acts of brutal rape, and, at age fourteen, is ignorant about what is happening to her body. Celie is, from the outset, dangerously insubstantial psychologically. Her parents have provided no training, no nurturing, no positive interaction. Worse, what parenting they *have* imposed has been extraordinarily negative. And the consequences of her mother's double betrayal — failing to protect Celie from incest, and then blaming her daughter for it — cannot be underestimated. Among other things, her feelings of isolation and helplessness produce profound insecurity.[10] Paula Bennett studies this effect, noting that in cases where the mother fails to intercede on behalf of her daughter, the mother is simply passing her own sexual victimization on to the next generation. Having lived with deprivation all her life, she transmits this sense of worthlessness to her daughter. The result typically leaves the daughter "mutilated beyond recognition."[11] Parental abuse has robbed Celie of self-esteem. There is virtually nothing in her life to ground her as a distinct personality — neither in her own eyes nor the eyes of most others. This lack of substance is emblematic of her early self as she struggles against a world that, from all sides, refuses her any definition.

Accordingly, the narrative begins with yet another negation of a self that is already only barely there. Celie writes, then strikes out, her one acknowledged saving grace in the very first sentence of the novel.

Dear God,
~~I am~~ I have always been a good girl [1].

Henry Louis Gates points out that, with the strikethrough, Celie "puts her present self (I am) under erasure."[12] Sensing that she is guilty, but unaware of what, exactly, she is guilty *of*, she cannot possibly comprehend her absolute victimization. She knows only that somehow, incest places her beyond the reach of "good girl" status. Celie comes by this ignorance honestly, having had little positive interaction with her biological mother, who abandoned her long before dying.

Yet Celie's fundamental humanity, evident throughout, extends even

5. Celie: Emergent Light

to the mother who was never her protector — who, on the contrary, actually *left* the home at one point to escape her husband's sexual demands, leaving Celie to fend for herself. Celie tells God that she is not angry. Instead, she pities her mother for having to live with her husband's lies. This empathy, this ability to forgive the unforgivable, along with her straightforward, uncomplicated love of Nettie, demonstrates that there is at least a foundation upon which this abused child can build. There is, in fact, a nugget of positive selfhood that will serve as the basis for further development. It also, however, signals a probable suppression of feelings on Celie's part, a psychological posture whose short-term benefits are heavily outweighed by their long-term dangers. The most apparent of these dangers is the consequent lack of affect, the inability to feel or to express emotion on anything approaching a psychically healthy level.

The question of Celie's mothering, like her being mothered, is not without complication. To say that she has been poorly mothered would understate the case. Celie never has children to raise. Although she gives birth to two children — sired by her "father" — she has no opportunity to raise them, as the father takes them from her immediately after are born. Later, when Celie marries Albert and inherits stepchildren, no true nurturing occurs. The four children — two male and two female — would be a handful for the most seasoned veteran, and a potential nightmare for a new young stepmother, but this is not all that prevents their bonding. Celie is by now emotionally repressed and therefore unable to give to or receive from them. She is, for all intents and purposes, an unpaid employee — a servant — simply doing her job, in an efficacious and objective manner. Notwithstanding the fact that everyone who knows them compliments her on her skills with the children, Celie admits to God, "*I don't feel nothing for them*" (30, emphasis mine). At the pivotal dining room scene, as Celie prepares to leave Albert (and the children), she tells them, "You was all rotten children. You made my life a hell on earth" (207). The function she served all those years was not mothering; it was damage control.

What little she *does* know about the state of motherhood is not promising. The very thought of a woman becoming pregnant makes her incomprehensibly sad. All that she has observed has taught Celie that a mother's life is one of thankless drudgery. Early on, she decided that a married woman had a chance at one good year of life, before the babies begin to come. What she knows, as a child of severe dysfunction, is that, conversely, mothers can also be woefully inadequate to meet the needs of the child. And she sees few role models who change this perception. Even Shug, for all her nurturing abilities, is no mother to her own three biological children, products of her and Albert's careless love. Shug seldom sees or mentions them, having left them to her mother's care.

Without Nettie, Celie would have heard virtually nothing good about herself in her young life. In an effort to sell her into marriage, her father punts, saying that she is a hard worker even though "she ugly" (9). When Shug Avery first lays eyes on her, she laughs. "You sure *is* ugly" (48). Later, at the explosive dinner table scene, a sputtering Albert counters Celie's pronouncements: "Look at you. You black, you pore, you're ugly, you're a woman.... Goddam, you ain't nothing" (213). While Albert indicts only himself with this outburst, he does concisely enumerate the characteristics of powerlessness as he and his society understand it. His condemnation stands as one of countless instances of ego-battering that Celie sustains.

"Show Me How"

The novel's epigraph, taken from the song "Do Like You" by Stevie Wonder, is key to understanding Celie's emotional development. The lyrics describe a young girl admiring her brother's prowess as a dancer and pressing him to teach her the art. "Show me! Show me!," she insists.

Walker elaborates on this theme of watching, mimicking, and learning in *The Color Purple* to have it embody Celie's basic *modus operandi*, indicating at once her awareness that she does not know how to navigate the treacheries of her world, and also her fierce determination to learn. "Show me"—voiced twice in quick succession to underline the importance and the immediacy of the need—is an imperative statement, and also an appeal, for Celie desperately wants to know how to *be*. Embedded in this posture is the implication that, despite her environment's efforts to erase her, Celie will not be invisible.

At the same time Celie's behavior models Horney's paradigm for children who are brought up in a neurotic family. Simply put, these children classically learn to deal with the world by moving toward people (complaisance); moving against people (aggression); or moving away from people (isolating themselves).[13] Celie is surrounded by neurosis among all of her "families"—in the larger White society, the enclosed Black community, and certainly her nuclear unit. So while she is not neurotic, her universe certainly *is*. Accordingly, she responds to it as if it were a mirror.

5. Celie: Emergent Light

The main "show me" that she wants is how to be a whole person. It is in this sense that, over the course of the novel, Celie gives birth to herself, nurtures and mothers herself, into womanhood. As her biological mother is not up to the task even when she is alive, Celie takes on a series of surrogate mothers. In significant ways, these surrogates raise her, and teach her how to become herself in the fullest sense. Her most significant teachers in this process of becoming are Nettie, Sofia, and Shug. With and through them, Celie's innate, then learned, ability to distinguish and to assimilate desired behavior ultimately allows her to achieve wholeness.

Nettie is the single most important person in Celie's life, and caring for Nettie is the closest thing to raising a child that Celie ever experiences. Because of the purity of their relationship, Celie's affection toward her sister is unadulterated and unconditional. Their sisterhood, so pivotal to Celie's subsequent psychic growth and development, makes all the difference between nothingness and substance. Nettie also mothers Celie, so that theirs is a reciprocal relationship, built on love and affection; they nurture each other freely and generously. Nettie shares her school lessons with Celie when Celie is consigned to the home because of her pregnancy. Celie protects Nettie with the fierceness of a mother bear. Her behavior is a striking contrast to her mother's enabling of—even complicity in—Celie's sexual abuse: When Nettie is similarly threatened by the father ("I see him looking at my little sister"), Celie puts herself directly in the line of fire ("I always git in his light" (4, 6). Knowing that this tactic will be only temporarily successful, she encourages Nettie, with only the best intentions, to escape from home in the only way that she can: by marrying Albert. Celie reasons that in this way, Nettie will at least be safe from their father's lust and have a little time before children and married-life drudgery set in. That Celie can imagine only one year of passable contentment out of an entire lifetime speaks volumes about the severe limitations of her dreams.

Celie urges Nettie to keep studying, preparing herself, learning for them both. And Nettie literally home-schools Celie when their father puts a halt to Celie's formal education once her pregnancy begins to show. But Celie, deeply burdened—figuratively *and* literally—with her father's sins, cannot concentrate. No matter how expertly Nettie instructs her on the earth's roundness, Celie cannot envision it. "I never tell her how flat it look to me" (11). An ironic, if unintended comment on the limits of Celie's horizons, her inability to perceive life in three dimensions does not prohibit a natural generosity of soul even as her own needs are not being met. At the same time, Nettie fights for Celie's education, pleading in vain for her father to let Celie stay in school. Later, when Nettie is temporarily living with Celie and Albert, she continues her teaching, encouraging Celie to think, and to work things out, for herself. Nettie's study is of the painstaking, focused, determined variety. She understands that her and Celie's way out of their structural and societal prison is through education. Her projection is accurate, although while Nettie's education is formal, Celie's is from life experience.

When Nettie leaves the country, her letters underscore a deep affection: "Always, no matter what I'm doing, I am writing to you. Dear Celie.... Dear, dear Celie" (161). Unfortunately these letters do not reach Celie until years after her marriage to Albert her betrayal of Sofia, and her early time with Shug. There is, consequently, a rupture in Nettie's nurturing, and Celie is long deprived of this vital connection. Worse, she is left with the ominous possibility that her sister might be dead: Celie and Nettie had agreed to write each other, vowing that only death would prevent them from communication. Their conversation encloses a sacred promise, the perceived breaking of which causes Celie to retreat even further into herself once Nettie has left.

Before Nettie's departure, Celie is pawned off in marriage by her father to Albert, whom she refers to as "Mr._____" until the closing pages of the novel. A widow with, he fudges, three children (he actually has four), Albert had wanted Nettie, not Celie, but is in no real position to bargain. His cleaning lady has quit, his mother refuses to help him any more, and he is desperate. Clearly, he needs a worker. Defeated in the face of the father's insistence that Nettie is not available, he reluctantly considers Celie only because she is his only immediate alternative: "Let me see her again.... He look me up and down. Turn round, Pa say" (11–12). With a cow as her dowry, the engagement is wrought, the narrative tone and language blatantly inviting comparison to a slave auction. Not too long afterward, Celie sees Nettie safely out of her dangerous family home. Then, déjà-vu, she must also see her safely out of *Celie's* own becoming-dangerous marriage home: Albert's lustful looks and sly comments to his attractive sister-in-law leave no doubt as to his intentions. Celie is alone in the world, primarily because she again sacrifices her needs for her sister's safety.

While Celie might lack formal education, she is shrewd and intelligent, and particularly vigilant where Nettie's welfare is concerned. Catching a glimpse of her biological daughter one day in town, Celie carries out reconnaissance with the skill of a seasoned detective. She approaches the well-dressed woman chaperoning the little girl, now about six years old, and engages her in conversation. Before the brief encounter ends, Celie knows the woman's name, her husband's occupation, that this couple adopted her children, and that they are apparently a family of some means. She is further impressed to see, for the first time, a woman with money of her own to spend as she chooses. Celie keeps these precious nuggets of information to herself until Nettie needs them. It is Celie who directs Nettie to Corrine and Samuel at a crucial moment. Nettie is thus hired as a nanny/assistant, and goes to Africa with the family. Not incidentally, Nettie's charges are Celie's two biological children.

The scene with Celie and Corrine is one of the few in *The Color Purple* that occur in the larger world outside their community. It parenthetically notes how commonplace and casual racism is — so much so that those affected barely seem aware of it, even as their self-identity shifts. Corrine, a bit haughty with Celie (her husband is "the *Reverend* Mr._____" [15]), is deferential to the White salesclerk, responding to his discourteous manner with a simple "Naw suh" or "Yessuh." The very tenor of her language changes from impeccable to unschooled when she redirects her comments from Celie to the clerk. When he short-changes her at the conclusion of her purchase, Corrine appears not to notice and Celie, who *does* notice, says nothing. Rarely spoken of, the debased position of Black men and women in society plays a huge part in their communal sense of self. Even small indignities, constantly piled atop one another like feathers, gather heft and weight over a period of time.

Marriage at first hand only reinforces the lessons Celie learned from her mother's unholy union — that a woman's life in matrimony, barring that possible first year of grace before the babies start coming, is a hard, thankless row to hoe. Moreover, in the familial hierarchy, the wife is at the absolute bottom of every consideration. Wives exist to care for the house and the children and to do their husband's bidding. They are otherwise virtually invisible, certainly not human: When Albert looks at her, he doesn't really *see* her. "It like he looking at the earth" (21). Men in Albert's world are fond of comparing their wives to children, but with far less indulgence. "Wives is like children," Albert schools Harpo (37). Men perceive that they are head of the house because women are incapable of making the tough decisions, doing the important work, thinking the intelligent thoughts. Women are treated badly — and rightly so — simply *because* they are women. When

Harpo asks his father why he whips Celie as he would a child, Albert responds matter-of-factly, "Cause she my wife" (23). Harpo mindlessly parrots his father years later, when, in classic fantasy mode, he tells Celie that he beats Sofia because "she my wife" (65). He does not add that whenever he so much as raises a hand to her, Sofia bludgeons him. The obstinacy of transgenerational behavioral patterns are clear as both father and son see (or want to see) cause and effect of wife-beating as obvious. Karen Horney's studies in the psychology of gender politics perceive what classic psychoanalytic theory fails to appreciate — namely, that patriarchal society, in its myopia, has *reversed* cause and effect. Women are not powerless because they are childish; they are perceived and treated as childish because they are powerless. And their powerlessness is the direct result of a long and deeply entrenched system of male supremacy.[14]

In Celie's marriage, sex and beatings are almost equally endured by rote, conversation is nonexistent, and laughter an alien concept, seldom expressed without the harsh undercurrent of derision. By the time Harpo, Albert's eldest son, reaches age seventeen and introduces the family to his fifteen-year-old intended, Celie is so solidly entrenched in her wifely role of bare expectations that she is unprepared for the force of nature that is Sofia Butler. She is consequently initially unable to appreciate just how much the younger woman can teach her.

Sofia

Sofia's first appearance in the novel leaves no doubt about her strength of purpose and mind. Attractive, smart, and physically strong, she is also about eight months pregnant when she and Harpo march together to meet with Albert. Celie is a silent, virtually invisible observer as Albert attempts to insult Sofia. His crudeness elicits shocked, cowardly silence from Harpo but only a hearty, defiant laugh from Sofia. She ends the meeting herself, with calm, strong words to both Albert and Harpo.

This initial encounter, so typical of Sofia, remains in Celie's mind as time passes and Sofia and Harpo marry, set up house in the shed behind Albert's house, have first one, then a second child, so that eventually Harpo seeks his dad's advice on wife control. He complains that Sofia never obeys him, talks back to him, refuses to acquiesce. Celie glimpses, however, a note of hidden pride in his voice even as he grumbles to his father. It is at this point that Albert offers his timeless lesson on wives being children and needing a good beating. While Harpo is burdened by Albert's neuroses as surely as Albert has been victimized by his own father's deeply contemptuous view of women, the younger man does show some minute sign of evolution. First, he has chosen to marry a woman who is more than a match for him, rather than a docile, compliant mate. Second, his incipient pride in the face of Sofia's defiance signals that he is not yet pathologically threatened by a woman's strength, as are his father and grandfather. Third, the fact that he actually *asks* his father — and later, in a pivotal scene, also Celie — what he should do about Sofia's inappropriate independence, suggests that wife-beating is not an automatic response for him.

But why, before taking action, would Harpo then go to his stepmother — a woman he knows his father routinely batters — for such advice? Does he expect approval or censure? While ideally, Celie would support Sofia as a natural ally and daughter-in-law, both women battling abusive and domineering husbands, Celie's upbringing forges a divide difficult to bridge that complicates the women's relationship. Celie admits in her letter to God that when Harpo complained to her about Sofia, she could have easily, but consciously did *not*, point out how happy Harpo is with Sofia just as she is. Instead, she thinks about how "every time I jump when Mr._____ call me, [Sofia] look surprise." (38). Humiliated by Sofia's pity, Celie makes a decision at this moment whose fallout will ultimately have a profound effect upon her emotional development. Her advice to Harpo is unequivocal.

"Beat her. I say" (38). These two clipped sentences encompass the single instance of unprovoked aggression on Celie's part in the entire novel. The syntactic isolation of "I say" from the damning "Beat her" indicates that Celie is taking deliberate and conscious responsibility for her words. Hence the desperate hope that Sofia never find out, and the relentless nightmares that plague Celie after this betrayal. Harpo's severely battered face the day after Celie's directive paints a much clearer picture than his transparent explanation: "That mule. She fractious, you know. She went crazy in the field the other day" (38). This turn of events tells Celie a couple of important things, *to wit*: her words have the power to invoke pain upon another. Also, Sofia fights back, giving as good as she gets, and then some. This means that Sofia knows not only *how* to fight, but *to* fight. Her response to threat is aggressive and decisive, an empowering stance that bears no resemblance to Celie's "flight" mode.

In the course of the novel, Celie adopts all three classic positions articulated by Horney that victims of neurotic environments assume (moving toward people, moving against people, and moving away from people). Her directive to Harpo reflects the second of those positions—moving against someone. The psychology behind this posture addresses, in Horney's words, "the need for vindictive triumph as an antidote to feeling humiliated." It allows the individual to maintain a certain level of detachment, since Celie perceives herself as having little or nothing in common with Sofia.[15] Their apparent commonalities pale dramatically beside their differences, best expressed by Celie's overarching perception that Sofia "don't act like me at all" (38).

The ensuing exchange between Sofia and Celie provides profound insight for Celie and is one of a handful of key instances that drive the leitmotif of redemption in *The Color Purple*. When Sofia confronts Celie, she does so more out of perplexity and disappointment than anger, returning the curtains that Celie had sewn for her as a symbol of their broken trust. Celie's initial denial is followed by her admission that she did, in fact, advise Harpo to beat Sofia, and she does so with a level of openness that is rare in her interaction with anyone other than Nettie. Armed with nothing but the truth, she admits her transgression with no attempt to excuse herself.

> "I say it cause I'm a fool. I say it cause I'm jealous of you. I say it cause you do what I cant."
> "What that?" she say.
> "Fight." I say [18].

This confession is as clear as any "Show me" in Celie's development: She wants to learn to respond to aggression proactively. The sharing is a revelation to Celie herself, opening her psyche to possibilities heretofore unconsidered. Earlier, when she and Nettie were discussing Celie's unruly stepchildren, Nettie had advised Celie that she had to fight. Celie's response even then is that she doesn't know how to fight. "All I know how to do is stay alive" (18). And therein lies the crux of the matter: Celie's objective is the narrowest, most atavistic impulse there is: to survive. Not having progressed past that point for herself—although she has for Nettie—the idea of actually engaging with life, tackling obstacles, has been beyond her purview.

Sofia gives Celie her first lesson on fighting, and it's *all* about gender: "All my life I had to fight ... my daddy ... my brothers ... my cousins and my uncles. A girl child ain't safe in a family of men" (42). As much as she loves Harpo, Sofia actually vows to kill him before standing passively by while he beats her. She opens up to Celie in understanding, sharing her own tale of paternal rape, the two children from this abuse muffled into the family under the guise that they are her mother's children. Sofia's strength comes from fighting against such depravity, and from having a group of like-minded, strong sisters who always band together against threat of such abuse. Sofia's anger is righteous and hard-earned. In turn, Celie shows uncanny adeptness at plumbing her own psyche as she grasps, through this exchange, that she never gets angry because she cannot *allow* herself to get angry.

"What you do when you git mad?" [Sofia] ast.
I think. I can't even remember the last time I felt mad [43].

Her mother and father had drilled into her the idea that anger — hers, not theirs — is bad, and, worse, that to disobey — to "dishonor" her father and mother — is against biblical teaching. She further understands that to show anger to, say, her husband, carries both physical and emotional risk. Since any incipient anger brings on feelings of guilt and fear, her solution has typically been to suppress all feeling, to make herself feel nothing. When Albert beats her, for example, Celie writes, "I make myself wood. I say to myself, Celie, you a tree" (23).

But now, here with Sofia, she is able to express, and to feel, real emotion. "I'm *so* shame of myself" (42), she earnestly offers, her inflection of the word "so" a rare departure from her usual monotone. Her rigid suppression of emotion has deprived her of (or, from her point of view, saved her from) the ability to feel. Ultimately, Celie's admission is met with a grace to which she is totally unaccustomed. Sofia draws Celie's laughter by encouraging this opening up of feelings (and behaviors), suggesting that Celie might consider knocking Albert around a little, just for a change of pace. Absent Nettie, there has been no joy to speak of in Celie's life, and laughter has been an uncommon experience: the last time she tried one on for size, the effort "like to split my face" (16). But this time it is cathartic, also releasing the guilt that has plagued her over this matter.

The women's exchange ends on a note of bonding through understanding, forgiveness, and healing — symbolized by their new collaboration. From the figurative tatters of the returned curtains, they decide to make a quilt, and Celie hastens to set the project in motion, gathering up her pattern book on the spot. Such creative piecing-together as quilt-making is a strong motif, not unrelated to the larger theme of redemption: More than one of *The Color Purple* characters uses their skills to combine damaged and disparate materials, making a beautiful whole. In much this way, Celie and her surrogate mothers build upon her foundation to enhance her psychological and emotional development.

From this single encounter, Sofia has imparted a wealth of information to Celie: Women can, and should, be strong. Abuse must not be tolerated. Women should support one another. And, importantly, men and women are not natural born enemies, but are, rather, socialized into rigid gender camps that must be challenged when they promote exploitation or aggression. Laughter is good for the soul. Honestly confronting an issue instead of suppressing resentment clears the air, and cleanses the spirit.

Like Noah's curse upon his son Ham because Ham witnessed his father's drunken nakedness,[16] Celie has resented Sofia simply for being witness to her debasement. Sensing Sofia's pity, feeling helpless in her marriage, and totally unskilled at fighting back, she does, she now realizes, the next best thing. If she cannot be a strong, confident wife like Sofia who, unlike Celie, would never even think of calling her husband "Sir," then she can at least plant a seed in Harpo's head that might make Sofia a bit more like she is — subservient, powerless, beaten down. This posture is, at bottom, the psychic need of misery for company in order to protect one's ego from feelings of shame and humiliation.[17] Such raw perception of one's own weakness is power in itself, as self-knowledge is crucial to positive psychological and emotional development.

And while Sofia is clear that not all actions are forgivable (she vows to kill Harpo, for example, if he tries to beat her again), the most crucial "show-me" that Celie gleans from her is how to seek forgiveness and how to forgive when warranted. The women's new and deeper bond with one another is founded upon the powerful balm of empathy, the sweet release that comes with forgiveness, and the exquisite grace of redemption. Redemption is a powerful thing, its essence lying in the ability to absolve, and therefore to empower, oneself.

Celie learns crucial lessons from Sofia about respect for others, but she does not yet extend that same beneficence to herself. When she questions Harpo to ensure that he no longer beats Sofia, she advises him that "some womens can't be beat. Sofia one of them" (66). She pointedly, if unconsciously, excludes herself from the category of unbeatable women. Her comment reflects not only a lack of personal self-esteem, but an inability to universalize the wrongness of wife-beating under any circumstance.

Shug

Sofia Butler and Shug Avery, both surrogates for Celie, are distinctly different personalities. Born Lillie, Shug retains this shortened version of the endearment "Sugar" as her signature on stage and in real life. The small-town legend that is Shug Avery goes against convention to design and construct her own persona, to make her own living, to ignore conventional societal- and role-restrictions. She is, pointedly, the woman who long ago captured the heart of Celie's heartless husband Albert. Shug is Celie's idol — an ideal — the woman she would be in her wildest dreams, if only Shug could "show" her how to be her.

In a second of three classic positions that Karen Horney outlines, Celie begins to move toward people. Specifically, long before she even meets her, while she is still an adolescent, Celie starts her gravitation toward Shug. Her attraction is not normal but an excessive, almost desperate reaching-out for affection and attention. Consistent with her feelings of helplessness and insecurity, nurtured by a dysfunctional family and society, Celie develops an unnaturally strong attachment to the ideal of Shug, uncharacteristically going to some length to acquire a photograph of her, upon which she fixates. Indeed, Celie's response to it borders on obsession. She stares at it hypnotically when awake and dreams of it when asleep. The picture of Shug in provocative dress, garish to some, only enhances her incredible beauty as far as Celie is concerned; never in her life has she beheld an image, or a woman, so magnificent. It is this image that "teaches" Celie, before she ever sees Shug in the flesh. Shug "shows" Celie, who does not even know where babies come from, how to be sexually appealing. Celie's heartbreaking parody of a femme fatale, in "horsehair, feathers, and ... high heel shoes" (8), in order to distract her father's lustful eye from Nettie, is an explicit (if inept) imitation of Shug in the picture.[18]

Something more than mere attraction drives Celie's fascination. When she hears that Shug is coming to town "with her orkestra," she carries the flyer announcing Shug's upcoming appearance like a talisman (26). Giddily but secretly infatuated, she is almost indulgent with Albert as he attends to his toilette before going to Shug's show. She even surprises him with a compliment, creating a rare moment between them, despite the irony of her husband's nervous care over his appearance for another woman's eyes. This rare moment of bonding occurs, in fact, over a shared attraction to Shug. Years later, when Albert, without explanation, brings a very ill Shug into their home, Celie delights in caring for her. Initially, it is Celie who mothers Shug. But the relationship soon shifts dramatically. In constant contact with Celie, Shug is able to perceive her attributes and a potential that few others appreciate.

A self-styled woman of the world whose three children with Albert are seldom mentioned, never seen, Shug is an unlikely nurturer to Celie. Yet, with an uncommon generosity of heart, she shares herself emotionally with Celie with such intimacy that their burgeoning friendship evolves, for a time, into a sexual relationship as well. Shug comes into Albert and Celie's home as Albert's longtime love who, he always believes, should have been his wife. Before she leaves, Celie and Albert's world is turned upside down. Shug, however, stays pretty much the same — unpredictable, powerful, uncontainable.

Shug, like Sofia, does not allow men to dominate her. But her major lessons to Celie lie in the area of emotional expression: affection, trust, sharing, friendship, respect, and intimacy. Even the most significant material gift that Shug gives to Celie — the priceless treasure trove of Nettie's letters — is, fundamentally, an emotional gift. As their friendship develops, Shug takes over the role of nurturer, protector, and caregiver. Still, at one point, Celie imagines an odd Oedipal triangle with Albert and Shug as parents, and herself as their child. The oppressiveness of Celie's world when Shug first enters it helps to explain this bizarre fantasy: "...I see myself sitting there quilting tween Shug Avery and Mr._____. Us three set together.... For the first time in my life, I feel just right" (60). Shug is perceptive enough to appreciate how emotionally undeveloped, how childlike, Celie's fragile ego is. Like so many characters in *The Color Purple* do, she projects caring — specifically, maternal care — to a secondary location, nurturing Celie, in place of her own children, and guiding Celie's evolution. Shug intercedes with Albert at every turn until Celie can fend for herself, much as a mother would mediate between a child and an unyielding father: Shug arranges that she and Celie — not Celie and Albert, or even Shug and Albert — will sleep together; she runs interference in the all-important issue of coaxing Nettie's letters out of Albert's hiding-place; she is instrumental in Albert's behavioral adjustment as a spouse. When Celie tells Shug about Albert's beatings, Shug, incredulous that her mild-mannered ex-love could be so cruel, con-

5. Celie: Emergent Light

soles Celie and vows to put a stop to it. Later, when Shug checks on the beating situation, Celie tells her, like a little girl reporting to her mother, that "he aint beat me much since you made him quit" (115). Shug's declaration that she doesn't feel the same about Albert since finding out that he is a wife-beater is also instructive to Celie. It's not just the Sofias of the world who do not deserve beating: *No* wife should be assaulted. Shug's very deliberate form of address to Celie signals that Celie deserves, and should demand, respect. She writes a song for "Miss Celie" and sings it publicly. Celie, needless to say, has never before been so honored. All these gifts from Shug work to strengthen Celie's badly damaged ego.

Shug "shows" Celie a great deal about relationships between men and women, including the fact that men are not fearsome, omniscient gods who must be appeased and obeyed. Even at her most ill, when Albert first brings her home, she disparages him to his face, and Celie realizes that this does nothing to diminish Albert's feelings for Shug. "I don't need no weak little boy can't say no to his daddy.... I need me a man" (49). Albert's hopeless love for Shug gives rise to a new perception from Celie, who has heretofore kept her eyes cast too far downward to see: "I notice his chin weak. Not much chin there at all" (50).

Celie's prior sexual encounters involved trauma (with her father) at worst or longsuffering boredom (with Albert) at best. But her sexual experience with Shug vitalizes her. The communal response to the homoerotic aspect of their relationship, however, is curious. As bell hooks points out: There *is* none.

> Patriarchy is exposed and denounced as a social structure ... specifically represented as black male domination of black females, yet it does not influence and control sexual desire and sexual expression. While Mr. Albert, dominating male authority figure, can become enraged at the possibility that his wife will be present at a jukejoint, he has no difficulty accepting her sexual desire for another female. Homophobia does not exist in the novel.[19]

hooks theorizes that Walker offers here a powerful suggestion that sexual desire can subvert the status quo, since Celie's relationship with Shug is the catalyst for her self-empowerment. Tuzyline Jita Allan concurs, in a somewhat different vein, that the women's relationship challenges patriarchy:

> [While] Pa can describe Celie as no longer 'fresh,' according to Shug, she is 'still a virgin....' That Celie's sexuality, like her humanity, can remain intact under a prolonged male siege is evidence that contradicts and invalidates her dominant image as pathological victim[20]

The difference between Celie's sexual experiences along gender lines is striking: besides being technically a virgin, according to Shug, because she has never known sexual pleasure, Celie's respective descriptions are unambiguous. Mr._____ "go to the toilet" on her as she lies there, receptive as a stone. With Shug the experience is not only active — and sensual — but, as Allan notes, elevated to a spiritual level ("It feel like I'm praying").[21] In Celie's case, there is also the matter of feeling safe that enables her sexual feelings for a woman. She fears men. One of her earliest letters relates that her father once beat her for looking at a boy in church, but that her father was wrong: "I don't even look at mens. That's the truth. I look at women, tho, cause I'm not scared of them" (6). On those rare occasions when she *does* hazard a glance at men, she finds, in a variation on the racial stereotype, that "most times mens look pretty much alike to me" (16). Pain-bringers all, in her experience, they are threatening, amorphous entities best avoided. That narrative placement of Celie's disclosure that she is not afraid of women, and that is *why* she looks at them, is almost immediately followed by her comment on the image in her treasured picture ("Shug Avery was a woman" [7]), is hardly coincidental.

The absence of homophobia in this novel *is* curious. It is a noteworthy exception, as other race- and gender-related biases are alive and well. Color consciousness in *The Color Purple* is so casual that its presence seems almost taken for granted. Yvonne Johnson refers to it as "incipient racism,"[22] which in itself is a signal that it is a comment by the Black community on self-loathing, turning against *itself*. Shug's very dark skin neutralizes, for some, the dazzling beauty that others see in her: "Shug Avery black as my shoe" (21), says Albert's sister. Albert's father, whose profound dislike of Shug prevented Albert from marrying her years ago, bluntly wonders what the attraction is. He cannot see past his own deeply set biases that center on her skin and her hair: "She black as tar, she nappy headed" (56). Conversely, Celie sees exquisite beauty in Shug's "long black body" (51). She also learns, from Shug's example, to love her natural, kinky hair. Shug redefines the value-laden term "good hair," which is often used in the Black community even today to describe naturally straight or wavy hair. Shug "shows" Celie that her own natural, thick, African hair *is* good hair — not because it is European, but because it is clean and expressive and meant to be worn proudly.

Shug possesses attributes that, in her rigidly gendered society, Celie cannot imagine connecting to womanhood. Shug's every gesture is bold. "She smile, like a razor opening" (50). Celie perceives that Shug "act more

5. Celie: Emergent Light

manly than most men" (276). What Celie *means* is that Shug is confident, unselfconscious, audacious. Like Sofia, Shug expands the possibilities and the scope of a woman's role. And Celie is attentive, if not yet equal, to these possibilities. When Shug encourages Celie to make herself a pair of pants for fieldwork, Celie's immediate response ("What I need pants for? I ain't no man" [152]) eventually gives way to a lively and lucrative pantsmaking enterprise. Shug "shows" Celie that people can construct their own tightly knit family unit based upon love and respect, rather than bloodline. When Celie learns that her biological father is long dead, Shug responds to her friend's shock and loss by assuring her, "Us each other's peoples now" (189).

The color purple symbolizes, among other things, all the world's beauty that Shug helps Celie appreciate through their many conversations. She tells Celie that God is a God of love and beauty and everyday miracles; that it probably irritates Him when people "walk by the color purple" in a field or elsewhere without noticing it (203). Shug's exuberance for life sets free some of the curiosity and wonder that Celie has learned too well to suppress. Left to her own devices, Celie considers that her eyes are only now opening up to the marvels that have always been within her grasp. The effect of this adjusted perspective reduces the force that is Albert's evil from supernatural and insurmountable to simply human. Celie's reiteration of "the color purple" signals how intently she listens to Shug. "I never truly notice nothing God make ... not the color purple (where it come from?). Not the little wildflowers. Nothing" (204). When these thoughts evolve from the beauty of nature into the beauty that might be waiting for her if her life were different, they find support in the women who have come to love Celie. Sofia and Shug, along with Squeak and Odessa, have come to constitute a powerful circle of womanhood in Celie's life, reminiscent of the community of women who band together in *for colored girls ...* by Ntozake Shange.[23] The strength of the collective engenders a sense of empathy as well as authority, serving her in other relationships as well.[24] Noting Harpo's dismissiveness toward his mistress, whom he calls Squeak, Celie advises her to make Harpo call her by her given name, Mary Agnes: "Then maybe he see you" (89).

The hallmark dinner table scene in *The Color Purple* is a series of unexpected announcements that amount to a declaration of independence on the part of the women, evoking sputtering disbelief from the men, and moving Celie further toward "becoming." Shug is the one to announce that Celie is going back to Memphis with her, but after this, Celie finds her own voice. And it is in rare form. She stuns the assembly when she unexpectedly unleashes astounding rage at Albert. His most egregious sin by far is, of course, "taking Nettie away from me" (206). Her first proud declaration of motherhood occurs at this moment, as well: "I got children. Being brought up in Africa" (206). Demonstrably well past the point of no return, Celie concludes her passionate outburst by bestowing a prophetic curse upon him: "Until you do right by me, everything you touch will crumble ... everything you even dream about will fail" (213). As she and Shug leave, she affirms her connection with the world in an uncompromising statement of existence. "I'm pore, I'm black, I may be ugly.... *But I'm here*" (214, italics mine).

"I'm Here"

Celie's departure and liberation from Albert's tyranny are a momentous step in her becoming, although her independence and her identity are somewhat by proxy. Along with the strength she has gained from Nettie's letters, Shug is the driving force behind this move, the one without whom Celie would have had no where to go and no idea of how to get there. Her first letter to Nettie from Shug's home carries a sort of postscript in the signature that relates both her new business and her reliance upon Shug:

Your sister Celie
Folkspants, Unlimited
Sugar Avery Drive
Memphis, Tennessee [221]

Years later, Celie faces her greatest challenge, much as she had when Nettie had left: learning to love herself *by* herself. She moves "away from people" when Shug redirects her affection to the handsome young Germaine. The main person Celie moves away from, in her isolation, is herself. While she has learned to see herself with love through Shug's eyes, once Shug leaves Celie is left with "Nothing here. Nothing special for nobody to love" (266). Her self-assessment is not objective, but rather, fraught with self-loathing because Shug is no longer there to affirm her. Without that anchor of affirmation and unconditional acceptance, Celie is not initially able to access positive feelings about herself.[25] It is a painstaking process that temporarily estranges her from others as she works through the process. When she does, her composure signals profound growth, and reflects a woman finally at peace with herself: "Just when I know I can live content without Shug ... [she] write me she coming home. Now. Is this life or Not? I figure this the lesson

5. Celie: Emergent Light

I was suppose to learn" (209). Indeed, this epiphany represents significant emotional maturity, an appreciation of the fact that Shug has her own life to live, an acceptance that the life of another is not subject merely to Celie's desires.[26] This hard-won lesson has been a lifetime coming. It is largely attributable to the unconditional love she receives from Shug and, once the letters are uncovered, from her sister Nettie.

Attaining Nettie's letters is tantamount to regaining Nettie herself. Once she has them in her possession, they perform their own miraculous alchemy, bringing Nettie to life and revitalizing her being. The letters transmit themselves directly into Celie's heart, emboldening her, and strengthening her sense of self. The knowledge and affection that she absorbs from them—especially, all that love expressed at once—is a watershed moment in Celie's development, profoundly affecting her psyche. Because Albert had maliciously hidden them for years, she receives them from Shug in a rush, all at once, so that at first they overwhelm her and actually threaten her sanity. They are initially read in haste, in desperation, in disbelief, but Celie is eventually able to digest and savor them. They "grow" her and help to offset the negative input she has been internalizing for years.

Through the written word and the force of her commitment to Celie, Nettie bolsters her sister's self-assurance. Speaking of Celie's biological daughter, she writes, "Celie, Olivia has your stubbornness and clear-sightedness" (163). Nettie's letters embrace Celie and affirm her in ways that only she understands. "God, I miss you, Celie. I think about the time you laid yourself down for me. I love you with all my heart" (133). Nettie is mindful of the extraordinary gift she holds of being placed with Celie's children. She considers it her sacred mission to oversee the care and welfare of Adam and Olivia, even as she respects Corinne's role as their adoptive mother. And she loves them not only as her niece and nephew, but as treasures from her absent, beloved sister. When Samuel finally asks her about Celie, she is unable to stop the torrent of words and emotions that accompany her memories. Both sisters use the second person plural "we" and "us" lavishly when speaking of themselves. They invariably refer to Adam and Olivia as "our children," underscoring their fierce connection and shared motherhood.

Before receiving the letters, Celie lacks topographical knowledge of the world. She has no idea where Europe or Africa are and cannot relate geographically to the places Nettie has traveled. She also lacks fundamental knowledge about how the world works. And that's the way she wants it.

Knowledge, in her worldview, is seldom power. "I know what I'm thinking bout ... Nothing. And as much of it as I can" (127). Importantly, Nettie "shows" the world to Celie in her letters, with information, observations, and reflections that open up Celie's universe, undermine her preconceptions, and broaden her horizons. Her writing virtually *wills* Celie to imagine, and even to experience, what she sees and experiences. In this way, Nettie is Celie's most influential teacher/mother. She presents the world not as a fearful, unknowable place but rather, a space unlimited in scope and possibility. At the same time she offers recognizable reference points. Relating the behavior of the Olinka tribe members at a barbecue she attended, Nettie writes that they act just like the folk back home. On a less carefree note, she reveals that Olinkan men, and, often, Olinkan women, share American men's misogynistic and sexist views, including the idea that women should not be educated. The Olinka, Nettie relates, believe that a girl or woman is nothing in and of herself. She only becomes someone if or when a man marries her and she has children by him. This is a lesson of numerous facets; above all, it "shows" Celie that she is not alone, that women all over the world are challenged by gender bias. Another of Nettie's letters informs Celie that the man they were raised to believe was their father is really their stepfather. This information is crucial to Celie's sense of herself, finally liberating her from the burden of incest she has carried since girlhood.

Nettie's advanced education and experience show in her writing. Her style is descriptive, instructive, even didactic at points, but not condescending. She writes as though they are having a conversation. Nettie often uses Celie's name in her text, conjuring her sister before her as a material presence. "It's hot here, Celie. Hotter than July." "Celie, do you know what a jungle is?" (154, 156). Such affirming constancy builds (and grows) Celie up, enabling her gradual emotional development.

When Celie discovers that her "pa" has left his large, beautiful home and successful business—a dry goods store—to her and Nettie, she takes a cementing step in her becoming. She moves into the house alone, but at the same time prepares it for a family. She writes Nettie that they now have a big, beautiful house for "us and our children," as well as for Nettie's husband Samuel and, of course, Shug, should she choose (352). Celie finally has within her grasp all that she has desired, deserved, and needed her entire life. In one of her last letters to Nettie she writes, "I am so happy. I got love, I got work, I got money, friends and time. And you alive and be home soon. With our children" (222).

5. Celie: Emergent Light

The end of *The Color Purple* paints a picture of life as it should always have been. Returning to her depressing old family home for Sofia's mother's funeral, she surprises her old friends with an air of self-possession they had not seen before in her. She laughs easily, telling a shocked Sofia that God understands what she means when she says that she and God "make love just fine" (227). Albert, bowed under Celie's curse and his own guilt over the years, has emerged a hard-working, sincerely religious man who cooks and cleans as fastidiously as if he were the woman of the house, in his old way of thinking. At his anxious instigation, he and Celie launch a new relationship that begins awkwardly, tentatively, but emerges as one of true mutual understanding and friendship. They talk bluntly about the past, unearthing ancient demons to come to terms with them, and then putting them to rest. Celie advises Albert that her expertise with thread and needle, for example, was honed as a creative diversion years ago when she lived with Albert "to keep from killing you" (261). Albert's contrition is genuine. Celie marvels that he actually sees her, listens to her, defers to her now. Albert confides to her, that, having undergone brutal soul searching and struggle to access his real, his best, self, this is the first time in his life that he feels "like a natural man" (267).

Celie and Albert make an intriguing picture in a scene of transgendered behavior as they both unselfconsciously smoke pipes and sew while talking. They are pleased to have finally discovered, during their talks, the secret of Shug's incredible appeal, which is exquisite in both its simplicity and its elusiveness: Simply put, Shug knows how to give love, and she is generous in her giving. Albert is humbled and surprised that his learning to love others, including his formidable daughter-in-law Sofia, is resulting in their coming to love him as well. In an extraordinary moment of metaphysical revelation, Albert confides, "I start to wonder why us need love. Why us suffer. Why us black. Why us men and women.... I think us here to wonder.... The more I wonder, he say, the more I love" (289–290). Remarkably, it is Albert who voices a central theme — the breaking down of artificial gender barriers — when he characterizes Sofia and Shug as "not like men" but, also, "not like women either." He is seeing, finally, that they simply dare to live outside the traditional, restricting role that society would impose upon them. With more than a touch of pride, he adds, "They hold they own. And it's different" (276). The surprising posture that Albert and Celie then assume crystallizes a hard-won place of reconciliation and the beginning of trust. "Then the old devil put his arms around me and just stood there on the porch with me real quiet. Way after while I bent my stiff neck onto his shoulder" (278). This picture lends an air of poignancy, but most importantly, of possibility to their unlikely reunion.

Near novel's end, Shug visits Celie's new home and is delighted with her old friend's distinctive eye for color. Celie's room is painted in brilliant shades of purple, red, and yellow. When Shug notices a purple frog on the mantelpiece, Celie's casual disclosure that the frog is "a little something Albert carve for me" elicits knowing laughter from both women, a tacit understanding that Albert, too, has evolved (261). The purple frog is in fact a private symbol for Albert and Celie that reflects a world of deferred growth and mellowing. Celie had once told Albert that, when men take off their pants, they all "look like frogs to me" (261). Following that conversation, she gently rejects Albert's proposal of marriage (an honest one this time), on the grounds that he is still, sadly, a frog.

As the novel approaches its close, Shug, Albert, and Celie are seated on a porch together again. But this scene is light-years away from the earlier bizarre Oedipal triangle that portrayed a cowed, frightened Celie sitting between parental figures Shug and Albert, piteously thinking that this was the way her life was supposed to be. This refigured scene is set on Celie's grand porch. She is now the woman, not the baby, of the house. The three of them — Shug, Albert, and Celie — share a profound regard for each other that has been wrought from a lifetime of lessons learned the hard way. "Me and him and Shug.... Sitting on the porch with Albert and Shug feel real pleasant" (292).

A moment does come in this scene when Albert and Shug must shore up Celie again, as they had done in the first porch scene all those years ago. But this time it is physical, not psychological support that she needs. And this time, it is not because she is inherently childlike or weak. It is the distant sight of approaching figures — a "dumpy little woman with her gray hair in plaits cross of top or her head" accompanied by Samuel, Olivia, and Adam and his wife — that takes her (and the reader's) breath away. "My heart is in my mouth and I can't move.... When Nettie's foot come down on the porch I almost die" (293). The sisters' fierce embrace ends a lifetime of separation. The air is hushed as the endless possibilities of this impossible moment render it surreal. Celie has grown herself up, and she has done so with increasing courage and resolve. Her natural gifts, including fierce determination, a profound capacity to love, an ability to find a bit of humor in all but the most depraved circumstances, a willingness — no, an *eagerness* ("Show me!")

5. Celie: Emergent Light

to learn life's important lessons from others, and a vital, unique worldview, round out her essence into a healthy, fully developed ego. Now her children have come home. She can finally be their mother.

The dismal opening of *The Color Purple* is in diametric opposition to its exuberant, hopeful finale. The characters that people this novel have faced and overcome enormous odds. Their failures, insecurities, and cruelties have been laid bare; their growth, successes, and redemption represent untold possibility. The world at the end of *The Color Purple* is one that Celie never even dared imagine in her abusive upbringing. It is her (and Walker's) dream of the world where the tired old warhorse of physical abuse has been exposed for the pathetic bully it is and unceremoniously laid to rest, just as it deserves. It is also a world where gender has lost the power to determine a person's right to respect, admiration, opportunity, and happiness. Skin color and hair texture simply *are*; they are not elements that contribute to or detract from an individual's attractiveness. It is in fact a world full of dark, proud, beautiful, kinky-haired women who have come to love themselves. At long last it is one in which Celie, her children, and her community are free to soar.

CHAPTER 6

Sethe: Beyond the Pale

This maternal portrait refuses to conform to, or be confined within, the frame. Its title does not refer to shading, but rather to an unknown, otherworldly dimension. Sethe's rendering is an amalgam of "too much." There is too much passion, too much love, too much heartache to be contained. The steel intensity of this mother's will suffuses the text with an insistence that forces color to the surface and overruns the frame. The narrative explicitly cautions against dwelling too long on this rendering: *This is not a story to pass on.* The text, and the subtext, warn in brilliant crimson that "motherlove ... is a killer."

In her lecture before the Swedish Academy in 1993, Toni Morrison shared the tale of an exchange between an old blind woman and a group of young people that ends with the old woman saying, "I trust you now.... Look. How lovely it is, this thing we have done — together."[1] The moral of this fable is a fitting response to Morrison's *Beloved*: the mutual trust that evolves between reader and writer as they both work to comprehend the world inside the text. The mother's tale in *Beloved* is a shared experience, fulfilled not only by the dynamism of the characters, but also by the writer's, and the reader's, collective imaginations.

Morrison's passionate sense of accountability to the unsung dead establishes a novelistic integrity that contributes to the power of the novel. "...the responsibility that I feel for the woman I'm calling Sethe, and for all of these people; these unburied, or at least unceremoniously buried.... the fear of not properly, artistically, burying them is extraordinary."[2] A great story, Walter Benjamin writes, cannot be told in only one way, nor can its essence be distilled in only one telling.[3] A richly overdetermined, multivalent text, *Beloved* is many stories at once, with myriad frames of reference.

6. Sethe: Beyond the Pale

I will call them my people, which were not my people; and her beloved, which was not beloved. — Romans 9:25[4]

The apparent opacity of Morrison's epigraph reveals itself during the unfolding of the narrative as coded language that, while leaving open a number of interpretive choices, offers profound and coherent insight into the text. *Beloved*'s narrative, as Lorraine Liscio notes, "refuses to behave,"[5] defying linearity by a staggering manipulation of time and space. *Beloved* makes clear the stunning degree to which freedom is a state of mind. The time-frame begins years after the Civil War and ends months later, with entire eras in between erupting in a narrative totally unrestrained by conventions of unity with regard to time, space, or action. The constant clash between past and present events and the image of the future as an unimaginable, unrealizable destination — as though it were a place rather than a matter of time — both link *Beloved* to, and distinguish it from, slave narrative. While the classic slave narrative focuses on the linear telling of events, or the "what happened," Morrison's novel offers the all-important *"whys"* that render ultimately conprehensible an otherwise barely indecipherable picture of the muddled world that was slave culture. While much of the canvas of the text is unclear, undefined, and even incomprehensible at first read, *Beloved* is in fact a profoundly coherent, analytical, and revelatory study. Its masterful application of often coded language results in a number of interpretive choices.

A historical novel, *Beloved* is also emphatically ahistorical in the sense that no celebrated figures or events are privileged, and dates are rarely given. Morrison's text, like a prototypical slave narrative, is abundant in silences and omissions.[6] In addition to imposed silences, some incidents are suppressed because the writer finds them to be beyond language — in Morrison's words, "unspeakable thoughts, unspoken" (187). *Beloved* overcomes the deafening silences that occur in slave narratives. Even its own deliberate silences convey information, giving voice to the "60 million and more" unheard dead to whom Morrison commemorates the novel. Ella and other free Black people in the novel know that escaped slaves are the walking wounded, especially on the level of the psyche. So when they encounter them, they listen on a deeper level — not so much to what they say, but rather, to what they "did not say; the questions they did not ask" (92).

The most compelling silence in slave narratives, and the one that I am most interested in examining, is the silence of the inner voice that comprehends, and that could disclose, the psychic processes of the slaves, especially the slave mother. Morrison's approach supplies the critical missing element. At the risk of "unsettling [and] confronting the reader with what must be immediately incomprehensible," she punctuates the narrative with "holes," disruptions, and a sense of fragmentation in order to represent the reality of slave and post-slavery life for the African American community.[7] *Beloved* plunges the reader into the world of the novel through a narrative that, while hardly airless, certainly does seem bottomless in its uncanny ability to convey not only the information, but also the visceral and psychological perception of what slave life was like, especially for slave mothers.

"Pool of red ... redbud trees ... red heart ... something red ... a cardinal feather ... red ribbon ... wet red hands" (8, 111, 113, 117, 180, 151). Red splatters the pages of the narrative at odd and frequent intervals, foreshadowing the blood-letting that will occur later on. While the mother/child canvas is vivid with wet, violent reds, other portions of the larger drawing are muted or faded, understated and unremarkable, even miniscule, as though they wish nothing more than to disappear completely from the canvas. Sethe is conspicuous among the vast cast of enslaved personalities by the very vividness and vivacity of her presence. It is this ardor, this forbidden love of life, that ultimately drives her to take the life of her daughter Beloved. Indeed, the act which some characterize as infanticide is perceived by others as a deliberate act of supreme love by a mother who loves her daughter more than her insane world allows. Sethe's daughter's name reflects unrestrained passion — a passion that has no place, no validity, and for which there is no salvation, in slave culture. Generally speaking, the other slaves "know better," and have turned the practice of leading inconspicuous, uneventful lives into a virtual art form. "Live small" is their motto, and Sethe seems to have trouble adjusting to the concept, having revealed a streak of rebelliousness more than once in the past. Repeat renegades like Sethe threaten the entire population with their intransigence.

Living Small

Baby Suggs withdraws to her bedroom to contemplate colors. Denver can't hear or speak for two years. Paul D wanders aimlessly for 18 years, his heart enclosed in a rusted tin can. Sethe expends critical amounts of energy burying memories. Sixo stops speaking. *Beloved* is a graphic tableau of a slave population restrained by the persistent and damaging authority of repressive societal — and, in consequence, psychological — imperatives. The definitive incident in *Beloved* considers the source of communal and familial, as well as material, patterns of learned behavior that enable such an unthinkable event as infanticide to occur in the first place.

In its scrupulous attention to the inner self, *Beloved* is uncommonly open to psychoanalytic examination. Anna Freud's *The Ego and the Mechanisms of Defense* is especially relevant to the world presented in *Beloved* because the behaviors it describes so precisely reflect the behavior of the enslaved community. Freud posits that ego defense mechanisms are designed to protect the ego from internal or external harm, but that mental soundness corresponds with ultimately relinquishing the defenses.[8] Far less value-laden than a great deal of the wider body of theory, Anna Freud's hypotheses nonetheless reflect the premise that external conditions are universally similar for individuals, and further, that these conditions are generally non-threatening. To extend the premise is to assume that one's social condition is manageable as long as one's internal processes are well developed. This assumption perceives a benign universe that excludes the history, and the experience, of African American men and women. Is it possible, or even advisable, for oppressed people to triumph over their defenses, when defense mechanisms are literally imperative to survival in a treacherous external world? If defense mechanisms protect the ego from pain, what secondary effects emerge when they succeed? More importantly, what results if they fail?

Freud perceives that individuals work on the psychic level to ward off internal pain and harm and to repel external threat through the ego. When the individual succeeds in working through and ultimately breaking down these defenses against the self and others, one achieves optimal mental health. At this point, reconciliation between the ego and the superego is favorably achieved. In other words, although defenses are useful in the short term, long-term mental soundness corresponds with the eventual relinquishment of defense mechanisms.[9] Freud's conclusion implies that external threats might be largely imagined, and/or that a healthy individual's force of will can right external, as well as internal, wrongs.

The stunning murder of a two-year-old daughter by her mother is the single event around which *Beloved* revolves. The text refuses easy justifications, facile psychological answers, and blame-letting. It concentrates instead on the inner workings of an entire social system whose pathology and dysfunction are of such stellar proportions that rational behavior by any of its members is virtually nonexistent. Indeed, what level of rationalization allows for the concept of human beings "owning" other human beings? Accountability is assessed for this circumstance without prejudice: slave culture as a whole, the slave holder, the enslaved, and, ultimately, the mother herself, all must answer for what occurs. Only the innocent, dead babe is exempt, and, at that, only initially. Incredibly, even *she* is called to task: at Beloved's "reincarnation," eighteen years after Sethe kills her, the now-adult "child" herself is in fact held accountable for the acts of naïveté, selfishness, and cruelty that she *would* have committed—especially against her mother—had she been truly "alive." A relentlessly comprehensive dissection of all factors that played a part in an event (and its aftermath) that should never have taken place, *Beloved* is a psychological *tour de force*.

Set around the 1860s–1880s in Kentucky and Ohio, *Beloved* brings the past to bear upon the present and illuminates the persistent grip of racial and gender hierarchies upon American society. Racial oppression is the overwhelming reality for the black community: Not one aspect of its existence is transcendent over this single, overriding circumstance. Classified as property, perceived as dumb, unfeeling beasts of labor, and beaten, bred, removed, sold, or killed at the owner's whim, slaves seek asylum by repressing their most natural impulses. Ego defenses are thus fundamental to the slave community for mental, emotional, and certainly physical endurance. Each instinct and desire must be internally processed and refined before public (and/or private) expression can occur. Behavior is literally dictated by the external world.

Primary mechanisms of defense by which the slave community of *Beloved* exists mirror Freud's outline to include distinct manifestations of repression, such as isolation, denial, inhibition of memory and knowledge, and alienation of affect, as well as subgroups of these defenses, including fantasy and avoidance.[10] Paradoxically forced to live by denying in themselves the very attributes by which human beings ordinarily express their existence, Black people engage primarily in reactions, as opposed to actions. They respond not to impulses, but to defense mechanisms. Voice, knowledge and thought, memory, ritual, feelings, are all suppressed.[11] Above all, excess is prohibited. "Everything depends on knowing how much" (87). If too much of *anything* occurs, everything that has been so carefully constructed crumbles; all is lost if one dares to tread outside the boundaries into prohibited territory. And the carelessness of one holds consequences for them all.

Beloved amplifies the primacy of external forces in the construction of the slaves' psyche, as well as the individual and collective consequences of acceding to the persistent authority of certain psychological imperatives. Perversely, the defense mechanisms that the slaves construct to protect themselves entrench them even more firmly into slavery. The slave community learns to suppress the desire for what they cannot have and to suppress the knowledge and the memory of what they have but do not want. These defenses effect a sublime paradox for the oppressed group by replicating the sanctions of slavery, with the result that behavioral patterns imposed from without are actually reinforced from within. Initially erected to ward off external danger, these mechanisms insidiously become a way of life. Yet without them, the slaves' lot would be unbearable. The dilemma is without middle ground: Acquiescence would lead to the loss of one's integrity, one's sense of self; rebellion would result in danger to, and often the forfeiture of, one's life. The emotional burden upon the oppressed group is exacerbated by its powerlessness. No matter what it does, it cannot eliminate the myriad dangers of everyday life. In an attempt to mitigate danger, however, they rely almost universally on defense mechanisms. By repressing their most natural and self-affirming impulses, slaves might physically survive, but their psyches are profoundly compromised. Unchecked, defenses evolve to a dangerous degree, effectively effacing the slaves as human beings even in their own eyes. When Garner asks Baby Suggs what name she goes by, she replies, "Nothing.... I don't call myself nothing" (142).

Beloved describes a world fragmented — not only in the metaphorical sense of Civil War binarisms of black and white, North and South, abolitionist and pro-slavery politics — but also in the lives of the slaves, which are marked by loss, rupture and division — before, during, and now here, after the war. Southern Whites are angry and frustrated in their defeat, and the black populace is set "free" without foundation, without resources, without real lives to replace the phantom existences they had experienced under slavery. Recurrent images reflect Morrison's depiction of "the trauma of racism ... and the severe fragmentation of the self."[12] "Throw-away," "junk-heaped" people, broken families, broken psyches, and broken bodies symbolize the terrible threat — and fact — of ego fragmentation that perpetuates the ex-slaves' psychological, if not physical, imprisonment. "Odd clusters and strays of Negroes wandered ... families of women and children, while elsewhere, solitary, hunted and hunting for, were men, men, men" (52).

Before the Civil War, slave culture ruled. There was no wandering; there was simply slave life. But Black people were not its only victims. Morrison, like Jacobs, charges White society with creating a monster that morally corrupts them even more profoundly than it does their slaves. She transposes the jungle metaphor used to stigmatize African so-called savages onto the slaveholders, charging *them* with hosting the "screaming baboon": "It was the jungle whitefolks planted them in. And it grew. It spread ... until it invaded the Whites who had made it" (198–9).

Paul Garner's Sweet Home is the only plantation depicted in *Beloved*. As the best instance of a brutal system, it invites the reader to imagine the worst. Small and apparently serene, Sweet Home probably comes closest to what might be called a humane slaveholding, an impossible contradiction in terms. Garner prides himself in his revolutionary approach to slave ownership: His slaves are not beaten; the male slaves have some say in certain life decisions — for example, "to buy a mother, choose a horse or a wife, handle guns, even learn reading." At Sweet Home, Garner brags, "My niggers is men every one of 'em," completely oblivious to the profound irony of his statement (195, 125, 10).

Mr. and Mrs. Garner justify their way of life by idealizing it as one big happy plantation family, notwithstanding the fact that slavery is anathema to family. The barring of legalized marital unions, the slaveholder's *droit du seigneur*, especially over his female slaves, the enforced estrangement of parents and children — even on the same plantation, and certainly through the selling and trading of slaves — and the inability of family members to protect one another, to name only a few prohibitions, nullify all claims to the institution of family in Western society. Rather, in this culture, a perverse Oedipal paradigm positions the slaveholder himself as all-powerful father, with his wife the non-nurturing, often evil stepmother, and the adult slave a sort of illegitimate child-laborer. No provisions are made for the nurturing of slave children, who are often unaware of their parentage. As acquisitive as his name suggests, Garner perpetuates his legacy and services his ego by naming his male slaves alphabetically after himself — e.g., Paul A, Paul B, Paul C, Paul D. Given his unlimited authority, his alphabetical namesakes are obviously unable to function both as his "children" and as grown men simultaneously.

Not only slaves, but also slaveholders, are infantilized in this culture, wherein the ruling class — wishing, like Peter Pan, never to grow up — institutionalizes its own pathology. The weakness of its collective ego allows the powerful id to overturn an immature superego, resulting in the archaic capitulation to childlike impulses.[13] Sexual and other physical aggressions are projected onto, and played out upon, the slaves with impunity. For all his innovations, Garner bows to the dictates of the pleasure principle as willingly as other slaveholders, indulging his supremacy for his own gratification, only in a somewhat different way. Baby Suggs perceives the gamesmanship in slavery, wherein the enslaved were "moved around like checkers," Black pawns for the amusement of the players (23).

The silence that invariably accompanies slave life is a part of everyday existence at Sweet Home. Baby Suggs barely talks, speaking only when she must, echoing the post-war silence of the enslaved and the formerly enslaved. The loss of voice is connected with other repressions — especially of memory and of emotion, both of which are scrupulously and resolutely observed in the slave community. Paul D as well keeps his thoughts to himself, and even *from* himself. Instead, he locks them "in that tobacco tin buried in his chest where a red heart used to be. Its lid rusted shut" (72). His dedicated aloofness helps to explain the incredible tension, as well as the extraordinary fluidity, between past and present. Speech and thought liquefy time, reanimating unwanted history so that it flows — or, rather, crashes — into today.

"Rememory" runs throughout the novel as an emphatic representation of past events that refuse to stay buried. Sethe's unwitting use of the word rememory for "memory" is nonetheless fitting, because it aptly describes the repeated resurfacing of anguished moments in her past: Her mother's hanging is a rememory, or "something she had forgotten she knew" (61). The slaves expend extraordinary amounts of energy to maintain the delicate balance that separates past from present. The future does not exist in slave life. To Sethe, and other enslaved people, the only function of the present is to beat back the past. Like Sisyphus, they labor mightily to obliterate unwanted memories, only to awake the next day to start the process all over again.

Knowledge is a dangerous commodity in the slave community, because it disallows fantasy, forgetting, and other defenses. While fantasy enables the individual to escape painful reality, it is a dangerous exercise for adults, since fantasy and reality are mutually exclusive states.[14] At the same time, it could be argued that the danger of psychosis is less threatening to slaves than the danger of utter hopelessness. Imagining, while perilously close to "fantasy," is virtually the only avenue that affords any hope: Sethe does not know, conclusively, what happened to Halle in his escape attempt, so she rejects the most likely probability (that he died 18 years ago). This daydream provokes

Denver's unrealistic expectations and tacitly eases mother and daughter into what is no doubt an empty expectation of Halle's eventual return. At the same time, however, it does stave off utter despair. Then too, fantasies promote sanity by helping the enslaved release hostilities in private and nonthreatening ways. Singing and laughing, they act out killing the "boss," bashing his head in and otherwise doing away with him, only to bring him back to life so that they can kill him again.

An even more powerful defense than fantasy, denial requires no conjuring of what is *not*; it merely rejects what *is*. Even unassailable evidence crumbles under a strong enough denial system: Sethe walks right by the hanged men in the trees at Sweet Home, refusing to accept Paul A's lynching because, although one of the bodies is clearly wearing Paul A's shirt, she does not recognize his head or his feet (both of which would be distorted as a result of hanging). As a child, Sethe had similarly denied the fact that the hanged woman on the ground is her mother because the mother's familiar field hat is not on the body. She does not speak directly of the unspeakable, instead using symbolic imagery to dilute the horror: Her rape is theft of her milk, and the horrible configuration on her back from severe beatings is an innocuous work of art — a "chokecherry tree" with a dizzying complex of branches (79). In much the same vein of denial, when Stamp Paid hands Paul D a news clipping of Sethe's trial, Paul D is glad that he can't read it. Paul D's defenses operate dynamically with one another, facilitating repression on multiple fronts. Besides being unable to read the article, he also resolutely refutes the clear evidence of Sethe's picture before him and, further, dissociates himself from any affect, in his desperate need to disavow Sethe's act: "There is no way in hell a black face could appear in a newspaper if the story is about something anybody wanted to hear.... He smoothed the clipping with his fingers and peered at it, not at all disturbed" (154–5). The terrible irony is that Paul D is *right*: except for the brief, deceptive flicker of opportunity that emerged for Black people during the Reconstruction era, a Black face in the newspaper could *only* transmit bad news. Paul D's investment in not knowing is so intense that he not only refuses to acknowledge what his own eyes show him; he also reaffirms his determination to remain illiterate. When Garner offers his male slaves the chance to learn to read, all but Halle refuse. Underlying Paul D's willful choice is a more general understanding that it is illegal for him to learn to read, that it would make him different from other slaves, and that he would be vulnerable to the laws and punishment of the world outside Sweet Home. Sixo, too, is afraid that read-

6. Sethe: Beyond the Pale

ing would provide him with information about the world that he would be better off not knowing.

Baby Suggs, Halle, Pauls A-D, and Sixo accommodate themselves to the small mercies of Sweet Home by adjusting their voices, their expectations, their emotions, and their desires accordingly. Their defenses thus develop, over time, into a permanent symptom that implies the acceptance of the world's view of them. Paul D, who had grown up thinking that Sweet Home was unique, and that he and the other alphabetized Pauls were the luckiest of slave men, eventually comes to realize, as has Baby Suggs all along, that Sweet Home is not fundamentally different from other plantations, nor is Garner so completely distinguishable from Schoolteacher. Certainly, Garner had been less physically abusive than most slaveholders. But his treatment of them, while manifestly progressive, reflects, on the latent level, the same sort of objectification, infantilization, and experimentation later enjoyed by his brutal successor, Schoolteacher. The difference is that Garner's experiment involves "turning niggers into men," while Schoolteacher's aim is to prove scientifically that they are animals. Under Garner, life had been less physically risky, but just as deadly to the spirit as on other plantations. Because he suppresses thought so effectively, it takes Paul D years to reason out the fact that not only his manhood, but also the entire fate of all the Sweet Home slaves depends exclusively on Garner. None of the slaves ever considered what Sweet Home life would be like if Garner were to die. "Everything rested on Garner being alive. Without his life each of theirs fell to pieces" (220-1). Life with Garner had not only made them feel special and fortunate; it had moved like bacteria to gradually blind them to reality. Slowly and softly it blunted their hopes, thoughts, and feelings, reconciling them to a life of restraint, to this genteel Sweet Home slavery. "They had been isolated in a wonderful lie ... *loving small and in secret*" (221, italics mine). "Everything depends on knowing how much." But how much is too much? Living such a precarious existence, wherein the whims of the slaveowner are subject to change from day to day, the slaves discover that the most prudent course of action is to expose as little of their humanity and their personality as possible, to live and love "small."

The sole exception to the rule against excess in the Black community is in the area of religion, and even there, rituals are observed within a strictly defined sphere of place, time, and behavior. Although the communal gatherings in the Clearing allow for dancing, crying, and laughing, even there the abandon is somehow muted, because "Baby Suggs, Holy, [doesn't] approve of extra" (87). On the singular occasion when the constraints are lifted, disaster visits the entire community, and the community is complicit. Baby Suggs's jubilation over Sethe and Baby Suggs's grandchildren's escape from Sweet Home is certainly cause for celebration. But the prohibitions against excess are so fierce that the community punishes itself for its indulgence. The party begins small and spontaneously, but grows into a veritable feast — unrestrained, joyful, exultant. The next day's stealthy condemnation is nothing less than a manifestation of the community's shameful realization that it had acted out, lost control, and Baby Suggs, spiritual leader and model of restraint, was the instigator. The neighborhood pipeline's deliberate failure to warn of imminent danger, an act of clear passive aggression, reflects the community's projection of its collective guilt and blame onto Baby Suggs and family. The signal announcing Schoolteacher's approach reaches 124 Bluestone too late for Sethe and the children to escape, and Sethe is propelled to act upon pure impulse.

Psychologically, the most disastrous aspect of slave conditioning lies in the area of affect. The slave community learns to suppress emotional attachments, including familial ties, because there is no assurance of the permanence of those connections. Family feeling is discouraged in a system where families can be ripped apart at any moment. Under profound impediments to a coherent family structure, the slaves respond by an alienation of affect. The mother/child relationship is especially complicated as a result. The mother, asserts Sigmund Freud, is "unique, without parallel, established unalterably for a whole lifetime as the first and strongest love-object and as the prototype of all later love-relations."[15] Yet slave mothers and their children are routinely separated. This estrangement virtually insures that the child will be inadequately nurtured and that his or her relationship with the mother will be impaired. Frederick Douglass writes of his mother's rare visits, accomplished by slipping away after a day's work to walk the long distance between the plantations that separated them. Consequently, Douglass does not "recollect of ever seeing my mother by the light of day." His dispassionate description does not conceal his own sense of early loss:

> It is a common custom ... to part children from their mothers at a very early age.... I do not know [why], unless it be to hinder the development of the child's affection toward its mother, and to blunt and destroy the natural affection of the mother for the child. This is the inevitable result.[16]

6. Sethe: Beyond the Pale

Even when they are not physically separated, the mother's often remote relationship with her child, deliberately established to defend against the eventual loss she so deeply fears, inflicts a narcissistic injury upon the child, whose ego development is consequently impaired. This cycle results in the overwhelming probability that this child will, as an adult, be unable to properly nurture his/her children. Clearly, transgenerational damage to the individual's ability to love, and specifically, to parent, are inherent liabilities of oppression, unless or until the cycle is willfully broken. Mothers in slavery understand that, by law, their babies are defined as property, and not *their* property. With each loss of a child, the heart is more and more broken until, finally, the mother learns to protect herself from such unbearable pain. After Baby Suggs's betrayal by a straw boss, whose child she bore in exchange for his promise not to sell her third child, she determinedly hardens her heart. In the end she bore seven children, and she sustained seven losses. "All seven are gone or dead. What would be the point of looking too hard at that youngest one?" (139). Ella, rational voice of the community, universalizes the sanction against emotional attachments. Her point of view is, simply, "Don't love nothing" (92), and this injunction pointedly and specifically refers primarily to family. This behavior conforms precisely to the slaveholder's intent for the benefit of his empire, i.e., that the Black family unit be unacknowledged, unconnected, impermanent, and emotionally distant from each other to facilitate the selling and buying of the enslaved.

Defense mechanisms, including silence, avoidance, denial, repression, and fantasy, operate dynamically in the world of the slaves. Far from imagined threats from the external world, however, the slaves are clearly responding to very real hazards. Their defenses, just as clearly, are learned responses to their external world. For mothers, this posture is particularly damaging. Baby Suggs warns Sethe against knowing or remembering too much, referring to her highly selective, intensely fragile memory of her seven (and probably eight) dead children.

Sethe: The Good Mother

Morrison wrote *Beloved* after hearing fragments of a story about, and becoming "obsessed" with, a slave woman who killed her children, "a woman [who] loved something other than herself so much."[17] Sethe's name encompasses the feminine pronoun "She" and echoes the name Seth, an Old Testament figure and the third son of Eve, whose name means "granted" or "appointed."[18] The story of Sethe is, like Eve's, a universal and symbolic woman's drama as well as a very personal story of one woman's life. And Sethe is surely appointed by Morrison to question, to problematize, and to illuminate accepted ways of thinking about love, mothering, accountability, and society.

Beloved complicates Anna Freud's theories on defense mechanisms. Sethe's attempt to kill her children rests squarely upon the fact that her defenses are inadequate to allow her to accept perpetual slavery for her children. Defense mechanisms protect Sethe to the extent that they help her to survive as a slave, but it is in fact the *insufficiency* of her defenses that empowers her to repudiate slave life. More important than their success are the consequences when Sethe's defenses fail: Overcoming them allows Sethe to seize freedom for her children, to dare to love them, and, finally, to try to kill them when faced with capture. Freud's contention that the individual's optimum goal is mental fitness, which will occur when one conquers one's defenses, is obviously an inadequate model for the reality of slave culture. An alternate psychoanalytic argument, that Sethe kills Beloved because she has been unable to individuate from her, has some basis in fact, but in the end is an incomplete analysis and altogether too facile. Certainly, attempts to merge, fluid ego boundaries, and other symptoms that indicate resistance to psychic separation occur in *Beloved*. But these phenomena must be examined within the context of external forces. To seek answers exclusively within the realm of the individual is to deny the circumstances of Sethe's society. Her culture *is* her preeminent threat, represented by Schoolteacher, who has come to reclaim her and her children into slavery.

Sethe's crime, legally speaking, is infanticide. The judgment of her own community, however, is far more subtle. She is censured not for the act itself, but for its signification. There had been, after all, any number of precedents to her act: Her own mother, raped by White crewmen, had thrown her newborn overboard during the Middle Passage. Ella's baby, spawned either by her slavemaster or his son, had died because she refused to nurse him. For slave mothers, rejection of the unwanted children they bear by White oppressors is one issue; the erection of defenses to spare themselves the anguish of loss of their own Black children is quite another. They do not generally kill them. Instead, they try to not cherish them too much. Sethe is conspicuous not because she kills her child, but because of the ferocity of her motherlove. The community's learned, assiduously guarded approach to such unrestrained emotion is summed up in Paul D's admonition to the woman he loves: "Sethe, your love is too thick" (164). Sethe's essential weakness, and her essential strength, is that her internal impulses are irreconcilable with her external world: She does not know how to love "small."

Sethe's derision of Paul D's restrained emotional philosophy prefigures Paul D's own eventual realization of the meanness and insubstantiality of "loving small," as he and the other slaves — except Sethe — learned to do at Sweet Home. Sethe is mutinous, not oblivious. She takes her children to Ohio not only to free them from slavery, but also so that she can open her heart freely to them. Her perception is psychologically astute: "Look like I loved em more after I got here. Or maybe I couldn't love em proper in Kentucky because they wasn't mine to love" (162). Describing her unrestrained feelings for her children since their escape to Ohio prompts Baby Suggs to drop to her knees. That the older woman actually prays for Sethe's repentance is a telling indicator of the slave community's awe and fear of such intense motherlove. And indeed, Sethe's attempt to kill her children, and her success in that attempt with Beloved, are a direct consequence of such reckless love. Emotional distance is encouraged, but loving one's children with abandon is a dramatic breach of the rules in both the Black and the White communities. For Schoolteacher, Sethe's act merely confirms his theory of the savage brutality of Black people. To the abolitionists who secured her release from prison, her desperate behavior underscores the awfulness of slavery. But insofar as her own people are concerned, the killing of Beloved marks an excess of emotion in a community that, above all, tolerates no excess. Where intense emotional attachments are disallowed, Sethe dares to presume that her children actually belong to her.

A significant factor motivating Sethe's behavior at the time of the killing is that slavery for her children is no longer an option she can accept, particularly after those crucial twenty-eight days of freedom. Her last memory of Sweet Home — of the hanged men in the beautiful sycamore trees, gentle men whose rebellious spirit had surfaced only once in their entire lives, and her gang rape by Schoolteacher's nephew and his friends — are irrevocably stamped upon her memory. Under no circumstances will she allow her children to undergo what she has suffered. Once she becomes a mother, her concerns center around not herself, but her children — her "beautiful, magical best thing." Sethe's defense mechanisms are insufficient to allow her to relinquish her children, but sufficient to mobilize her into action against impending danger. In her desperate need to free them from slavery, she actualizes her determination to see them dead rather than alive in bondage. Carolyn Mitchell sees Sethe's act as a spiritual, if not a moral, decision, because Sethe understands that "simply to embrace life at any cost is not freedom."[19] "Worse [than killing *Beloved*] — far worse — is ... that anybody White could take your whole self" (251).

Sethe's case is not unique, but it *is* rare. Why do her defenses fail to develop when so many slave women are able to uphold the protective shield against loving their children too much? The particular circumstances of Sethe's life provide some answers. In the first place, until the later incident with Schoolteacher's nephew, Sethe is spared the sexual and emotional abuse that Baby Suggs, her mother, Nan, Ella, and other slave women had endured. Young and hopeful when she comes to Sweet Home, she has not yet learned to love "small," and the little mercies at Sweet Home prevent her from fully perceiving the degradation of her slave status. The only slave woman on the plantation, she is revered by the slave men, who have sex with farm animals rather than impose upon her while they respectfully wait for her to choose a mate from among them. This farm is to be her new beginning, a chance for her to build and nurture a real family. Sethe's familial experience while at Sweet Home is rare in that she is allowed to choose her husband, and in that she, Halle, and their children remain an unbroken unit. Even the early disappointments of her wedding ritual — a "bedding" for slaves, the term an accurate representation of White society's assessment of the significance of Black wedlock — do not discourage her. But Sethe's mild resentment of Mrs. Garner's laughter in response to her desire for a real wedding, her insistence on a dress for the occasion, and the poignant "honeymoon" trip into the cornfields with Halle — all necessary to her sense of ceremony — disclose a rebellious spirit given to "excess" and, therefore, at terrible risk.

Sethe never knew her father and remembers her mother only as one of an undifferentiated group of women field workers, all of whom she called simply "Ma'am." Vital and spirited, Sethe is driven to be a good-enough mother in part because of an intense awareness of her own lack of nurturing from her mother, who was not allowed to nurse Sethe because of the fieldwork she was assigned. "I'll tend [*Beloved*] as no mother ever tended a child, a daughter" (200), she vows. Her determination to be a "better" parent than her mother reflects an inability to comprehend and interpret the reasons for her mother's apparent detachment when Sethe was a child, and her inability to concede the realities of her environment. But after Garner dies, Schoolteacher awakens Sethe to the harsher side of slavery. He makes her realize how little control she exercises over her life and over those of her children. Just as she equates giving milk with nurturing, Sethe uses the image of stolen milk to represent assault when she relates to Paul D the story of her rape by multiple attackers. Even as he questions her on specifics, her mind remains fixed on one point only. Above the brutality of the cowhide beating she sustained and the fact that she was pregnant when the young men raped her, the most egregious aspect of this assault, as Sethe repeatedly insists, is that "they took my milk" (16–17). This focus, and Sethe's repeated response, are as much an illustration of the seriousness with which she regards maternal nurturing as they are her inability to specifically articulate the abuse that she suffered at the hands of Schoolteacher's nephew and his friends. The writing of the "master's narrative" is represented by Schoolteacher, who watches impassively as he compiles his report on the incident. Sethe, of course, has no voice. Her narrative would wait over a century to be written.

Sethe's account of the assault enables Paul D to reconstruct that long-ago day, and to explain why Sethe's husband Halle never met her and the children to escape with them. Apparently, while she is being raped and Schoolteacher is expanding his scientific narrative animalistic on slave behavior, Halle, hidden from view, witnesses the assault. Paul D knows that Halle was watching, hiding, in the loft when Sethe was forced inside. Besides that, he only knows that "something broke him." Paul D's last sighting of Halle is indeed that of a broken man, insensible, still crouched by the butter churn, with butter plastered "all over his face" (68–9).

Unable to cope with either his wife's rape or with his absolute powerlessness and inability to protect her as he witnesses her brutal abuse, Halle regresses to infancy on the psychological level. Probably no longer sane, he attempts to nurse *himself* while he watches Sethe being forced to "nurse" grown White men. But the butter is too aged, too thick, bred of rancid milk. It can not restore what he and Sethe have lost.

Maternal milk is an important theme in *Beloved* that Morrison deploys on a number of levels in addition to the mother's nursing of her child, including the oral aggression of slaveholders, the infantilization of slaves, and the mother's method of telling her story by de-stabilizing the master's (Schoolteacher's) order.[20] Just as Harriet Jacobs's slave narrative depicts the incompatibility between kinship ties and freedom, Morrison's novel illustrates this dilemma through the act of nursing. Beloved's feeding, as Sethe tells Paul D, is necessarily interrupted in order for the escape plan from Sweet Home to proceed. But nothing would stop this mother from nourishing her daughter. "I had to get my milk to my baby girl. Nobody was going to nurse her like me" (16). This "rememory" serves as metaphor for maternal nurturing that is disrupted or invalidated by slavery. The jarring conflation of nurturing and rape images, as well as Sethe's anxiety that Beloved will not be properly nourished, suggest Sethe's motherly dilemma. Her hope of properly nurturing them is compromised by her fear for their safety. That Sethe specifically alludes to nurturing not just her "child," but her "baby girl" reflect the gender-specificity of her concern in the above quote. This focus underscores an explicit fear — that is, the naked vulnerability of female slaves, especially to sexual abuse. This scene of compelling imagery defies Sethe's earlier expectations about nursing her baby and saturates with dark irony Sethe's statement that she will "tend [Beloved] as no mother ever tended a child." With Schoolteacher approaching to reclaim her family, moments after she "tends to Beloved," and in fact has been nursed *by* Beloved, after a fashion — when her child's blood gushes over her — Sethe's consciousness grasps a baffling thought in the midst of this extraordinary tableau: that baby Denver, whom she would have killed moments before, now needs nursing — immediately. Baby Suggs, afraid for the children, struggles with her daughter-in-law for possession of baby Denver, but Sethe, relentless in single-minded determination, easily overpowers the older woman. So Denver "took her mother's milk right along with the blood of her sister" (152). The scene reflects the mind's incredible ability to dissociate itself from unbearable circumstances by re-focusing on some other imperative. But it also, importantly, bears out Sethe's resolve to not have her girl-children "dirtied" by forces outside her control. An intimate awareness of the sexual hazards for female slaves surely accounts for Sethe's intent to kill her daughters before she kills her sons.

Schoolteacher's nephew's rape doesn't "break" Sethe; rather than causing her submission, it triggers rebellion. Finally fully aware of the dangers inherent in slavery, she is not, at this point, able to stop loving her children, or to love them "small," so her only recourse at this point is to escape, or die trying. Her passion for her children has developed virtually unchecked because at Garner's Sweet Home she had felt free enough to love and nurture them. Her twenty-eight days of freedom in Ohio were critical to her state of mind. Like the cycle of the moon, they had brought her full circle, lulling her into the dream of a relatively safe and normal life as mother and protector.

But even after a desperate escape north, the fugitive slave law ensnares

6. Sethe: Beyond the Pale

them by licensing Schoolteacher to follow them to Ohio and reclaim them. Such incredible disadvantage, in such an overwhelmingly punitive external environment, illuminates the central horror of the narrative, of her life, and of her world: They could not live free. In a flash, this insight pushes Sethe beyond the pale.

> She saw them coming and recognized Schoolteacher's hat. And if she thought anything it is No. No. Nono. Nonono.... [She] carried, pushed, dragged them through the veil, out, away, over there where no one could hurt them [163].

The apocalyptic moment is heralded by the chapter's opening words, "When the four horsemen came" (148). Morrison refashions Schoolteacher and his men from Sweet Home into the preternatural rider-conquerors from the Book of Revelation:

> Now I saw when the Lamb opened one of the seven seals, and I heard one of the four living creatures say, as with a voice of thunder, 'Come!' And I saw, and behold, a white horse, and its rider had a bow; and a crown was given to him, and he went out conquering and to conquer.... When he opened the fourth seal, I heard the voice of the fourth living creature say, 'Come!' And I saw, and behold, a pale horse, and its rider's name was Death. —Revelation 6:1–8.

To Sethe, Death Himself is riding up the hill on His white horse to claim her children, bringing with Him other abominations that would irrevocably harm them. The vision of this approaching crisis gives rise to a desperate maternal impulse that overrides the prohibitions of her culture. Sethe is unable to reconcile her internal impulses with her external world. With exquisite devotion, Sethe protects her children from Schoolteacher, but fails to protect them from herself. Her triumph over her defenses results in her loving her daughter to death.

The irony of Sethe's act is sublime. Her resolution of the dilemma stands on paradoxical ground: Had she loved her children less, had she reconciled herself to her children's enslavement, had she accepted the probable impermanence of her family unit, she would have acted with less vehemence and more restraint. However, her children would then have been re-enslaved, and this is a condition she finds worse than death. There seems to be no middle ground for Sethe. She can locate no mediating space between the rock and the hard place. Slavery and maternity are, simply, profoundly incompatible. Nothing good can come of a situation where a mother is not free to love her children without restraint.

In Sethe's brutal world, all traditional concepts and conventions are turned inside out. Syncretic phrasing underscores the impossible contradictions of the slave's existence: Just as Paul D passive-aggressively allows his imprisonment to "dr[i]ve him crazy so he would not lose his mind" (41), Sethe thinks that when Beloved returns, it'll be "nice to think ... about all I ain't got to remember no more" (182). Life and death blur and become confused, assuming exceptional meaning under slavery. "Life [is] dead," Paul D thinks, when the chain gang of slaves seems to have sapped every ounce of vitality from his spirit (109). Baby Suggs had been more prepared for Halle's death than she had for his life. To Sethe, dying is easy; "being alive is the hard part" (7). In the same sense, Sethe kills her baby so that it can live: "If I hadn't killed her she would have died" (200).

These reversals are hardly mere rationalizations. Just as Beloved's return from the dead demonstrates the fluidity between life and death in *Beloved*, so too does Sethe actually believe that "the veil" behind which her children will be safe is a benevolent universe, not actually removed from the world in which she lives. Indeed, it is a line of such exquisite thinness that separates the two worlds as to be virtually nonexistent. When Paul D argues that Sethe should not be so protective of Denver, asking reasonably what will happen to Denver when Sethe dies, Sethe replies, "Nothing! I'll protect her while I'm live and I'll protect her when I ain't" (45).

Sethe learns to live and love smaller after the killing in order to maintain her sanity and safeguard her equilibrium, like other slave women. At the same time she is different, because her psychological processes have evolved differently. Even the other slaves are aware that Sethe's defenses have not developed to the degree that the community considers safe. "The Misery" of that fateful post-celebration day culminates in Beloved's death, a dramatic consequence of impulses that, suddenly heightened by external threat, temporarily overwhelm Sethe's defense mechanisms. As a result, the ego defenses that Sethe could not access prior to killing her daughter are now instantly, savagely propelled into high gear. As they kick in, her selfhood disintegrates and Sethe's mind simply "shut[s] down" (201). Her eyes, depicted as "two wells" because of their profound emptiness, are a true mirror to her psyche at this time (9).

Before the killing Sethe is spirited, determined, loving, and unafraid to feel. This very spiritedness is what motivates her to escape slavery at all costs. After the killing, Sethe's tendency toward "excess" disappears, as does her fighting spirit, open nature, easy affection, and will to survive. The new Sethe would never have killed her children. But the new Sethe would also not have had the courage to escape and free them from slavery, or the audacity to love them as deeply as she did. Sethe's new-found maternal restraint leaves her three remaining children starved for nurturing. Sadly, this circumstance precipitates alienation within, and eventually the fragmentation of, the family unit.

The Return of the Repressed

If Beloved had not returned in corporeal form, despite the poltergeist activities inside Baby Suggs's home, Sethe might be clinically diagnosed as suffering only from persecutory anxiety, manifested by the imaginary conjuring of her dead daughter. But this is no figment of her imagination: Beloved's (un)timely rebirth, straight out of the water—fully grown and fully dressed—is a fact. It is also most certainly a direct response to the newly-configured family unit of Paul D, Sethe, and Denver, who have just spent an enjoyable day together at the fair. The outing marks a breakthrough for mother and daughter, a tentative reaching-out to the world beyond their home, a possible beginning of the healing process after eighteen years of sorrow and isolation. The irrepressible memories that Sethe holds, and tries to suppress, about Beloved are partly responsible for Beloved's reappearance. But it is specifically the current potential for Sethe's *recovery* from her daughter's killing, and the arrival of Paul D (a would-be suitor) at 124 Bluestone, that invoke Beloved's rage, and her manifestation in flesh and blood, on this particular fair-going day.

All this time after the killing, Sethe's perpetual state of mourning has apparently been sufficient to appease the angry spirit of her daughter. During these intervening years Sethe has been the soul of propriety. While she has been tried and acquitted by a jury *not* of her peers on the charge of destruction of property, and the legal consequences of her deed are behind her, its impact on her psyche has been overwhelming. Beloved's killing opened the floodgates to all her repressed nightmares. Sethe's former curiosity and engagement with the world have been replaced by a conscious disregard of everything save mechanical labor. Physical labor for Sethe is more a distraction than a chore at this point in her life, all the better for accomplishing her *real* goal, which is the "serious work of beating back the past" (72). Before the carnival, and Beloved's return, Sethe directs her energies entirely to repressing memories, leaving no room for anything else. Like

Baby Suggs, she has become more concerned with *not* knowing what is going on — especially within herself. Her development of rigid defense mechanisms subsequent to the murder of Beloved operates in tandem to widen the gap between her and the rest of the world, and even between her external and her internal self. Her conversation with Paul D about the house describes precisely her mechanism for dealing with inner thoughts and memories:

"How are [things]?"
"We get along."
"What about inside?"
"I don't go inside" [45-6].

Sethe's maternal impulses diminish in direct proportion to the increasing organization of her defenses. As she distances herself from her children, sons Howard and Bugler conspire in whispers and then run away from home to escape the vortex of fear and silence precipitated by her unutterable act. Sethe's sense of isolation following the trial is exacerbated by Baby Suggs's and Denver's reciprocal apathy and seclusion. Denver, starved for nurturing, responds to Sethe's remoteness by regressing into a silent, pre-adolescent state. Baby Suggs's withdrawal to her room signals, in effect, a renunciation of a lifetime's worth of faith and community. In her desperate need to avoid more pain, she locates a safe, and isolating, avocation: She decides to contemplate colors because they are harmless. "Blue don't hurt nobody. Yellow neither" (179). When she finally "exhaust[s]" blue, she dies. Before this, the three generations of women — grandmother, mother, daughter — hold onto their sanity by isolating themselves from the community, from one another, and even from their inner selves. Their defense mechanisms are functioning beautifully, but the family is verging on collapse.

Beloved's murder induces Sethe's detachment and withdrawal from the mothering process, which contributes to Denver's extremely fragile ego. Profound psychic fragility prompts Denver to erect her own defenses. Her decision to stop speaking and hearing for two years is a direct response to a classmate's inquiry about her mother's crime, an artful compromise between her conscious and unconscious mind, between knowledge of the truth and an inability to confront it.[21] Because of inconsistent and insufficient nurturing, Denver exhibits an arrested development that situates her psychically in childhood. Her twelve-year, self-imposed isolation within the walls of her home signal her retreat from society and, also, a rejection of maturity. Her idea of the world reflects her internal, as well as external, fears. Forced outside by a crisis, Denver stands barely outside the front door, contemplating the horrors that exist past the narrow boundaries of 124 Bluestone. What many would view as a prison is to her the only safe haven, because beyond her home is only threat and pain, places where "things so bad had happened" that it would be suicidal to approach them again (143–4).

Avoidance, a more primitive defense even than denial, is extremely efficacious and, in Denver's case, severely crippling. Avoiding speech and hearing, like avoiding the outside world — especially the killing shed where The Misery occurred — is Denver's uncomplicated response to even the *possibility* of encountering dangerous external situations. Her fear of being "swallowed up" and "eaten alive by the dark" (123) corresponds to the issues of oral anxiety that preoccupy her. While being ingested reflects an infantile fear of her mother[22] — a fear *not* entirely built upon fantasy — her sustained, excessive eating also suggests that she is nurturing herself in the absence of maternal nurturing. "Denver's imagination produced its own hunger and its own food, which she badly needed because loneliness wore her out" (28–9). The very real threat of ego fragmentation is manifested in her obsession with part objects, her extremely liquid boundaries, and in her desolated center. "She does not know which part of her is an arm, a foot or a knee.... She has no self" (123).

Denver's confused and conflicted feelings for Sethe surface as a result of her alternating denial and admission of Sethe's attempt to kill her when she was a child. They also reflect a neglected child's frustration and pain. Denver's loneliness is so intense that she actually looks forward to visitations from the ghost of her sister, and she has expectations of her father as well. Her childlike fantasy that Halle will materialize one day to complete the family circle significantly excludes her mother. What is most bizarre is that it also excludes any living people besides herself: Her ideal family is composed of herself, her (probably dead) father, and her dead sister: "I bet he's trying to get here. If Paul D could do it my daddy could too. Angel man. We should all be together. Me, him and Beloved" (209). Denver's Oedipal fantasy, triggered by her resentment of Sethe's first potential romance in over eighteen years, illuminates the paucity, and the brooding darkness, of her interior existence. Her desperate thirst for love and affection, and the damage caused by this unmet need, give rise to her regression, her fantasies, her oral anxieties, and her withdrawal, situating her more in the land of the dead than of the quick.

Sethe, who had once nursed Denver under the most extreme circumstance possible — immediately after killing Beloved, with bounty hunters fast approaching — doesn't have the time now to consider her daughter. The kind of nurturing that Denver so desperately needs, and is not getting, is not only emotional, but also the sustenance of memory, the reconstruction of her past. She is spiritually undernourished because of her mother and grandmother's repression of the past; only when Beloved comes back is Denver's need adequately addressed.

Sethe, however, seems to be taking fragile, tentative steps toward ego reparation. Even in her weakened psychic state, her ability to love still borders on what some ex-slaves consider "excess." Encountering her again a lifetime after Sweet Home, Paul D feels — and fears — the quiet, restrained love that she radiates towards Denver. Children of slaves, especially, should be loved only a little bit. "Risky, thought Paul D, very risky.... To love anything that much is dangerous" (45). How different they are! What is far too much for him is only temporarily acceptable to Sethe, but still much too small for Denver. Also, the breach between mother and daughter has continued too long to be easily mended. Now rejecting her mother's stories, Denver welcomes her sister's memories. Once nursed with Beloved's blood, Denver is now nursed by her sister's seductive presence. Beloved's own wretched hunger for companionship would swallow her up if she *could* be consumed. They are both severely malnourished, and they now both blame Sethe. Denver is resentful, but Beloved's anger has been seething longer than time. More than sister now, Beloved effectively becomes surrogate mother to Denver as they exchange family history; unlike Sethe, Beloved does not fail her: "Denver is seeing it now and feeling it — through Beloved" (78). Between them, they recreate the past, even from Sethe's point of view. Still, they do not forgive their mother.

Just as Liscio connects Sethe's maternal "writing" through the mother's milk with Julia Kristeva's concept of the semiotic, Rebecca Ferguson closely compares *Beloved*'s first stream of ideas with the pre–Oedipal semiotic.[23] Beloved's fragmented discourse signals not only her recent rebirth, however, but also the symbolic experience of the Middle Passage, a horrific place and event that Morrison, like others, characterizes as *nowhere*: Beloved, who exists in the eternal present ("All of it is now" [210]), represents the "gap between Africa and Afro-America and the gap between the living and the dead and the gap between the past and the present."[24] "I don't want that place. This is the place I am," Beloved, smiling, tells Denver, indistinctly alluding to her journey from Africa on the slave ship to Ohio by way of water. The disjointed utterances depict the miserable conditions on the ship — jammed masses of starving humanity, rats, disease, filth, death — delineate even more sharply Beloved's disposition in both the life-state and the death-state. Her duality recalls Amy Denver's warning to Sethe as the younger White woman rubs Sethe's swollen, burning feet during Sethe's escape: "It's gonna hurt, now.... Anything dead coming back to life hurts" (35).

> I am always crouching the man on my face is dead the men without skin bring us their morning water we have none someone is thrashing ... we are all trying to leave our bodies behind ... it is hard to make yourself die forever [210].

Beloved's rebirth is a fulfillment of Denver's fantasies. But more importantly, her reincarnation represents Sethe's judgment against herself. A questing agent seeking accountability for the act that deprived her of life, Beloved is the very embodiment of the return of the repressed.

The symbol of Sethe's profoundest love, greatest fear, and deepest anguish, Beloved returns in corporeal form because Sethe can no longer repress the memory of the child she killed. For all the repression that she constantly enacts, there persists in her a force that will not succumb to total denial of reality, nor does she deny personal responsibility for her action. Denver marvels at her mother's poise and equanimity, her refusal to look away, when life has offered dreadful scenes best not viewed by the naked eye: a man's fatal beating, the carnage as a mother pig eats her own young. That Sethe could face especially this second, appalling scene, in view of what she had done to (for) Beloved and what she had tried to do to (for) her other children, is a testament to the strength of her self-possession and the depth of her self-recrimination. By reconstructing her "re-memory," Sethe reverses her long-ago dismemberment of her child. By remembering Beloved, Sethe in effect re-*members* Beloved.

Sethe's daughter returns in an uncanny blend of past and present, child and woman, desire and revulsion, life and death. Physically she is a young woman of about twenty, as though she had never died. But apart from verbal abilities, she is developmentally arrested in childhood, as she would have been at the time of her death. Like a child, she is narcissistic and uninhibited, totally unencumbered by conventional restraints. Sethe greets Beloved's reappearance with serenity and relief because she is worn out by the guilt and the constant output of energy required to forget about killing her: "Now I can look at things again because she's here to see them too" (201). Ironically, now that she can begin to reconnect with life because Beloved has come home, Beloved's return has been prompted by the distinct desire to disconnect Sethe *from* life. Even more than this, however, Sethe feels that she deserves this visitation. She is desperate to know that Beloved understands why she killed her. Beloved's re-birth initially gives Sethe a deceptive sense of the rightness of her act and of having been forgiven by her daughter and invites Sethe's unfruitful fantasy that her living sons will return to her just as Beloved had. Unremembered is her earlier acceptance that Howard and Bugler fled because they are terrified of her, that she will never see them again.

Before Beloved's reincarnation Sethe has never denied the murder itself. Rather, to help accommodate her unflagging conviction that she did what she had to do, Sethe's memory has refashioned the murder into the "perfect death of her crawling-already baby" (99). But Beloved's adult self, her increasingly bitter pain and rage, her innocent yet deadly bewilderment over why she was killed, undermine the perfection of Sethe's illusion. The awful, raw, jagged gash upon Beloved's neck testifies to Sethe's mark upon her daughter — much like the slavemaster's whip marks Sethe's — and explodes Sethe's ultimate fantasy. Beloved's death, *not* beautiful, is ugly, bloody, abhorrent. And Beloved, unable to perceive anything but her own victimization, forces her mother into a stark accounting. Sethe's crippled defense mechanisms struggle at full power under Beloved's compelling authority. "Tell me your diamonds," she pressures, referring to Sethe's rhinestone earrings (58). And she wants every detail. So childlike, and so demanding, with that chilling grimace on her face that passes for a smile, Beloved relentlessly extracts endless stories from Sethe and ingests them as though starved for sustenance. They become a way to feed her, just as she feeds Denver with her own tales. And she is insatiable. Sethe obliges, somewhat like a detached, robotic Scheherazade, but unlike the fabled dancer, she is not playing for time, nor is she concerned about saving her own life. She wants only forgiveness. Beloved, ever childlike, is certainly not predisposed to forgive; nor does she appreciate the concept of compromise. Whereas Beloved shares stories with Denver, she only *takes* from Sethe. Her appetite for her mother, sharpened by the starvation conditions from which she emerged on this side of the veil, is voracious. Beloved

> never got enough of anything ... made demands ... took the best of everything ... ate up her life, took it, swelled up with it.... The bigger Beloved got, the smaller Sethe became.... Locked in a love that wore everybody out [242–3; 250–1].

6. Sethe: Beyond the Pale

Beloved's behavior is the essence of pure impulse, a classic representation of narcissistic desire and rage, a consequence of the psychic (and physical) injury she sustained at her mother's hands. As she probes for, and ultimately demands, answers, accountability, and retribution, all Sethe's walls of defense crumble. Sethe makes no attempt to temper her daughter's appetite: "Anything Beloved wanted, she got" (240). A free spirit, so to speak, Beloved has Sethe at a distinct disadvantage. Beloved's cunning manipulation of Paul D, Sethe's would-be knight in rusted armor, is only a sample of the weapons that comprise her vast arsenal. She easily dispatches him, first seducing him, then expelling him from 124 Bluestone when she no longer needs him, now that she has what she wants — a "baby" in her ghostly belly. These strategies are calculated to accomplish one goal: to punish Sethe, to take from Sethe what Beloved feels she lost when Sethe took her life.

The projection and role reversal the two women undergo reflect a genuine need, or at least a willingness, to experience what the other has felt and lived. It also expresses their mutual identification of the other as protector as well as oppressor. Sethe identifies with Beloved out of a sense of profound guilt and remorse; Beloved identifies with Sethe through an anguished conviction of having been betrayed and through a child's spiteful longing to overtake a life in compensation for the one that has been taken from her. Beloved wants to re-enact the killing, only with the roles reversed. Sethe, childlike, makes no move to stop her. As Beloved begins to strangle her mother in the clearing, it is only Denver's intervention that stops her. Left to her own devices, Beloved, Unholy, would have transformed Baby Suggs, Holy's spiritual space into a killing field without compunction.

A measure of Beloved's increasing power, and of the ego fragmentation of the entire family, is reflected in the narrative rupture that occurs in *Beloved* once the three women are alone in the house. This breach reflects other images of impending disintegration as Sethe's tenuous hold on authority and denial are broken down under Beloved's relentless demands. Identities blur and become confused as Sethe and Denver endeavor to possess and to contain the ethereal aura that calls herself Beloved, privileging her existence at the expense of their own:

> I am Beloved and she is mine. I am not separate from her ... her face is my own [210, *Denver's chapter*].
>
> Beloved, she my daughter. She mine.... She come back to me, my daughter, and she is mine [200–204, *Sethe's chapter*].

Sethe and Beloved's highly complex relationship involves a tangled web of emotions that reconfigure the parent/child relationship. Entirely defenseless, almost eager to be judged and found guilty, Sethe becomes passive in direct proportion to Beloved's increasing aggression. At this point the question of psychological individuation *is* pertinent, because Sethe now regresses to the stage where she actually seeks merger with, and consumption by, her daughter. Locked in a bizarre shadow-dance, mother and daughter form a curious symbiosis of two incomplete entities, virtually undifferentiated, willfully fusing. Beloved blatantly imitates Sethe in all things, and Sethe passively accepts her emerging doppelgänger. The resemblance becomes so uncanny that sometimes "it is difficult for Denver to tell who is who" (241).

Sethe's use of pronouns, as she shifts the direction of her speech from a third party to herself, reflects her fixed and constant movement further and further away from others and deeper and deeper inside herself through Beloved, her alter ego: "I am Beloved and she is mine; you are me ... I am you" (200, 217). This willful merging signals that the spiritually devastated mother, who had never sought forgiveness from anyone, now desperately seeks absolution and, failing that, punishment, from the one person to whom she feels accountable. But her spectral daughter wants only to *become* Sethe. "Beloved accused her.... How could she have left her? And Sethe cried..." (241).

Sethe's murder of Beloved violates, yet, incredibly, sanctions, the mother's role. Sethe's perception that fluid boundaries exist between life and death informs the dichotomy of her decision: She had wanted to kill her children because of a passionate resolve to keep them from harm. Her plan, after all, had been "to take us all to the other side where my own ma'am is" (203). Beloved has done no less by coming back to be with Sethe. As she expresses to both Denver and Sethe, her profound sense of betrayal by Sethe is more the result of maternal abandonment than it is of her mother's killing her: "She left me behind. By myself" (75).

Denver's behavior since Beloved's first death shows that Sethe must also be accountable to *her* for maternal neglect. Denver's passivity during Sethe and Beloved's emotional struggle denotes not a lack of awareness of the implicit threat that Beloved represents to Sethe, but rather, her own conflicted feelings toward her mother, and a vague sense of obligatory loyalty toward her sister as well: although it is not clear to her on a conscious level, Denver suffers from survivor's guilt because she survived the shed and Beloved did not. Gnawing at the fringes of her psyche is the idea that "a bill

6. Sethe: Beyond the Pale

was owing somewhere.... But who she owed or what to pay it with eluded her" (77).

But before Denver takes action, she is forced to accept that the drama in which Sethe and Beloved are engaged is literally a life-or-death struggle. Only when Denver acknowledges her own complicity in the haunting of 124 Bluestone — that is, her conjuring of the ghost — does she begin to assume a measure of responsibility. Her call for help is Denver's first break from a self-imposed isolation of twelve years. And the community responds because it, too, is responsible for Beloved's return. The malice it exhibited eighteen years ago in failing to warn Sethe of the slave hunters' approach has come back to haunt them as well. And the terrifying excesses that Beloved demands are beyond the community's ability to cope. Beloved has forced them to know that, even as they reject the past for a "safer" present, they cannot obliterate it. The present is somehow always accountable to the past; Sethe's trouble is, in effect, their trouble. The ominous implications of a dead baby giving birth to a (?baby?) mobilize the community to break its own rule — to behave with "excess" and become involved in collective concerns. And it is the communal effort that succeeds where all else has failed. Ella, center of consciousness of the community, "didn't like the idea of past errors taking possession of the present" (256). Sethe's action had been appalling, but Beloved's behavior is egregious. Her blatant, audacious behavior, "unleashed and sassy" (256), will no longer be tolerated.

Thus in a very significant way, Beloved is the positive catalyst that forces the breakdown of defense mechanisms and the resurfacing of a unified front within the community. She is the agent that compels a reckoning for each individual's personal choices. Her attempted re-enactment of the killing in the clearing was initiated through rage and pain, but the re-enactment that Beloved provokes at the end of the novel performs an extraordinary service for Sethe: Beloved gives her mother the opportunity to relive the most significant act of her life. The language of denial and obstruction that fell from Sethe's mouth eighteen years ago ("Nonono") echoes uncannily with her words and thoughts when the scene replays itself. But something is different. Sethe has found the answer to that haunting question that has been with her since she killed Beloved: Could she have done something different? She turns her weapon not toward her children this time, but to the White man on horseback. "And if she thinks anything, it is no. No no. Nonono. She flies.... Beloved is smiling.... Sethe is running away from her, running" (262). The fundamental difference in the drama this time is profound. *This* time, danger is perceived within, rather than without, the household; this time, the community has come out of hiding; it is present *en masse* and ready to assist. Eighteen years earlier, Sethe had overcome her defenses to act on impulse. Powerless and alone, her passionate rage against Schoolteacher had transformed into passionate desperation. Now again she acts on impulse, but with one significant difference. And this difference indicates a crucial shift in her psychic organization. This time, Sethe focuses her unbridled rage directly upon the Pale Horse, Pale Rider who have come — again, she thinks, to re-enslave and abuse her children. "Now [Sethe] is running into the faces of the people out there.... And above them all, the man without skin, looking" (262). That the rider is not Schoolteacher but Mr. Bodwin, a kind man and staunch abolitionist, does not diminish the importance of Sethe's reconfigured response to what she perceives as danger to her children. A purely Morrisonian touch, the irony of this situation illustrates the myriad possibilities, nuances, and complications to which Sethe must now adapt, now that she has decided to return to the land of the truly living.

In the aftermath of Sethe's misguided attempt on Bodwin's life, while the community makes its first overtures to reestablish relations with Sethe's family and Denver begins to come into her own, Paul D and Stamp Paid actually share a joke. Fully aware that Bodwin is the lead abolitionist of the community, the one most responsible for Sethe's acquittal when the prosecutor and countless others would have seen her hanged, they revel in the irony. Gallows humor, certainly, but for once, unreserved: "Every time a whiteman come to the door she got to kill somebody?" (265). More important is the recognition, through Sethe's act, of their own psychic imbalance.

> "Damn. That woman is crazy. Crazy."
> "Yeah, well, ain't we all?"
> They laughed then. A rusty chuckle at first [265].

Rusty because so long untried, the robust, lingering laugh that eventuates is a cathartic release of long-built tensions, anxieties, and repressions. This sharing between them indicates that the release of defenses at this point is not only an individual, or even a familial process, but a communal undertaking, nudging them gently toward more healthy responses to life's exigencies.

Margaret Atwood explores the meaning of Morrison's epigraph, noting that while it might initially seem to suggest that Beloved was not really deeply loved, or that Sethe was not really accepted by her community, its larger con-

6. Sethe: Beyond the Pale

text provides a fuller, more promising message than the verse itself seems to bestow:

> *I will call them my people, which were not my people; and her Beloved, which was not Beloved....*

The passage is from a chapter in which the Apostle Paul ponders, Job-like, the ways of God toward humanity. The passage proclaims not rejection, but reconciliation and hope. It continues:

> *And it shall come to pass, that in the place where it was said unto them, Ye are not my people; there shall they be called the children of the living God.*[25]

This fuller passage conveys a sense of a redemptive future, a place and a condition that the ex-slaves have been unable to imagine. Similarly, the dénouement, following Beloved's banishment (vanishment), offers muted but cautiously hopeful signs of Sethe's eventual reemergence as a restored individual. Sethe's final words ("Me? Me?") privilege her integrity as a whole person in a way that she has heretofore been unable to envision. The expectant note in Sethe's voice must be delicately balanced, however, against the constant danger of both the internal, and the external, worlds in which she exists. Sethe's story maintains that pain must be re-lived, worked through, and exorcised in order to be relieved.

In Sethe's universe, mothering is a formidable undertaking. Sethe's choice to kill her daughter is framed by both internal and external imperatives, based upon the demands of her passion in view of the dangers of her powerful external world. From her restricted frame of reference, in a life of such small mercies, Sethe gives her daughter the only gift she has to give. Sethe is a good mother. The problem is that the environment in which she and her children exist is not a good universe. From Sethe's frame of reference, life is slavery, but death brings true freedom. This is her reality, where moments of exquisite beauty coexist with chilling horror. *Beloved* is a terrible story. It is also a love story. Above all, it *is* a story to pass on.

These are all stories to pass on.

Chapter Notes

Introduction

1. Fernando Suman, *Race, Culture, and Psychiatry* (London: Routledge, 1989), 19–21.

2. Thomas J. Otten, "Pauline Hopkins and the Hidden Self of Race," *EHL* 59 (1992), 237.

3. Jeffrey Berman, *Narcissism and the Novel* (New York: New York University Press, 1990), 17.

4. Barbara Johnson on Nella Larsen's *Quicksand* and Heinz Kohut, The Carpenter Lectures at the University of Chicago, April 26, 1990.

5. Alice Walker, *In Search of Our Mothers' Gardens* (New York: Harcourt Brace Jovanovich, 1983), 233.

6. Marianne Hirsch, "Maternal Narratives," in *Reading Black, Reading Feminist*, ed. Henry Louis Gates, Jr. (New York: Meridian, 1990), 416. Hirsch notes that "unlike many contemporary white women writers who define their artistic identity as separate from or in opposition to their mothers," Black women writers have begun determinedly retracing their matrilineal line, spiritually and literarily.

7. Washington, Mary Helen, "I Sign My Mother's Name: Alice Walker, Dorothy West, Paule Marshall," *Mothering the Mind*, eds. Ruth Perry and Martine Watson Brownly (New York: Holmes and Meier, 1984), 161.

8. Hirsch, 417.

9. *Ibid.*, 417.

Chapter 1

1. Harriet Jacobs. *Incidents in the Life of a Slave Girl, Written by Herself, The Classic Slave Narratives*, ed. Henry Louis Gates, Jr. (New York: New American Library, 1987). All page references to Jacobs's text are from this edition.

2. The work of Jean Fagan Yellin has put to rest extra-textual issues raised by numerous critics, including John Blassingame, noted author of *The Slave Community*, regarding the authorship and authenticity of Jacobs's narrative. See her introduction on p. xv of *Incidents*.

3. In all subsequent references to the author I use, as does she, her pseudonym, Linda Brent.

4. Jean Fagan Yellin, "Texts and Contexts of Harriet Jacobs's *Incidents in the Life of a Slave Girl: Written by Herself*," *The Slaves' Narrative*, eds. Charles T. Davis and Henry Louis Gates, Jr. (Oxford: Oxford UP, 1985), 263.

5. John W. Blassingame, *The Slave Community: Plantation Life in the Antebellum South* (New York: Oxford University Press, 1972), 234.

6. D. W. Winnicott, *Playing & Reality* (London: Routledge, 1971), 10.

7. Sigmund Freud, *An Outline of Psycho-Analysis*, rev. ed., ed. James Strachey (New York: W. W. Norton & Company, 1969), 45.

8. Nancy Chodorow, *The Reproduction of Mothering: Psychoanalysis and the Sociology of Gender* (Berkeley: University of California Press, 1985), 223–4.

9. Heinz Kohut, *The Analysis of the Self: A Systematic Approach to the Treatment of Narcissistic Personality Disorders* (New York: International Universities Press, 1971), 49.

10. Hortense Spillers, "Mama's Baby, Papa's Maybe: An American Grammar Book," *Diacritics* (Summer 1987), 77.

11. Hazel Carby, *Reconstructing Womanhood: The Emergence of the Afro-American Woman Novelist* (New York: Oxford University Press, 1987), 57.
12. Ralph Ellison, *Invisible Man* (New York: Vintage, 1990), 156.
13. Yellin, "Texts and Contexts," 263.
14. Deborah Grey White, *Ar'n't I A Woman? Female Slaves in the Plantation South* (New York: W. W. Norton, 1985), 89.
15. Sigmund Freud, *Outline of Psycho-Analysis*, 336.
16. Anna Freud, *The Ego and the Mechanisms of Defense*, revised edition, trans. Cecil Baines (New York: International Universities Press, 1966), 89–91.
17. Claude Meillassoux, *The Anthropology of Slavery: The Womb of Iron and Gold*, trans. Alide Dasnois (Chicago: University of Chicago Press, 1991), 127.
18. Winnicott, *Playing and Reality*, 10.
19. *Ibid.*
20. *Ibid.*, 67.
21. Frederick Douglass, *Narrative of the Life of Frederick Douglass, an African Slave*, in *The Classic Slave Narratives*, ed. Henry Louis Gates, Jr. (New York: New American Library, 1987), 256.
22. Julia Kristeva, *Black Sun: Depression and Melancholia*, trans. Leon S. Roudiez (New York: Columbia University Press), 41.
23. D. W. Winnicott, *The Maturational Processes and the Facilitating Environment* (London: Hogarth, 1965), 54.
24. D. W. Winnicott, *The Child and the Outside World: Studies in Developing Relationships*, ed. Janet Hardenberg (New York: Basic Books), 137.
25. Heinz Kohut, *The Search for the Self: Selected Writings of Heinz Kohut: 1950–1978*, ed. Paul H. Ornstein (New York: International University Press, 1985), 637, Volume 2.
26. *Ibid.*
27. Ellison, 3.
28. *Ibid.*, 13, 580.
29. Winnicott, *The Child and the Outside World*, 15.

Chapter 2

1. Pauline E. Hopkins, *Contending Forces: A Romance Illustrative of Negro Life North and South* (Oxford University Press), 1988. All page references to Hopkins's text are from this edition.
2. See, for example, Mary Helen Washington, ed., *Invented Lives: Narratives of Black Women, 1860–1920* (Garden City, NY: Doubleday, 1987), p. 76. Washington's view that "in spite of [Hopkins's] attempts to give women autonomy and power ... [she was] influenced by the 'Cult of True Womanhood'" is echoed by other critics. This term, that designates genteel and traditional values for women in a patriarchal society, was originated by Barbara Welter in her article "Cult of True Womanhood, 1820–1860," which appeared in *American Quarterly*, 18 (Summer 1966).
3. Claudia Tate's *Domestic Allegories of Political Desire* (New York: Oxford University Press, 1992), her "Allegories of Black Political Desire" in *Conjuring*, eds. Marjorie Pryse and Hortense J. Spillers (Bloomington: Indiana University Press, 1985), and Hazel Cabry's *Reconstructing Womanhood* (New York: Oxford University Press, 1987) discuss the reemergence of *Contending Forces*. See also, for example, Judith R. Berzon's *Neither Black Nor White: The Mulatto Character in American Fiction* (New York: New York University Press, 1978), 201–2; Richard Yarborough's introduction to the 1988 Oxford University Press edition of the novel, Sandi Russel's *Render Me My Song* (New York: St. Martin's, 1990) and Jane Campbell's *Mythic Black Fiction* (Knoxville: University of Tennessee Press, 1986). These and other critics mirror Berzon who charges that, among other flaws, the plot of *Contending Forces* is "incredible and incredibly complicated," the characters "totally unconvincing and lifeless," the novel itself "dreadfully written ... stilted ... [and] 'preachy,'" though she acknowledges its "historical, if not literary, importance." Tate's *Domestic Allegories* examines the novel's plot, language, and structure within the context of nineteenth-century conventions and provides clarifying perspectives on, for example, Hopkins's use of the sentimental romance format, the term "mulatto," and gender, societal, and institutional conventions during that era. Such scrutiny effectively neutralizes many objections about this novel by critics who read it through contemporary eyes.

Notes — Chapter 3

4. Eric Foner, *Reconstruction: America's Unfinished Revolution, 1863–1877* (NY: Harper & Row, 1988), 199–123. Eric Foner details staggering accounts of violence against newly freed slaves during Reconstruction, noting that "gender offered no protection to black women."

5. Claudia Tate, "Allegories of Black Female Desire; or, Rereading Nineteenth-Century Sentimental Narratives of Black Female Authority," in *Changing Our Own Words: Essays on Criticism, Theory, and Writing by Black Women*, ed. Cheryl Wall (New Brunswick, NJ: Rutgers University Press, 1989), 123.

6. Melanie Klein, *Introduction to the Work of Melanie Klein*, second edition, ed. Hanna Segal (New York: Basic Books, 1974), 30–36.

7. Klein, *The Selected Melanie Klein*, ed. Juliet Mitchell (New York: The Free Press, Macmillan, 1986), 225.

8. W. E. B. DuBois, *The Souls of Black Folk* (NY: Signet, 1969 [1903]), p. 45.

9. Thomas J. Otten, "Pauline Hopkins and the Hidden Self of Race," *ELH* 59 (1992), 243.

10. Klein, *The Selected Melanie Klein*, 182.

11. *Ibid.*, 20–21.

12. *Ibid.*, 187–188.

13. *Ibid.*, 156–167. The Kleinian depressive position is not synonymous with clinical depression, but rather a necessary process toward healing the "split" parts of the ego and achieving ego integration.

14. Klein, *The Selected Melanie Klein*, 190.

15. Klein, *Love, Guilt, and Reparation*, 319.

16. *Ibid.*, 83–4. Sappho's position reflects conscious denial of psychic and physical reality.

17. Washington, 81.

18. Claudia Tate, "Allegories of Black Female Desire," 119; endnote, 233.

19. Christian, 200.

20. Nancy Cott, *The Bonds of Womanhood: "Women's Sphere" in New England, 1780–1835* (New Haven: Yale University Press, 1977), 168, 160.

21. Carroll Smith-Rosenberg, *Disorderly Conduct: Visions of Gender in Victorian America* (New York: A. A. Knopf, 1985), 75–6.

22. Winnicott, 1–5, 12. Winnicott describes a transitional object as a possession whose function is to help an individual defend against anxiety and by providing a firm sense of security, and a temporary safeguard. While the term "object" is generally disparaging if used in reference to a human being, its psychological connotation does not distinguish between animate and inanimate entities.

23. *Ibid.*, 1–5.

24. Cott, 168.

25. *Ibid.*

26. Klein, *Introduction to the Work of Melanie Klein*, viii–ix.

27. Klein, *Love, Guilt, and Reparation*, 318. In Kleinian terms, the child's helplessness, as well as his openness to and acceptance of love, can elicit gratitude from the mother, as well as her strong wishes, heretofore submerged, to make reparation on his, as well as her own, behalf.

28. Klein, *The Selected Melanie Klein*, 210, 227–8. Complete reparation is, like complete wisdom, an ideal state toward which human beings constantly strive but never fully reach. The psychic reduction of guilt, persecution, and anxiety permit love and hate to be better synthesized in the individual psyche, facilitating healing of the "split" through acceptance of the whole personality. The more integrated the ego becomes, the more it can withstand. The ideal result of the process of reparation is enhanced ego strength and enrichment through awareness, acceptance, and synthesis.

29. Tate, 148–9.

Chapter 3

1. Nella Larsen, *Quicksand and Passing* (New Brunswick, NJ: Rutgers University Press). All page references are from this edition.

2. Margaret Just Butcher, *The Negro in American Culture*. Revised (New York: Signet, 1957), 140.

3. Hoyt Fuller, Introduction, *Passing* by Nella Larsen (New York: Collier, 1971), 18.

4. Fairly recent studies — particularly by Deborah McDowell (introduction, *Quicksand and Passing*), Hazel Carby (*Reconstructing Womanhood*), Hortense Spillers (*Conjuring: Black Women, Fiction, and Literary Tradition*),

Ann Allen Shockley (*Afro-American Women Writers, 1746–1933*) and other African-American women literary critics — help bring to light previously unexamined aspects of *Passing* that reconfigure traditional assessments of its dimensions, and its depth, as a literary text.

5. *The Random House College Dictionary*. Revised edition (New York: Random House, 1980), 971.

6. Deborah McDowell, Introduction, *Quicksand and Passing* by Nella Larsen (New Brunswick, NJ: Rutgers University Press, 1986), xiii.

7. Hazel Carby, *Reconstructing Womanhood: The Emergence of the Afro-American Woman Novelist* (New York: Oxford University Press, 1987), 174. Carby refers to Helga Crane, *Quicksand*'s heroine, as "the first truly sexual Black female protagonist in African-American fiction." Larsen pioneered depictions of Black female sexuality in African-American literature and sustains themes of sexuality in *Passing*.

8. Cary D. Wintz, *Black Culture and the Harlem Renaissance* (Houston: Rice University Press), 212–13.

9. William H. Robinson, ed., *NOMMO: An Anthology of Modern Black African and Black American Literature* (New York: Macmillan, 1972), 16.

10. William H. Grier and Price M. Cobbs, *Black Rage*. (New York: Basic Books, 1992), 81. Grier and Cobbs address the stultifying nature of racism that prevents the African-American family from performing "its most essential function ... protection of its members."

11. E. Franklin Frazier, *The Black Bourgeoisie* (New York: Macmillan, 1957), *passim*. Frazier maintains that pathology among the Black bourgeoisie occurs at an extraordinary level precisely because this group is so profoundly psychologically insubstantial.

12. Jeffrey Berman, *Narcissism and the Novel* (New York: New York University Press, 1990), 33. Kohut's insight into "penis envy" as a cultural construct promulgated by a male-oriented society is one example of his more progressive thinking. One strength of his work is a grasp of certain cultural biases that have historically influenced psychoanalytic theory. For example, he views homosexual relationships to be as capable of maturity and object love as heterosexual relationships.

13. Heinz Kohut, *The Analysis of the Self* (New York: International Universities Press, 1971), 26–7; Heinz Kohut, *The Search for the Self: Selected Writings of Heinz Kohut: 1950–1978*, ed. Paul H. Orstein (New York: International University Press, Inc., 1978), 10; Kohut "Narcissism and Object Love," *The Kohut Seminars on Self Psychology and Psychotherapy with Adolescents and Young Adults*, ed. Miriam Elson (New York: W. W. Norton, 1987), 28.

14. Charles B. Strozier, Introduction, *Self Psychology and the Humanities: Reflections on a New Psychoanalytic Approach*, by Heinz Kohut (New York: W. W. Norton, 1985), xxvii. While Charles Strozier claims that Kohut's cultural discourse "recover[s] for historians what is most usable in psychoanalysis," Barbara Johnson, conversely, finds that Kohut understates the importance of, and even neglects, external social factors throughout his analyses of the inner self. (Barbara Johnson, Carpenter Lecture, University of Chicago, April 26, 1990.)

15. Heinz Kohut, *Self Psychology and the Humanities*, xxix; "Idealization and Cultural Selfobjects," 225, 237. While Kohut defines White Western cultural selfobjects as "artists, historians, [and] intellectuals," he represents African-American cultural selfobjects exclusively as male sports figures.

16. Heinz Kohut, "Psychoanalysis in a Troubled World," *The Search for the Self*, 512. Vol. 2.

17. Kohut, *The Kohut Seminars on Self Psychology and Psychotherapy*, 15. See, for example, his work on cultures and historical figures in World War II Nazi Germany.

18. Frantz Fanon, *Black Skin, White Masks: The Experience of a Black Man in a White World* (New York: Grove Press, 1967), 41–44.

19. Kohut, *The Search for the Self*, 629; Kohut, *Analysis of the Self*, 65 and passim.

20. Kohut, *Analysis of the Self*, 45–49.

21. Bone, 106.

22. Kohut, *Analysis of the Self*, 152.

23. Heinz Kohut, *How Does Analysis Cure?*, ed. Arnold Goldberg and Paul Stepansky (Chicago: University of Chicago Press, 1984), 37.

24. Melanie Klein, *The Selected Melanie Klein*. Juliet Mitchell, ed. (New York: The Free Press, 1986), 216–17 and passim. "Split-

ting" describes the ego activity of rejecting one's "bad" parts and privileging the "good" parts in order to escape persecutory anxiety.

25. Kohut, *Analysis of the Self*, 66; 645.

26. Kohut, *Search for the Self*, 60–62. A "selfobject," even when distinguished by the self as a separate individual, is recognized only in relation to the needs of the self.

27. Elisabeth Young-Bruehl, ed., *Freud on Women: A Reader* (New York: W. W. Norton, 1990), 195. The quote is excerpted from Sigmund Freud's 1914 essay "On Narcissism."

28. Kohut, *The Kohut Seminars*, 29. The mere existence, in psychoanalytic terms, of "objects" (in this case, children) in one's life does not insure a person's, even a mother's, capacity to love.

29. McDowell, xxix.

30. Kohut, *Search for the Self*, 432. The idealized parent imago is the individual upon whom the narcissistic self fixates to supply the missing self-confirming segments of its psychic structure. The construct is archaic, and is not a true representation of object love.

31. Klein, 216–17.

32. Spillers, 252.

33. Kohut, *Search for the Self*, 645–657.

34. bell hooks, *Black Looks: Race and Representation* (Boston: South End, 1992), 9.

Chapter 4

1. Gwendolyn Brooks, *Maud Martha*, *Blacks* (Chicago: The David Company, 1987). All page references to Brooks's novella are from this edition.

2. Deborah E. McDowell, "The Changing Same," *Reading Black, Reading Feminist: A Critical Anthology*, ed. Henry Louis Gates, Jr. (New York: Meridian, 1990), 113; Christian, Barbara, "Nuance and the Novella: A Study of Gwendolyn Brooks's Maud Martha," *Black Feminist Criticism: Perspectives on Black Women Writers* (Elmsford, NY: Pergamon, 1985), 239, 247.

3. Gwendolyn Brooks, Jefferson Lecture in the Humanities, May 11, 1994, Chicago State University.

4. Irene L. Gendzier, *Frantz Fanon: A Critical Study* (New York: Pantheon, 1973), 10–12.

5. Frantz Fanon, *Black Skin, White Masks: The Experiences of a Black Man in a White World*. Trans. Charles Lam Markmann (New York: Grove Press, 1967), 81. Fanon asserts that "the neurotic structure of an individual is simply the elaboration, the formation, the eruption within the ego, of conflictual clusters arising in part out of the environment and in part out of the purely personal way in which that individual reacts to those influences."

6. D. W. Winnicott, *Playing & Reality* (London: Routledge, 1986), 139.

7. Fanon, 100. It should be noted throughout that Fanon's references to "the Black man" generally refer to both men and women, in accordance with narrative conventions of his era. At the same time, it is important to understand — especially here, in a study focused upon the gender-specific role of mothering — that his writings do not provide an essential distinction between the particular nature of life experience for Black men and for Black women; his essay entitled "The Woman of Color and the White Man," for example, restricts itself to broad generalities rather than an in-depth study of the Black woman.

8. *Ibid.*, 13, 104, 213. Of his own culture, for example, Fanon says, "It is not just this or that Antillean who embodies the neurotic formation, but all Antilleans. Antillean society is a neurotic society.... Hence we are driven from the individual back to the social structure. If there is a taint, it lies not in the 'soul' of the individual but rather in that of the environment."

9. *Ibid.*, 151–2; 188; 213; 216; 60.

10. *Ibid.*, 10, 12, 16, 221. The psychiatrist himself rejects the concept of one monolithic Black culture, citing the re-acculturation that various African peoples have undergone within disparate societies in consequence of their historical dispersion across the globe. Oppressed groups *do* have in common, among other realities, the psychological "racial prisons" within which they are locked, long after physical enslavement/colonization has ended. A grossly unequal racial balance of power creates "a massive psychoexistential complex."

11. Fanon, 109.

12. William H. Grier and Price M. Cobbs, *Black Rage* (New York: Basic Books, 1968), 41.

13. Harry B. Shaw, "Maud Martha: The War with Beauty," *A Life Distilled: Gwendolyn Brooks, Her Poetry and Fiction*, eds. Maria K. Mootry and Gary Smith. (Urbana: University of Illinois Press, 1987), 254–269.

14. Heinz Kohut, *The Analysis of the Self: A Systematic Approach to the Psychoanalytic Treatment of Narcissistic Personality Disorders* (New York: International Universities Press, 1971), 37.

15. Heinz Kohut, *The Search for the Self: Selected Writings of Heinz Kohut: 1950–1978*, ed. Charles B. Strozier (New York: W. W. Norton, 1985), 678.

16. Heinz Kohut, *Self Psychology and the Humanities: Reflections on a New Psychoanalytic Approach*, ed. Charles B. Strozier (New York: W. W. Norton, 1985), 225.

17. Fanon, 85, 152.

18. Kohut, *Analysis of the Self*, 706.

19. *Ibid.*, 49.

20. Fanon, 44.

21. *Ibid.*, 63.

22. James Weldon Johnson, *Autobiography of an Ex-Colored Man*, ed. William L. Andrews (New York: Penguin, 1990), 144.

23. Fanon, 56.

24. Mary Helen Washington, "'Taming All That Anger Down': Rage and Silence in Gwendolyn Brooks's *Maud Martha*," *Black Literature and Literary Theory*, ed. Henry Louis Gates, Jr. (New York: Methuen, 1984), 251.

25. Melanie Klein, *Love, Guilt, and Reparation & Other Works, 1921–1945* (USA: Delacorte, 1975), 318.

26. Washington, "'Taming All That Anger Down,'" 254.

27. "Update on *Part One*: An Interview with Gwendolyn Brooks," *CLA Journal* (21, 1977), 26.

28. Kohut, *Search for the Self*, 629.

29. Washington, "'Taming All That Anger Down,'" 255–7.

30. E. Ann Kaplan, *Motherhood and Representation: The Mother in Popular Culture and Melodrama* (London: Routledge, 1992), 37.

Chapter 5

1. Alice Walker, *The Color Purple* (New York: Pocket Books, 1982). All page references to Walker's novel are taken from this edition.

2. Calvin Hernton, *The Sexual Mountain and Black Women Writers* (New York: Doubleday, 1987), p. 33. Hernton notes that while Tony Brown declared "that he had not seen the film nor read the book and would never do so," he nonetheless published several articles and devoted more than one of his syndicated television shows (*Tony Brown's Journal*) to denounce the novel and the film — particularly, the portrayal of Black men in both media.

3. *Ibid.*, 35–6.

4. Deborah McDowell, "'The Changing Same': Generational Connections and Black Women Novelists," *Modern Critical Views: Alice Walker*, ed. Harold Bloom (New York: Chelsea House, 1989), 140–150.

5. Mary Helen Washington, "An Essay on Alice Walker," in *Alice Walker: Critical Perspectives Past and Present*, eds. Henry Louis Gates, Jr., and K. A. Appiah (New York: Amistad, 1993), 39. Washington adds that "though Walker does not neglect to deal with the external realities of poverty, exploitation, and discrimination, her [work] most often focus[es] on the intimate reaches of the inner lives of her characters."

6. Karen Horney, *Our Inner Conflicts: A Constructive Theory of Neurosis* (New York: W. W. Norton, 1972), 13–19. While she acknowledges the groundbreaking contributions of Sigmund Freud to psychoanalysis, Horney notes that Freud's postulations on feminine psychology triggered her focus on cultural factors, basically because the failure of Freud to take them into account resulted in some serious foundational miscalculations that affect the larger body of his work

7. Karen Horney, *Neuroses and Human Growth* (New York: W. W. Norton, 1991), p. 43.

8. William H. Grier and Price M. Cobbs, *Black Rage* (New York: Basic Books, 1992, ©1068), 40.

9. Lynn Davidman, *Motherloss* (Berkeley: University of California Press, 2007), 48.

10. Horney, *Our Inner Conflicts*, 41; Horney refers to this state as *basic anxiety*.

11. Paula Bennett, "The Mother's Part: Incest and Maternal Deprivation in Woolf

and Morrison," in *Narrating Mothers: Theorizing Maternal Subjectivities*, eds. Brenda O. Daly and Maureen T. Reddy (Knoxville: University of Tennessee Press, 1991), 125, 135-6.

12. Henry Louis Gates, "Color Me Zora: Alice Walker's (Re) Writing of the Speakerly Text," in *Alice Walker's The Color Purple*, ed. Harold Bloom (Philadelphia: Chelsea House, 2000), 39.

13. Horney, *Our Inner Conflicts*, 42-3, chapters 3-5, *passim*.

14. Horney, *Feminine Psychology* (New York: W. W. Norton, 1967), 145. Speaking specifically of male writers, philosophers, and medical professionals, Horney notes that "individual minds ... from Aristotle to Moebius have expended an astonishing amount of energy and intellectual capacity in proving the superiority of the male principle."

15. Horney, *Inner Conflicts*, 43, 101.

16. Genesis 9:20-27. RSV.

17. Karen Horney, *Our Inner Conflicts*, p. 101.

18. Lauren Berlant, "Race, Gender, and Nation in The Color Purple," *Modern Critical Interpretations: Alice Walker's The Color Purple*, ed. Harold Bloom, 7.

19. bell hooks, "Reading and Resistance: The Color Purple" in *Alice Walker: Critical Perspectives Past and Present*, eds. Henry Louis Gates, Jr., and K. A. Appiah (New York: Amistad, 1993), 285.

20. Tuzyline Jita Allan, "The Color Purple: A Study of Walker's Womanist Gospel," in *Alice Walker's The Color Purple*, ed. Harold Bloom, 131.

21. *Ibid*.

22. Yvonne Johnson, "Alice Walker's The Color Purple," in *Alice Walker's The Color Purple*, ed. Harold Bloom, 216.

23. Ntozake Shange, *for colored girls who have considered suicide when the rainbow is enuf* (New York: Collier, 1989).

24. Janet L. Surrey, "The 'Self-in-Relation': A Theory of Women's Development," *Women's Growth in Connection: Writings from the Stone Center*, eds. Judith V. Jordan et al. (New York: The Guilford Press, 1991), 57.

25. Karen Horney, *Neuroses and Human Growth: The Struggle Toward Self-Realization* (New York: W. W. Norton, 1991), 120-4.

26. Judith V. Jordan, "The Meaning of Mutuality," *Women's Growth in Connection*. 82.

Chapter 6

1. Toni Morrison, *Lecture and Speech of Acceptance, Upon the Award of the Nobel Prize for Literature, Delivered in Stockholm on the Seventh of December, Nineteen Hundred and Ninety-Three* (New York: Alfred A. Knopf, 1994), 9-30.

2. Gloria Naylor, "A Conversation: Gloria Naylor and Toni Morrison," *Conversations with Toni Morrison*, ed. Danille Taylor-Guthrie (Jackson: University Press of Mississippi, 1994), 209.

3. Karen E. Fields, "To Embrace Dead Strangers: Toni Morrison's *Beloved*." *Mother Puzzles: Daughters and Mothers in Contemporary American Literature*, ed. Mickey Pearlman (New York: Greenwood, 1989), 169. Fields references Benjamin's "The Storyteller" in *Illuminations* (New York: Schocken, 1969).

4. Toni Morrison, *Beloved* (New York: New American Library, 1987), 1. All subsequent page references to the text are taken from this edition.

5. Lorraine Liscio, "*Beloved*'s Narrative: Writing Mother's Milk," *Tulsa Studies in Women's Literature*, 11:1, Spring 1992, 37.

6. Toni Morrison, "The Site of Memory," *Out There: Marginalization and Contemporary Cultures*, eds. Russell Ferguson et al. (New York: The New Museum of Contemporary Art, 1990), 301-2. Morrison regrets the imposed silence that restrained the pens of slave narrators, and especially the meager account of inner thoughts and feelings, leaving massive breaches in the historical and psychological perception of American slavery: "Over and over, the writers pull the narrative up short with a phrase such as, 'But let us drop a veil over these proceedings too terrible to relate.' In shaping the experience to make it palatable to those who were in a position to alleviate it, they were silent about many things, and they 'forgot' many other things.... Most importantly — at least for me — there was no mention of [the slaves'] interior life."

7. Toni Morrison, "Unspeakable Things

Unspoken: The Afro-American Presence in American Literature," *Michigan Quarterly Review*, 28:1, Winter 1989, 31-2. Of the opening, Morrison writes, "It is abrupt, and should appear so. No native informant here. The reader is snatched, yanked, thrown into an environment completely foreign, and I want it as the first stroke of the shared experience that might be possible between the reader and the novel's population. Snatched just as the slaves were from one place to another, from any place to another, without preparation and without defense."

8. Anna Freud, *The Ego and the Mechanisms of Defense*, Revised edition, trans. Cecil Baines (New York: International Universities Press, Inc., 1966), 60.

9. *Ibid.*, 60-63.

10. *Ibid.*, 31-49.

11. *Ibid.*, 60-61. Freud postulates that the ego's need for synthesis and harmony is attained only when the threat of punishment from the outside world is neutralized.

12. Toni Morrison, "Unspeakable Things Unspoken," 16.

13. Anna Freud, 141-2.

14. *Ibid.*, 72-77.

15. Sigmund Freud. *An Outline of Psycho-Analysis*. Revised edition, ed. James Strachey (New York: W. W. Norton, 1969), 45.

16. Frederick Douglass, *Narrative of the Life of Frederick Douglass, an African Slave*. *The Classic Slave Narratives*, ed. Henry Louis Gates, Jr. (New York: New American Library, 1987), 315-16.

17. Naylor, 206-7.

18. Mae B. Henderson, "Toni Morrison's *Beloved*: Re-Membering the Body as Historical Text," *Comparative American Identities: Race, Sex, and Nationality in the Modern Text*, ed. Hortense Spillers (New York: Routledge, 1991), 78.

19. Carolyn A. Mitchell, Carolyn A. "'I Love to Tell the Story': Biblical Revisions in *Beloved*," *Religion & Literature*, 23:3, Autumn 1991, 29.

20. Liscio, 33-35. Sethe's repeated charge that the boys "took my milk" sustains Liscio's argument that Sethe's milk corresponds with the prelinguistic mode of expression that Julia Kristeva refers to as the semiotic, through which the mother addresses her preeminent concerns of protecting her children and of retaining control over her reproductive powers.

21. Anna Freud, 42-50.

22. Melanie Klein, *The Selected Melanie Klein*, ed. Juliet Mitchell (New York: The Free Press, MacMillan, 1986), 50-1, 96, 208.

23. Rebecca Ferguson, "History, Memory and Language in Toni Morrison's *Beloved*," *Feminist Criticism: Theory and Practice*, ed. Susan Sellers (London: Harvester Wheatsheaf, 1991), 116-117.

24. Marsha Darling, "In the Realm of Responsibility: A Conversation with Toni Morrison," *Conversations with Toni Morrison*, 247.

25. Atwood, Margaret. Review of Toni Morrison's *Beloved*, The New York Times Book Review, September 13, 1987, reprinted in *Toni Morrison: Critical Perspectives, Past and Present*, eds. Henry Louis Gates, Jr., and K. A. Appiah (New York: Amistad, 1993), 35.

Bibliography

Alford, Fred C. *Melanie Klein and Critical Social Theory*. New Haven and London: Yale University Press, 1989.
Allport, Gordon W. *The Nature of Prejudice*. Abridged edition. Garden City, New York: Doubleday Anchor Books, 1958.
Anderson, Linda. *Plotting Change: Contemporary Women's Fiction*. London: Edward Arnold, 1990.
Atwood, Margaret. Review of Toni Morrison's *Beloved*. *The New York Times Book Review*, September 13, 1987. Reprinted in *Toni Morrison: Critical Perspectives, Past and Present*. Ed. Henry Louis Gates, Jr., and K. A. Appiah. New York: Amistad, 1993.
Baker, Houston A., Jr. *Blues, Ideology, and Afro-American Literature: A Vernacular Theory*. Chicago: University of Chicago Press, 1987.
———. "To Move without Moving: Creativity and Commerce in Ralph Ellison's Trueblood Episode." *Black Literature and Literary Theory*. Ed. Henry Louis Gates, Jr. New York and London: Methuen, 1984. 221–248.
———. *Workings of the Spirit: The Poetics of Afro-American Women's Writing*. Chicago and London: University of Chicago Press, 1990.
Bennett, Lerone, Jr. *Before the Mayflower: A History of the Negro in America, 1619–1964*. Revised edition. Baltimore: Penguin Books, 1973.
Berman, Jeffrey. *Narcissism and the Novel*. New York: New York University Press, 1990.
Bernal, Martin, *Black Athena: The Afroasiatic Roots of Classical Civilisation*. Vol. 2. New Brunswick, NJ: Rutgers University Press, 1991.
Berzon, Judith R. *Neither Black Nor White: The Mulatto Character in American Fiction*. New York: New York University Press, 1978.
Blassingame, John W. *The Slave Community: Plantation Life in the Antebellum South*. New York: Oxford University Press, 1972.
Bloom, Harold. *A Map of Misreading*. Oxford: Oxford University Press, 1975.
———, ed. *Alice Walker's The Color Purple*. Philadelphia: Chelsea House, 2000.
———, ed. *Modern Critical Views: Alice Walker*. New York: Chelsea House, 1989.
Bone, Robert. *The Negro Novel in America*. New Haven: Yale University Press, 1968.
Bontemps, Arna, ed. *The Harlem Renaissance Remembered*. New York: Dodd, Mead, 1972.
Botkin, B. A., ed. *Lay My Burden Down: A Folk History of Slavery*. Chicago: University of Chicago Press, 1945.
Braxton, Joanne M., and Andrée Nicola McLaughlin, eds. *Wild Women in the Whirlwind:*

Afra-American Culture and the Contemporary Literary Renaissance. New Brunswick, NJ: Rutgers University Press, 1990.

Brooks, Gwendolyn. *Annie Allen*. Blacks. Chicago: The David Company, 1987. 77–140.

———. *Family Pictures*. Blacks. Chicago: The David Company, 1987. 481–497.

———. *Maud Martha*. Blacks. Chicago: The David Company, 1987. 141–322.

———. *Report from Part One*. Detroit: Broadside, 1972.

———. *A Street in Bronzeville*. Blacks. Chicago: The David Company, 1987. 17–75.

Bulham, Hussein Abdilabi. *Frantz Fanon and the Psychology of Oppression*. New York and London: Plenum, 1985.

Butcher, Margaret Just. *The Negro in American Culture*. Revised. New York: Signet, 1957.

Cade, Toni, ed. *The Black Woman: An Anthology*. New York: New American Library, 1970.

Campbell, Jane. *Mythic Black Fiction: The Transformation of History*. Knoxville: University of Tennessee Press, 1986.

Carby, Hazel V. "On the Threshold of Woman's Era:" Lynching, Empire, and Sexuality in Black Feminist Theory. *"Race," Writing, and Difference*. Ed. Henry Louis Gates, Jr. Chicago: University of Chicago Press, 1985. 301–316.

———. *Reconstructing Womanhood: The Emergence of the Afro-American Woman Novelist*. New York: Oxford University Press, 1987.

Chodorow, Nancy. *Feminism and Psychoanalytic Theory*. New Haven and London: Yale University Press, 1989.

———. *The Reproduction of Mothering: Psychoanalysis and the Sociology of Gender*. Berkeley: University of California Press, 1978.

Christian, Barbara. *Black Feminist Criticism: Perspectives on Black Women Writers*. Elmsford, NY: Pergamon, 1985.

———. "The High and the Lows of Black Feminist Criticism," in *Reading Black, Reading Feminist: A Critical Anthology*, ed. Henry Louis Gates, Jr. New York: Meridian, 1990.

———. "Nuance and the Novella: A Study of Gwendolyn Brooks's Maud Martha," in *Black Feminist Criticism: Perspectives on Black Women Writers*. Elmsford, NY: Pergamon, 1985.

Collins, Patricia Hill. *Black Feminist Thought: Knowledge, Consciousness, and the Politics of Empowerment*. Cambridge, MA: Unwin Hyman, 1990.

Cooke, Michael G. *Afro-American Literature in the Twentieth Century*. New Haven: Yale University Press, 1984.

Cott, Nancy. *The Bonds of Womanhood: "Woman's Sphere" in New England, 1780–1835*. New Haven, Yale University Press, 1977.

Daily, Gary W. "Toni Morrison's *Beloved*: Rememory, History and the Fantastic." *The Celebration of the Fantastic: Selected Papers from the Tenth Anniversary International Conference on the Fantastic in the Arts*. Donald E. Morse, Marshall B. Tymm, Bertha Csilla, eds. Westport, CT: Greenwood, 1992.

Daly, Brenda O., and Maureen T. Reddy. *Narrating Mothers: Theorizing Maternal Subjectivities*. Knoxville: The University of Tennessee Press, 1991.

Darling, Marsha. "In the Realm of Responsibility: A Conversation with Toni Morrison." In *Conversations with Toni Morrison*. Ed. Danille Taylor-Guthrie. Jackson: University Press of Mississippi, 1994.

Davidman, Lynn. *Motherloss*. Berkeley: University of California Press, 2007.

Davidson, Basil. *The African Slave Trade: Precolonial History, 1450–1850*. Boston: Little, Brown, 1961.

Davidson, Cathy N., and E. M. Broner, eds. *The Lost Tradition: Mothers and Daughters in Literature*. New York: Frederick Ungar, 1980.

Davies, Carole Boyce. "Mother Right/Write Revisited: *Beloved* and *Dessa Rose*." *Narrating Mothers: Theorizing Maternal Subjectivities*. Ed. Brenda O. Daly and Maureen T. Reddy. Knoxville: University of Tennessee Press, 1991. 44–57.

Davis, Thadius. "The Browsing Reader." *The Crisis* 36. July 1929:234.

Delaney, L. A. *Struggles for Freedom: Six Women's Slave Narratives*. Oxford and New York: Oxford University Press, 1988.

Dengler, Carl N. "Slavery and the Genesis of American Race Prejudice" in *The Origins of American Slavery and Racism*. Ed. Donald L. Noel. Columbus, Ohio: Merrill, 1972.

Douglass, Fredrick. *Narrative of the Life of Frederick Douglass, an African Slave. The Classic Slave Narratives*. Ed. Henry Louis Gates, Jr. New York: New American Library, 1987.

Du Bois, W. E. B. *The Souls of Black Folk*. New York: Signet, 1982.

———. *Suppression of the African Slave Trade to the United States of America, 1638–1870*. New York: Schocken Books, 1969.

Edelman, Hope. *Motherless Daughters: The Legacy of Loss*. New York: Delta, 1995.

Edwards, Audrey; Polite, Craig K. *The Psychology of Black Success*. New York: Anchor, 1993.

Ellison, Ralph. *Invisible Man*. New York: Vintage, 1990.

Fanon, Frantz. *Black Skin, White Masks: The Experiences of a Black Man in a White World*. Trans. Charles Lam Markmann. New York: Grove Press, 1967.

———. *The Wretched of the Earth*. Trans. Constance Farrington. New York: Grove Press, 1963.

Ferguson, Rebecca. "History, Memory and Language in Toni Morrison's *Beloved*." *Feminist Criticism: Theory and Practice*. Ed. Susan Sellers. London: Harvester Wheatsheaf, 1991. 109–127.

Ferguson, Russell, et al., *Out There: Marginalization and Contemporary Cultures*. New York: The New Museum of Contemporary Art, 1990.

Fernando, Suman. *Race, Culture, and Psychiatry*. London: Routledge, 1989.

Fields, Karen E. "To Embrace Dead Strangers: Toni Morrison's *Beloved*." *Mother Puzzles: Daughters and Mothers in Contemporary American Literature*. Ed. Mickey Pearlman. New York: Greenwood, 1989.

Fine, Reuben. *A History of Psychoanalysis*. New York: Columbia University Press, 1979.

Foner, Eric. *Reconstruction: America's Unfinished Revolution, 1863–1877*. New York: Harper & Row, 1988.

Frazier, E. Franklin. *The Black Bourgeoisie*. New York: Macmillan, 1957.

Fredrickson, George M. *The Arrogance of Race: Historical Perspectives on Slavery, Racism, and Social Inequality*. Middletown, CT: Wesleyan University Press, 1988.

Freud, Anna. *The Ego and the Mechanisms of Defense*. Revised edition. Trans. Cecil Baines. New York: International Universities Press. 1966.

Freud, Sigmund. *Beyond the Pleasure Principle*. Trans. James Strachey. W. W. Norton, 1961.

———. *A General Introduction to Psycho-Analysis*. Translated by Joan Riviere. New York: Pocket Books, 1963.

———. *Inhibitions, Symptoms and Anxiety*. Trans. Alix Strachey. Revised and newly edited by James Strachey. New York: W. W. Norton, 1959.

———. *The Interpretation of Dreams*. Trans. and ed. James Strachey. New York: Avon, 1965.

———. *An Outline of Psycho-Analysis.* Revised edition. Ed. James Strachey. New York: W. W. Norton, 1969.
———. *Sexuality and the Psychology of Love.* Ed. Philip Rieff. New York: Collier Books, 1963.
———. *Totem and Taboo: Some Points of Agreement Between the Mental Lives of Savages and Neurotics.* Trans. James Strachey. New York: W. W. Norton, 1950.
Friere, Paulo. *Pedagogy of the Oppressed.* Trans. Myra Bergman Ramos. New York: Continuum Publishing, 1993.
Fuller, Hoyt. Introduction. *Passing.* By Nella Larsen. New York: Collier Books, 1971.
Gates, Henry Louis, Jr., ed. *Black Literature and Literary Theory.* New York and London: Methuen, 1984.
———, ed. *"Race," Writing, and Difference.* Chicago: The University of Chicago Press, 1986.
———, ed. *Reading Black, Reading Feminist: A Critical Anthology.* New York: Meridian, 1990.
———, and K. A. Appiah, eds. *Alice Walker: Critical Perspectives, Past and Present.* New York: Amistad, 1993.
———, and ———. *Toni Morrison: Critical Perspectives, Past and Present.* New York: Amistad, 1993.
———, and Charles T. Davis, eds. *The Slave's Narrative.* Oxford: Oxford University Press, 1985.
Gendzier, Irene L. *Frantz Fanon: A Critical Study.* New York: Pantheon, 1973.
Genovese, Eugene D. *Roll, Jordan, Roll: The World the Slaves Made.* New York: Vintage, 1976.
Giddings, Paula. *When and Where I Enter: The Impact of Black Women on Race and Sex in America.* New York: Bantam, 1988.
Gilbert, Sandra M., and Susan Gubar. *Madwoman in the Attic: The Woman Writer and the Nineteenth-Century Literary Imagination.* New Haven: Yale University Press, 1984.
Gilmore, Al-Tony, ed. *Revisiting Blassingame's The Slave Community.* Westport, CT; London, England: Greenwood, 1978.
Grier, William H., and Price M. Cobbs. *Black Rage.* New York: Basic, 1992.
Hall, Edward T. *Beyond Culture.* New York: Anchor, 1976.
Hansberry, Lorraine. *To Be Young, Gifted and Black.* Adapted by Robert Nemiroff. New York: Signet, 1969.
Harding, Vincent. *There Is a River: The Black Struggle for Freedom in America.* New York: Harcourt Brace Jovanovich, 1981.
Hawks, Joanne V., and Sheila L. Skemp, eds. *Sex, Race, and the Role of Women in the South.* Jackson: University Press of Mississippi, 1983.
Hegel, G. F. W. *The Phenomenology of Mind.* New York and Evanston: Harper & Row, 1967.
Henderson, Mae B. "Toni Morrison's *Beloved*: Re-Membering the Body as Historical Text." *Comparative American Identities: Race, Sex, and Nationality in the Modern Text.* Ed. Hortense J. Spillers. New York: Routledge, 1991.
Hernton, Calvin C. *The Sexual Mountain and Black Women Writers: Adventures in Sex, Literature, and Real Life.* New York: Doubleday, 1990.
Hirsch, Marianne. "Maternal Narratives." *Reading Black, Reading Feminist: A Critical Anthology.* Ed. Henry Louis Gates, Jr. New York: Meridian, 1990.

Hopkins, Pauline. *Contending Forces: A Romance Illustrative of Negro Life, North and South*. New York: Oxford University Press, 1988.
Hogan, Patrick Colm. "The Politics of Otherness in Clinical Psychoanalysis: Racism as Pathogen in a Case of D. W. Winnicott." *Literature and Psychology*. 30:4, 1992.
hooks, bell. *Ain't I a Woman? Black Women and Feminism*. Boston: South End, 1981.
_____. *Black Looks: Race and Representation*. Boston: South End, 1992.
_____. *Sisters of the Yam: Black Women and Self-Recovery*. Boston: South End, 1993.
Horney, Karen. *Feminine Psychology*. New York: W. W. Norton, 1993.
_____. *Neuroses and Human Growth: The Struggle Toward Self-Realization*. New York: W. W. Norton, 1991.
_____. *The Neurotic Personality of Our Time*. New York: W. W. Norton, 1964.
_____. *Our Inner Conflicts: A Constructive Theory of Neurosis*. New York: W. W. Norton, 1972.
Huggins, Nathan Irvin, ed. *Voices from the Harlem Renaissance*. New York: Oxford University Press, 1976.
Hughes, Judith M. *Reshaping the Psychoanalytic Domain: The Work of Melanie Klein, W. R. D. Fairbairn, and D. W. Winnicott*. Berkeley: University of California Press, 1989.
Hull, Gloria T. *Color, Sex, and Poetry: Three Women Writers of the Harlem Renaissance*. Bloomington: Indiana University Press, 1987.
Hurston, Zora Neale. *Their Eyes Were Watching God*. Urbana: University of Illinois Press, 1978.
Jackson, Anna Mitchell. "A Theoretical Model for the Practice of Psychotherapy with Black Populations." *The Journal of Black Psychology*. 10:20.
Jacobs, Harriet. *Incidents in the Life of a Slave Girl, Written by Herself. The Classic Slave Narratives*. Ed. Henry Louis Gates, Jr. New York: New American Library, 1987.
Janeway, Elizabeth. "On Female Sexuality." *Women and Analysis*. Ed. Jean Strouse. New York: Grossman, 1974.
Johnson, Barbara. "Is Male to Female as Ground Is to Figure?" *Feminism and Psychoanalysis*. Ed. Richard Feldstein and Judith Roof. Ithaca and London: Cornell University Press, 1989. 255–267.
_____. "Metonomy, Metaphor and Voice in *Their Eyes Were Watching God*." *Black Literature and Literary Theory*. Ed. Henry Louis Gates, Jr. New York and London: Methuen, 1984.
_____. "The Re(a)d and the Black." *Reading Black, Reading Feminist: A Critical Anthology*. Ed. Henry Louis Gates, Jr. New York: Meridian, 1990. 145–154.
Johnson, James Weldon. *Autobiography of an Ex-Colored Man*. Ed. William L. Andrews. New York: Penguin, 1990.
Jordan, Judith V. et al., eds. *Women's Growth in Connection: Writings from the Stone Center*. New York: The Guilford Press, 1991.
Jordan, Winthrop. *White Over Black: American Attitudes Toward the Negro, 1550–1812*. New York: W. W. Norton, 1977.
Kaplan, E. Ann. *Motherhood and Representation: The Mother in Popular Culture and Melodrama*. London and New York: Routledge, 1992.
Kardiner, Abram, and Lionel Ovesey. *The Mark of Oppression: Explorations in the Personality of the American Negro*. Cleveland and New York: Meridian, 1967.
Kellner, Bruce, ed. *The Harlem Renaissance: A Historical Dictionary for the Era*. New York: Methuen, 1987. xxiii, 214.

Kent, George E, "Patterns of the Harlem Renaissance." *The Harlem Renaissance Remembered.* Ed. Arna Bontemps. New York: Dodd, Mead, 1972.
Klein, Melanie. *Introduction to the Work of Melanie Klein.* Second edition. Ed. Hanna Segal. New York: Basic, 1974.
_____. *Love, Guilt, and Reparation & Other Works, 1921–1945.* USA: Delacorte, 1975 .
_____. *The Selected Melanie Klein.* Juliet Mitchell, ed. New York: The Free Press, Macmillan, 1986.
Klineberg, Otto. *Race and Psychology.* Paris: UNESCO, 1951.
Knowles, Louis L., and Kenneth Prewitt, eds. *Institutional Racism in America.* Englewood Cliffs, NJ: Prentice-Hall, 1969.
Kohut, Heinz. *The Analysis of the Self: A Systematic Approach to the Psychoanalytic Treatment of Narcissistic Personality Disorders.* New York: International Universities Press, 1971.
_____. *How Does Analysis Cure?* Ed. Arnold Goldberg and Paul Stepansky. Chicago: University of Chicago Press, 1984.
_____. *The Kohut Seminars on Self Psychology and Psychotherapy with Adolescents and Young Adults.* Ed. Miriam Elson. New York: W. W. Norton, 1987.
_____. *The Restoration of the Self.* New York: International Universities Press, 1977.
_____. *The Search for the Self: Selected Writings of Heinz Kohut: 1950–1978.* Ed. Paul H. Orstein. New York: International University Press, 1978. Volumes 1–2.
_____. *Self Psychology and the Humanities: Reflections on a New Psychoanalytic Approach.* Ed. Charles B. Strozier. New York: W. W. Norton, 1985.
Kristeva, Julia. *Black Sun: Depression and Melancholia.* Trans. Leon S. Roudiez. New York: Columbia University Press, 1989.
Larsen, Nella. *Quicksand* and *Passing.* New Brunswick, NJ: Rutgers University Press, 1986.
Lederer, Wolfgang. *The Fear of Women.* New York and London: Grune & Stratton, 1968.
Lerner, Gerda, ed. *Black Women in White America: A Documentary History.* New York: Vintage Books, 1973.
Liscio, Lorraine. "*Beloved*'s Narrative: Writing Mother's Milk." *Tulsa Studies in Women's Literature.* 11:1. Spring 1992. 31–46.
Lorde, Audre. *Sister Outsider: Essays and Speeches.* Freedom, CA: Crossing, 1984.
McDowell, Deborah. Introduction to *Quicksand* and *Passing* by Nella Larsen. New Brunswick, NJ: Rutgers University Press, 1986. ix–xxxv.
_____, and Arnold Rampersad, eds. *Slavery and the Literary Imagination.* Baltimore: Johns Hopkins University Press, 1989.
McKay, Nellie Y., ed. *Critical Essays on Toni Morrison.* Boston: G. K. Hall, 1988.
Meillassoux, Claude. *The Anthropology of Slavery: The Womb of Iron and Gold.* Trans. Alide Dasnois. Chicago: University of Chicago Press, 1991.
Melhem, D. H. *Gwendolyn Brooks and the Heroic Voice.* Lexington: University of Kentucky Press, 1987.
Miller, Jean Baker. *Toward a New Psychology of Women.* Second Edition. Boston: Beacon, 1986.
Millett, Kate. *Sexual Politics.* Garden City, New York: Doubleday, 1970.
Mitchell, Carolyn A. "'I Love to Tell the Story': Biblical Revisions in *Beloved*." *Religion & Literature.* 23:3, Autumn 1991.
Mitchell, Juliet. *Psychoanalysis and Feminism.* New York: Vintage, 1974.
Mootry, Maria K., and Gary Smith, eds. *A Life Distilled: Gwendolyn Brooks, Her Poetry and Fiction.* Urbana and Chicago: University of Illinois Press, 1987.

Morgan, Edmund S. *American Slavery, American Freedom: The Ordeal of Colonial Virginia*. New York: W. W. Norton, 1975.

Morrison, Toni. *Beloved*. New York: New American Library, 1988.

———. *Lecture and Speech of Acceptance, Upon the Award of the Nobel Prize for Literature, Delivered in Stockholm on the Seventh of December, Nineteen Hundred and Ninety-Three*. New York: Alfred A. Knopf, 1994.

———. "The Pain of Being Black. Interview with Bonnie Angelo." *Time Magazine*. May 22, 1989: 120.

———. *Playing in the Dark: Whiteness and the Literary Imagination*. Cambridge: Harvard University Press, 1992.

———. "The Site of Memory." *Out There: Marginalization and Contemporary Cultures*. Ed. Russell Ferguson et al. New York and Cambridge: The New Museum of Contemporary Art and MIT Press, 1990. 299–305.

———. *Song of Solomon*. New York: Signet, 1977.

———. "Unspeakable Things Unspoken: The Afro-American Presence in American Literature." *Michigan Quarterly Review*, 28:1, Winter 1989.

Mucci, Clara. "The Blank Page as a Lacanian 'Object a': Silence, Women's Words, Desire, and Interpretation between Literature and Psychoanalysis." *Literature and Psychology*. 30:4, 1994. 23–35.

Myrdal, Gunnar. *An American Dilemma*. New York: Carnegie, 1943.

Noel, Donald L., ed. *The Origins of American Slavery and Racism*. Columbus, Ohio: Merrill, 1972.

Otten, Thomas J. "Pauline Hopkins and the Hidden Self of Race." *ELH, a Journal of English Literary History*. 59:1, Spring 1992. 227–56.

PMLA Program of the 1992 Convention, New York, New York, 27–30 December. MLA: New York, Volume 107, number 6, 1992. Section 505.

Prince, Mary. *The History of Mary Prince, a West Indian Slave. The Classic Slave Narratives*. Ed. Henry Louis Gates, Jr. New York: New American Library, 1987.

Pryse, Marjorie; Spillers, Hortense J., eds. *Conjuring: Black Women, Fiction, and Literary Tradition*. Bloomington: Indiana University Press, 1985.

Rich, Adrienne. *Of Woman Born: Motherhood as Experience and Institution*. New York: W. W. Norton, 1986.

Rigney, Barbara Hill. "'A Story to Pass On': Ghosts and the Significance of History in Toni Morrison's *Beloved*." *Haunting the House of Fiction: Feminist Perspectives on Ghost Stories by American Women*. Eds. Lynette Carpenter and Wendy K. Kolmar. Knoxville: University of Tennessee Press, 1991. 229–235.

———. *The Voices of Toni Morrison*. Columbus: The Ohio State University Press, 1991.

Robertson, Claire C., and Martin A. Klein, eds. *Women and Slavery in Africa*. Madison: The University of Wisconsin Press, 1983.

Robinson, William H., ed. *NOMMO: An Anthology of Modern Black African and Black American Literature*. New York: Macmillan, 1972.

Roses, Elena Lorraine; Randolph, Ruth Elizabeth. *Harlem Renaissance and Beyond: Literary Biographies of 100 Black Women Writers, 1900–1945*. Boston: G.K. Hall, 1990.

Russell, Sandi. *Render Me My Song: African-American Women Writers from Slavery to the Present*. New York: St. Martin's, 1990.

Samuels, Wilfred D.; Hudson-Weems, Clenora. *Toni Morrison*. Boston: Twayne, 1990.

Sato, Hiroko, "Under the Harlem Shadow: A Study of Jessie Fauset and Nella Larsen."

The Harlem Renaissance Remembered. Ed. Arna Bontemps. New York: Dodd, Mead, 1972. 63–89.

Saxton, Alexander. *The Rise and Fall of the White Republic: Class Politics and Mass Culture in Nineteenth-Century America.* London and New York: Verso, 1990.

Shange, Ntozake. *for colored girls who have considered suicide when the rainbow is enuf.* New York: Collier, 1989.

Shockley, Ann Allen. *Afro-American Women Writers, 1746–1933: An Anthology and Critical Guide.* Boston: G.K. Hall, 1988.

Six Women's Slave Narratives. Oxford and New York: Oxford University Press, 1988.

Smith, Sidonie. *Where I'm Bound: Patterns of Slavery and Freedom in Black American Autobiography.* Westport, CT: Greenwood Press, 1974.

Smith-Rosenberg, Carroll. *Disorderly Conduct: Visions of Gender in Victorian America.* New York: A. A. Knopf, 1985.

Snitow, Ann. Review of Toni Morrison's *Beloved. The Village Voice Literary Supplement,* September 1987. Reprinted in *Toni Morrison: Critical Perspectives, Past and Present.* Eds. Henry Louis Gates, Jr., and K. A. Appiah. New York: Amistad, 1993.

Spillers, Hortense. Afterword. *Conjuring: Black Women, Fiction, and Literary Tradition.* Eds. Marjorie Pryse and Hortense Spillers. Bloomington: Indiana University Press, 1985. 249–261.

———. "Gwendolyn the Terrible: Propositions on Eleven Poems." *A Life Distilled: Gwendolyn Brooks, Her Poetry and Fiction.* Eds. Maria K. Mootry and Gary Smith. Urbana: University of Illinois Press, 1987. 224–238.

———. "Mama's Baby, Papa's Maybe: An American Grammar Book." *Diacritics.* Summer 1987. 65–81.

———. "'An Order of Constancy': Notes on Brooks and the Feminine." *The Centennial Review,* 29:2, Spring 1985. 223–248.

———. "Psychoanalysis and Race," Critical Inquiry Lecture. April 9, 1993. The University of Chicago.

———, ed. *Comparative American Identities: Race, Sex, and Nationality in the Modern Text.* New York: Routledge, 1991.

Sprengnether, Madelon. *The Spectral Mother: Freud, Feminism, and Psychoanalysis.* Ithaca and London: Cornell University Press, 1990.

Stampp, Kenneth M. *The Peculiar Institution.* NY: Vintage, 1956.

Starling, Marion Wilson. *The Slave Narrative: Its Place in American History.* Boston: G. K. Hall, 1981.

Stein, Gertrude. "Melanctha." *Three Lives.* New York: Random House, 1909.

Stepto, Robert B. *From Behind the Veil: A Study of Afro-American Narrative.* Urbana: University of Illinois Press, 1979.

Sterling, Dorothy. *We Are Your Sisters: Black Women in the Nineteenth Century.* New York: W. W. Norton, 1984.

Strozier, Charles B. Introduction. *Self Psychology and the Humanities: Reflections on a New Psychoanalytic Approach.* By Heinz Kohut. New York: W. W. Norton, 1985.

Tate, Claudia. "Allegories of Black Female Desire: Or, Rereading Nineteenth-Century Sentimental Narratives of Black Female Authority." *Changing Our Own Words: Essays on Criticism, Theory, and Writing by Black Women.* Ed. Cheryl Wall. New Brunswick, NJ: Rutgers University Press, 1989.

———. *Domestic Allegories of Political Desire: The Black Heroine's Text at the Turn of the Century.* New York: Oxford University Press, 1992.

———. "Pauline Hopkins: Our Literary Foremother." *Conjuring: Black Women, Fiction, and Literary Tradition.* Eds. Marjorie Pryse and Hortense J. Spillers. Bloomington: Indiana University Press, 1985. 53–66.

Taylor-Guthrie, Danielle, ed. *Conversations with Toni Morrison.* Jackson: University Press of Mississippi, 1994.

Thomas, Alexander; Sillen, Samuel. *Racism and Psychiatry.* New York: Brunner/Mazel, 1972.

"Update on *Part One*: An Interview with Gwendolyn Brooks," *CLA Journal,* 21, 1977.

Wade-Gayles, Gloria. *No Crystal Stair: Visions of Race and Sex in Black Women's Fiction.* New York: Pilgrim, 1984.

Walker, Alice. *The Color Purple.* New York: Pocket Books, 1982.

———. *In Search of Our Mothers' Gardens.* New York: Harcourt Brace Jovanovich, 1983.

Wall, Cheryl, ed. *Changing Our Own Words: Essays on Criticism, Theory, and Writing by Black Women.* New Brunswick, NJ, and London: Rutgers University Press, 1991.

Washington, Booker T. *Up from Slavery.* New York: Bantam, 1963.

Washington, Mary Helen, "The Darkened Eye Restored': Notes Toward a Literary History of Black Women." *Reading Black, Reading Feminist.* Ed. Henry Louis Gates, Jr. New York: Meridian, 1990. 30–43.

———. "I Sign My Mother's Name: Alice Walker, Dorothy West, Paule Marshall." *Mothering the Mind.* Eds. Ruth Perry and Martine Watson Brownly. New York: Holmes and Meier, 1984.

———. *Invented Lives: Narratives of Black Women, 1860–1960.* New York: Garden City, NY: Doubleday, 1987.

———. "'Taming All That Anger Down': Rage and Silence in Gwendolyn Brooks's *Maud Martha.*" *Black Literature and Literary Theory.* Ed. Henry Louis Gates, Jr. New York: Methuen, 1984. 249–262.

Welter, Barbara. *Dimity Convictions: The American Woman in the Nineteenth Century.* Athens: Ohio University Press, 1976.

Wheatley, Phyllis. "On Being Brought from Africa to America." *Crossing the Danger Water: Three Hundred Years of African-American Writing.* Ed. Deirdre Mullane. New York: Anchor, 1993. 41.

White, Deborah Grey. *Ar'n't I A Woman? Female Slaves in the Plantation South.* New York: W. W. Norton, 1985.

White, E. Frances. "Listening to the Voices of Black Feminism." *Radical America* 18, nos. 2–3. Spring 1985.

White, Joseph L. *The Psychology of Blacks: An Afro-American Perspective.* Englewood Cliffs, NJ: Prentice-Hall, 1984.

Winnicott, D. W. *The Child and the Outside World: Studies in Developing Relationships.* Ed. Janet Hardenberg. New York: Basic, 1957.

———. *The Child, the Family, and the Outside World.* Middlesex, England: Penguin, 1964.

———. *The Maturational Processes and the Facilitating Environment.* London: Hogarth, 1965.

———. *Playing & Reality.* London and New York: Routledge, 1986.

———. *Winnicott on the Child.* Cambridge, MA: Perseus, 2002.

Wintz, Cary D. *Black Culture and the Harlem Renaissance.* Houston, TX: Rice University Press, 1988.

Wolman, Benjamin B. *The Unconscious Mind: The Meaning of Freudian Psychology.* Englewood Cliffs, NJ: Prentice-Hall, 1968.

Yarborough, Richard. Introduction. *Contending Forces*. By Pauline Hopkins. New York: Oxford University Press, 1988. xxvii–xlviii.

Yellin, Jean. Introduction. *Incidents in the Life of a Slave Girl, Written by Herself.* By Harriet A. Jacobs. Cambridge, MA: Harvard University Press, 1987. xiii–xxxiv.

———. "Texts and Contexts of Harriet Jacobs' *Incidents in the Life of a Slave Girl: Written by Herself.*" *The Slave's Narrative*. Eds. Charles T. Davis and Henry Louis Gates, Jr. New York: Oxford University Press, 1985.

Young-Bruehl, Elisabeth. *Anna Freud: A Biography*. Summit, 1988.

———. *Freud on Women: A Reader*. New York: W. W. Norton, 1990.

Index

abandonment 13–14, 22, 27, 29, 32, 39, 47, 116, 164
Adler, Alfred 89
affect 65, 117, 125, 142, 148
African American family 39, 47, 61, 89, 121
Allan, Tuzyline Jita 129–130
alter ego 56, 86, 164
anxiety 25, 47, 59, 68, 74, 171*n*22; racial 89; sexual 18
Apostle Paul 167
Atwood, Margaret 166
Autobiography of an Ex-Colored Man 100

beating 11, 147, 122–129; *see also* physical abuse
beauty (standards of) 91–92, 98–100, 115, 130
Benjamin, Walter 138
Bennett, Paula 116
The Black Bourgeoisie 66, 172*n*11
Black Laws 24, 113
Black Rage 91
Black Skin, White Masks 88–89, 94, 99, 101
Blassingame, John 10, 169*ch1n*2
Bone, Robert 69
bourgeoisie 66; *see also* class consciousness
Brent, Linda *see* Jacobs, Harriet
Brooks, Gwendolyn 4, 87, 106
Brown, Tony 111, 174*n*2

Carby, Hazel 14, 170*n*3, 171*ch3n*4
castration 14
Chodorow, Nancy 12
Cixous, Hélène 109
class consciousness 64, 66, 69, 72–3, 86, 92–93, 100; *see also* bourgeoisie
Cobbs, Price 91
color consciousness 64, 66, 79, 88, 91, 93, 95, 99–100

Cott, Nancy 53–54
Cult of True Womanhood 14, 32, 36, 38, 51, 54, 170*n*2

dandelion 95–96, 110
dark skin 72–73, 87, 92–93, 98–99, 106, 130, 137; *see also* color consciousness
Davis, Bette 94–95, 110
death wish 25, 28, 86, 164
defense mechanisms 13, 45–46, 58, 94, 141–143, 147, 149, 151, 156, 162, 165–166; avoidance 142, 159; denial 13, 22, 25, 37, 56, 70, 92, 95, 111, 142, 146, 159, 161; dissociation 47, 49; fantasy 142, 145; isolation 96, 142, 158; repression 37, 62, 65, 68–70, 82–84, 95, 107, 109, 117, 142–145, 145–146, 157–158, 160–161, 166
depression 47, 68–69,75
depressive position 47, 171*n*13
developmental stages 68
disease 18
displacement 90
"Do Like You" 118
double consciousness 46
Douglass, Frederick 25, 148
DuBois, W.E.B. 46

ego 23, 46, 48, 63, 65–67, 79, 86, 94, 96–97, 141; boundaries 82; damage 59, 73–74, 79, 81, 86, 94, 97–98, 100, 106, 116, 118, 129, 149, 159; development 74, 78–79, 96, 114, 117–118, 124, 133, 137, 158; fragmentation 69, 82, 140, 143, 159, 163; reparation 46, 48, 56, 125, 160, 171*n*28
The Ego and the Mechanisms of Defense 141–142, 144, 150, 160
Ellison, Ralph 31; *see also Invisible Man*
envy 43, 45, 54–55

Index

Eve 150
eyes 80

Fanon, Frantz 88–90, 94, 99–101, 173n7
female friendships 40, 50–55
Ferguson, Rebecca 160
Fernando, Suman 5
for colored girls who have considered suicide when the rainbow is enuf 131
Frazier, E. Franklin 66
Freud, Anna 141, 150
Freud, Sigmund 5, 11, 45, 67, 77, 88, 148
Fugitive Slave Law 32
Fuller, Hoyt 64

garret 10, 13, 23, 26–32
Gates, Henry Louis 116
gender: bias 4–5, 43, 64, 101, 112–115, 122, 130; 137; roles 41, 53, 66, 88, 94, 102, 131
glass 81
gold 83
"good-enough mothering" 3, 9, 11, 23–24, 35, 37, 64, 92, 152
"good" hair 98–99, 101, 130, 137
gray 87, 95–96, 101, 103
Grier, William 91
guilt 21, 45, 47, 56–57, 59, 79, 111, 116, 125, 135

Hall, Stanley 5
Ham 126
hanging *see* lynching
Harper, Frances 112
Hegel, Georg Wilhelm Friedrich 89
Hernton, Calvin 111
Hirsch, Marianne 6, 169*Intro.n*6
homoeroticism 50, 52–53, 65, 80–81, 128–129
homophobia 111, 130
homosexuality 5, 52–53, 172n12; *see also* homoeroticism
hooks, bell 86, 129
Hopkins, Pauline 4, 6
Horney, Karen 111, 113–114, 118, 122, 124, 127, 174n6, 175n14
Hurston, Zora Neale 6
hysterical reaction 28

id 58, 63, 81, 144
idealization 43; object 15, 68, 77, 81–85; parent imago 81, 173n30
In Search of Our Mothers' Gardens 5
incest 116–117, 125

individuation 50, 64
infanticide 140–141, 150
infantilization 28, 144, 147, 153, 161
inner voice, interiority 95, 97, 102, 105–108, 139
Invisible Man 16, 31

Jacobs, Harriet 4, 9
Jim Crow laws 24, 113
Johnson, Barbara 5, 172n14
Johnson, Yvonne 130
Jung, Carl 5, 89
jungle metaphor 18, 144

Klein, Melanie 36–37, 45, 47–48, 86
knowledge 142
Kohut, Heinz 63, 66–68, 70, 81, 93–94

language 40–41, 50, 57, 64–65, 69, 84, 86, 95, 101–102, 105, 115, 121, 139, 156, 163, 165
Larsen, Nella 4, 6, 63
lesbian relationships 52, 128; *see also* homoeroticism
Liscio, Lorraine 139, 160, 176n20
Locke, Alain 64
lynching 39, 65, 69, 92, 145–146, 151

marriage 41–43, 51, 59–61, 69, 75–6, 78, 83, 101–104, 112, 120–121
matrilineal line 11
McDowell, Deborah 6, 65, 81, 112, 171*ch*3n4
Meillassoux, Claude 24
memory 68, 74, 77, 96–97, 142, 160–161; suppression of 70, 86, 140, 145, 161
Middle Passage 150, 160–161
milk (mother's) 146, 153–154, 160, 176n20
mirroring 28, 29, 58, 66, 68, 73–75, 77–78, 83, 93–94, 106
misogyny 112, 114, 123, 134
Mitchell, Carolyn 152
mixed race 33, 37, 44, 65, 70, 75
Morrison, Toni 4, 138, 149–150, 175n6
mulatto 10, 22, 37; *see also* mixed race

narcissism 5, 64, 66, 67, 68, 70, 71, 74, 77, 86, 161, 163; injury 27, 29, 39, 68, 74, 149; personality disorder 67, 78, 85; rage 68, 71, 76, 95, 163
neurosis 114, 114, 118, 123–124, 173n7
Noah 126

"object" (psych.) 53, 81, 171n22, 173n28;

188

Index

mediating object 12; object hunger 97; object love 67, 78, 148; transitional object 54–55
objectification 89–90
obsession 80, 127
Oedipal: fantasy 159; neuroses 89; paradigm 74, 144; triangle 128, 136
Olinka tribe 134
orality 54; aggression 153; anxiety 159; infantile 18
Otten, Thomas 46

paranoid-schizoid position 47
part objects 72, 159
passing 30, 44, 57, 71, 82–84, 86
patriarchy 129
penis envy 45, 172n12
persecution anxiety 47–48
physical abuse 39, 111, 146–147; see also beating
pleasure principle 145
pre–Civil Rights era 88
projection 22, 52, 60, 90, 93, 128, 148, 163
psychosis 86, 145
purple 131, 136

race 29
racial identity 29, 37, 71, 84
racism 66, 75–76, 90, 108, 121, 142 passim
rage see narcissistic rage
rape 37, 39, 45, 48, 116, 146, 150; see also sexual assault
Reconstruction era 36, 146, 171n4
red 83, 140, 145
redemption 112, 115, 124, 137, 167
religion 15, 50, 113, 135, 147
"rememory" 145, 152, 161
Revelation (Book of) 155
Robinson, William H. 65

Sappho 44, 52
Scheherazade 162
self-esteem 107–108, 116, 121
self-loathing 45, 71–72, 79, 93, 102, 130, 132
self-object 77, 85, 97–98, 173n26; cultural 94, 172n15; idealized 97
Seth 149
sex 68, 71, 76, 102, 122, 128–129
sexism 93, 114–115, 122, 135; see also gender bias
sexual abuse 54, 61, 116, 119; in slave culture 17, 20, 27, 39, 144, 152; see also rape

sexuality 54, 128; Black female 52–55, 172n7
Shange, Ntozake: *for colored girls who have considered suicide when the rainbow is enuf* 131
Shaw, Harry B. 91
Shockley, Ann Allen 172n4
The Signifying Monkey 20; see also trickster figure
silence 29, 63, 68, 73, 107–108, 111, 139, 145, 158, 175n6
Sisyphus 145
skin color 82, 95, 130, 137; see also color consciousness
slave auction 112, 120
slave narrative 10, 17, 153, 139
slavery 9–35, 138–167 passim; culture 3, 16–17, 20, 23–25, 30, 38, 113, 142, 150; family 24, 26, 31–33, 38, 140, 148–149; fathers 16
Smith-Rosenberg, Carroll 53
Spillers, Hortense 12, 84, 171ch3n4
"splitting" 45–48, 56–57, 61, 83, 86, 173n24
Stein, Gertrude 68
superego 63, 81, 93, 141, 144
surrogate mothers 12–14, 16, 48, 58, 114, 119, 126–127, 160

Tate, Claudia 40, 52, 170n3
tradition 96, 103, 105
tragic mulatto" 64–65
trickster figure 20–21

voice 92, 94, 102, 104–110, 115, 131, 139, 142, 145, 153

Walker, Alice 4–6, 112, 137; *In Search of Our Mothers' Gardens* 5
Washington, Mary Helen 6, 50, 101, 109, 112, 170n2
Welter, Barbara 170n2
White, Deborah Grey 17
White, E. Frances 6
wife- or woman-beating see beating
Winnicott, D. W. 9, 11, 23, 24, 28, 34, 88
Wintz, Cary D. 65
Wonder, Stevie: "Do Like You" 118
The Wretched of the Earth 88

Yellin, Jean Fagan 9, 169ch1n2

www.ingramcontent.com/pod-product-compliance
Lightning Source LLC
Chambersburg PA
CBHW032102300426
44116CB00007B/852